25·00

Running a Limited Company

Sixth Edition

Running a Limited Company

Sixth Edition

David Impey, MA
Solicitor

Nick Montague, FCA

JORDANS

Published by
Jordan Publishing Limited
21 St Thomas Street
Bristol BS1 6JS

British Library Cataloguing-in-Publication Data

A catalogue record for this book is available from the British Library.

ISBN 978 1 84661 087 5

Typeset by Letterpart Ltd, Reigate, Surrey

Printed in Great Britain by Antony Rowe Limited, Chippenham, Wiltshire

CONTENTS

PREFACE

Running a limited company can be a complicated business. A company is a legal entity and the law makes many demands on the company itself and those who run it. These legal requirements must be fulfilled if the company and its officers are to avoid getting into trouble. Such problems may be avoided if the director and secretary have the basic information they need to carry out their duties and run the company smoothly.

This book is intended to serve as a practical guide to the requirements faced by an officer or shareholder of a private company limited by shares registered in England and Wales, Scotland or Northern Ireland. It aims to complement the professional advice which the company's officers will receive from their solicitors and accountants, though it is not intended as a substitute for such advice. Indeed, many of the matters covered should not be considered without professional advice.

What this book will do is enable the reader to gain a better understanding of the way in which his or her business affairs are organised in the form of a limited company. It explains how to carry out the simpler operations which the company and its officers have to perform by law, and gives an indication of what the company's advisers will do in more complex situations. It will enable the officer to approach an outside adviser, armed with the information the adviser will require, thereby enabling a more economical service to be provided to the company.

These principles apply equally whether considering the application of the laws of England and Wales, the laws of Scotland or the laws of Northern Ireland, to the company. Much of the law of each jurisdiction is identical, but there are areas in which the law in one or more of them is different. Sometimes the different law applies only to companies registered in that jurisdiction. Sometimes it applies to all companies, wherever registered, which carry out a transaction governed by the law of that jurisdiction. The text makes clear the differences between rules in each jurisdiction and the extent to which the differences affect not only companies registered in that jurisdiction, but also other companies.

Many people only seek the help of experts in times of difficulty. In terms of a company's future survival, that may already be too late. The key is in knowing when advice is needed and when it is not. Chapter 13 looks at the company's need to use lawyers, accountants and bankers. It analyses the do-it-yourself versus buy-it-in decision, sets out the wide range of services on offer, and suggests how to get the most out of using professionals.

An informed director or, for private companies that have one, an informed secretary is not only better equipped to perform his or her duties with confidence in the normal course of events, but also has a better grasp of the more technical problems which are beyond the scope of his or her experience. He or she is more likely to know when and how to act and when not to act alone.

Since the last edition of this book, a new Companies Act 2006 has received royal assent, and is being brought into force in phases. This lengthy piece of legislation – at 1300 sections and 16 schedules, the longest Act that Parliament has ever produced – re-enacts, amends and adds to previous company law, creating some significant new changes. Those made by the Act to date are incorporated into the text of this edition, and future changes are flagged up. Changes already in force include 'codified' directors' duties; significant changes to the way shareholders of a private company make decisions; wider powers for companies and their shareholders to communicate electronically; new rules about disclosure of company details on electronic documents and websites; and new rules restricting public access to a private company's register of shareholders, to name just a few.

Those to come include making the company secretary optional for private companies; new rules about conflicts between directors' interests and those of their company; and the introduction of a new right for anyone to object to a 'company name adjudicator' if a company name is too similar to a business name in which they have goodwill.

Generally, where references are made to decisions of the Secretary of State for Business, Enterprise and Regulatory Reform (or, in Northern Ireland, the Department of Economic Development), these are in fact decisions taken on his behalf by the relevant Registrar of Companies unless the contrary is stated in the text.

Throughout the rest of this book the personal pronoun 'he' is used. Its use is intended to encompass references to both males and females.

The law is stated as at 1 April 2008.

David Impey
Nick Montague

April 2008

NOTE ON THE RATING SYSTEM

A unique feature of this book is its star-rating system which indicates the degree of need to take professional advice. One star means advice is desirable; two stars means it is strongly recommended; and three stars means it is crucial. Where a topic is given a no-star rating, it may usually be undertaken without professional advice – but remember, when in doubt, ask an expert.

In this context, the importance of taking advice from a Scottish qualified professional in relation to Scottish matters and from a Northern Irish professional in relation to Northern Irish matters cannot be overstated.

CHAPTER 1

WHAT IS A COMPANY?

1.1 THE FUNDAMENTAL PRINCIPLE

There is one fundamental principle of company law from which all the rules and laws governing companies are derived. A company is recognised by the law as being a person. In legal jargon, a company has a separate and independent legal personality, distinct from its shareholders and directors.

1.2 'PERSONS' AND 'INDIVIDUALS'

It follows that every time the word 'person' appears in an Act of Parliament, or is used by a lawyer or accountant, it includes not only a natural person, but also a company. (It also includes a limited liability partnership, although these entities are not covered in this book.) The word 'individual', on the other hand, would refer only to a natural person. The strict legal meanings of these words will be used throughout this book.

Whilst an individual and a company are both recognised by the law as a person, a company is subject to many rules and limitations which either do not apply to an individual, or are different versions of the rules and limitations which apply to individuals. This book aims to help in understanding the reason for these rules and limitations.

1.3 'BUSINESS' AND 'COMPANY'

A distinction must be drawn between the words 'business' and 'company'. A business is simply a collection of assets and/or an activity. The assets or the activity should be thought of as quite distinct from the person or persons who own them, or carry it on – the two are separate. The person or persons carrying on the business may be either an individual, several individuals, a company or a limited liability partnership.

However, confusion is often caused because people commonly use the word 'company' to refer to their business. This is inaccurate.

To confuse the meaning of 'business' and 'company' can be an expensive mistake. For example, an individual who wants to sell his *business* may put an advertisement in the newspaper which says *'company for sale'*. This is inaccurate, and will not impress a potential purchaser.

Similarly, a person who buys a defective item from a business owned by an individual, but who instructs his solicitor to sue 'the company' which sold it to him will confuse his solicitor – this is bound to make the exercise more expensive!

1.4   BUSINESS NAMES

The situation is made more complicated by the fact that an individual, or a company, may own and carry on a business, and give it a name which is different from his or its own. This is called a 'business' or 'trading' name. To confuse matters further, it is quite lawful for a business name to include the words 'company' or '& company', even if the business is not carried on by a company.

To avoid this confusion, and really find out who carries on a business, look at documents such as business letters, order forms, invoices, official emails, website(s) and other documents (electronic or otherwise) of the person carrying on the business. While such documents may have the owner's business name displayed prominently on them, the name of (and certain other details about) the owner himself, itself or themselves must also appear somewhere on such documents (unless there are more than 20 people carrying on the business, in which case the document must state an address at which a list of the names of those persons is available for inspection), and it must be legible. If the person carrying on the business is a company, the name of the company will therefore appear. It is easy to recognise a company name because it will end in 'Limited', 'Ltd', 'public limited company' or 'plc' (or their Welsh equivalents). It is an offence for any person other than a company to use a name which ends in any of these words or initials.

Documents of customers, suppliers, etc, should always be checked to make sure you know who you are dealing with – do they make it clear who is carrying on the particular business? Is it an individual, or individuals, or a company? See Chapter 16 in respect of disclosure both on documents and at premises.

In this book, the word 'name', when applied to a company, means its true corporate name, and not any business name which it might use.

A final word of warning. It is increasingly common to find oneself doing business with foreign entities. Some of these entities share many characteristics with our own limited companies – even to the extent that they may include, for example, 'Limited' or 'Ltd' in their names. However, any similarities should not disguise the fact that these are *not* UK companies, and due caution should be exercised in dealings with them.

Again, Chapter 16 will help recognise whether a company is in fact a UK company or is a foreign entity.

1.5 STARTING UP AS A SOLE TRADER OR IN PARTNERSHIP

Many businesses are started by individuals themselves rather than within the legal structure of a limited company. An individual who carries on a business alone is called a 'sole trader' or 'sole proprietor'. Where two or more persons carry on a business together they are called 'partners' and their relationship is called a 'partnership'. Under English and Northern Irish law, it is very important to realise that a partnership is *not* itself a person, as a company is. The word 'partnership' is just a description of the relationship between two or more persons.

Nevertheless, there are two special circumstances in which the word 'partnership' is used but the body referred to does have a legal personality of its own – it is a legal person distinct from the partners of whom it is composed.

First, in Scotland a partnership has always been recognised as a legal person in its own right. This does not mean that a Scottish partnership is really a company. It is still a partnership and shares the vast majority of its characteristics with an English partnership – it is just that Scottish partnership law is slightly different in this respect.

Second, a new form of legal entity was introduced throughout the UK on 6 April 2001, called a 'Limited Liability Partnership'. Despite the inclusion of the word 'Partnership' in the name of this new entity, it is in fact a legal person distinct from its members. This book does not deal with Limited Liability Partnerships, which can be a complex and specialised subject. Where the term 'partnership' is used, it refers to an ordinary partnership.

1.6 FORMING A COMPANY AND TRANSFERRING THE BUSINESS

After a while, if the business grows, the sole trader or partners who carry on the business may form a company, and become its shareholders and directors. The business will then be sold to the company by the sole trader or partners – this is quite possible because the company is a separate legal person from the sole trader or partners, even if they are its directors and shareholders.

In return for selling the business to the company, the sole trader or partners will receive shares in the company. This will constitute all, or a part of, their payment from the company for the business it is buying from them. In the case of partners who sell their business to a company, they will usually take a proportion of shares in the company which corresponds to the proportion of profits of the partnership to which they were entitled – what their lawyer would call their 'profit-sharing ratio'.

For example:

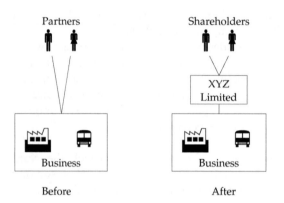

Figure 1 – Sale of business to company which pays by issuing shares

Before the transaction, the business is carried on by the partners. Afterwards, it is carried on by the company. It appears that the partners have relinquished control of the business to the company and have lost the right to income from it; it is no longer their business. However, the shares in the company are owned by the partners, and the shares will usually confer rights which enable the shareholders to control the company and derive an income from it. For example, the shareholders have the right to vote on important matters relating to the company's affairs and to tell it and its directors what to do. They have the right to a dividend from the company if the business generates profits for the company. They also have the ultimate right to appoint and remove its directors – the people who manage the business of the company for them.

Alternatively, a company may be formed in order to start a business from scratch, rather than to buy an existing business. In that case, the shareholders will usually put cash into the company in payment for its shares. This (together with any money the company may borrow from, for example, a bank) provides the company with the means to start up and carry on the new business.

1.7 ACQUISITIONS ***

Another common transaction is for an existing company to acquire control of an existing business from an individual, a partnership or a company with which it has no previous association or links, either as its only business, or in addition to its existing business(es).

There are a number of commercial and tax considerations as to the form and structure which such an acquisition should take in the particular circumstances. These mean that professional advice is always required.

1.8 WHY A COMPANY? THE TWO MAIN REASONS

Forming a company and complying with the requirements of the Companies Acts is a burden. Companies must be registered, and are subject to continuing disclosure requirements. One of the most significant burdens on a company is the need for its directors to prepare annual accounts. The accounts are filed with the registrar of companies and are therefore available for inspection by the public, although the abbreviated accounts which may be filed by smaller companies only provide a limited amount of information. Sole traders and partners do not have to suffer these burdens. So why should a company be formed at all?

The answer lies in the benefits which arise from the separate legal personality of the company in certain circumstances. The two main benefits which can arise from the company's legal personality are tax benefits and the benefits of limited liability. There are others, which will be looked at later.

1.8.1 Tax

The tax benefits can arise from the fact that the company is subject to its own special tax rules. If a business is carried on by a sole trader, he pays income tax on any profits, and capital gains tax on capital gains. The rule is exactly the same in partnership in that the partners' profits and gains are charged to income and capital gains tax in separate assessments. However, a company which carries on business pays only one tax, on both profits and gains. This tax is called 'corporation tax'.

The rates of income and capital gains tax and the rates of corporation tax are different. Not only are the rates different, but the profits and gains which are subject to tax are also worked out differently. The taxes are also assessed and payable at different times.

The amount of profit which directors and shareholders wish to distribute from the company is also relevant when comparing the tax bill in the two different circumstances. Profits and gains which are taxed to corporation tax going into the company can also be taxed to income tax coming out of it, and into the pockets of its directors (as remuneration) and shareholders (as dividends), so the comparison between the two circumstances is more complicated than it first appears.

However, the general result of the differences between the two tax regimes is that the more profitable a business becomes, the more likely it is that corporation tax rules will produce a lower overall tax bill than the income and capital gains tax rules.

This is why a business often begins by being owned by a sole trader or partners but, when it grows larger, is transferred by them to a company formed for that purpose.

At what stage should a sole trader, or partners, form a company and sell their business to it in return for a shareholding in the new company?

Unfortunately, there is no overall magic figure at which a sole trader or partner automatically knows that a company should be formed – each case will depend upon many circumstances, and will require a complicated calculation.

Particular sole traders or partners will need professional advice as to the appropriate time to form their own company. However, the bigger the profits, and the more sharply they are rising, the more likely it is that a company will be appropriate. Involving the professional adviser in the business on a regular basis is crucial to ensure that the company is formed at the right time.

1.8.2 Limited liability of a company's shareholders

The second main benefit flowing from the company's separate legal personality is that of limited liability.

Limited liability means that, in the case of a company whose business is not doing well, and is getting into financial difficulties, the shareholders of the company are not obliged to help the company pay its debts and discharge its liabilities. The business does not belong to them, it belongs to the company. It is the company which has the debts and liabilities, not its shareholders. The company and its shareholders are separate legal persons. The shareholders do, of course, have to pay the company any money owing in respect of their shares. However, if the shares are fully paid for (and, in the case of a private company, they invariably are), no further money is payable by the shareholders under company law. In these circumstances, the *liability* of each shareholder for the debts of the company is said to be *limited* to the amount outstanding (if any) on his shares. In legal jargon, the shareholders have limited liability.

It is interesting that the common expression a 'company with limited liability' is not strictly accurate. It is not the company which has limited liability, it is its shareholders. The company's liability for the debts of its business is unlimited, and it may end up insolvent (unable to pay its debts) if the debts of its business are sufficiently large.

Of course, a sole trader, or partners, carrying on business are in the same position as the company. They carry on the business themselves, and must pay the debts of the business personally if things go wrong – their liability is unlimited, and they may end up insolvent.

Indeed, if a business is carried on by partners, their liability for the debts of the business carried on by them is said to be 'joint and several' under English and Northern Irish law. This means that one partner can be sued for the whole amount owed by all the partners; for example, if the others cannot afford to pay or have disappeared. It is not enough for the one partner to simply pay his proportion of the debt. So one partner may have to pay all the partnership debts either because he is richer than the others, or simply because he is available to be sued, and they are not. Of course, in those circumstances, he is entitled to sue his partners for reimbursement, but if they have no money, or have disappeared, this remedy will be useless.

The laws of England and Wales and Northern Ireland differ from those of Scotland in this respect. Since a Scottish partnership *is* a legal person, the partners cannot be sued directly for a liability of the partnership. However, once liability has been established against the partnership, the individual partners may still be liable, jointly and severally, without limit, for the debts and liabilities of the partnership in those proceedings. Ultimately, therefore, in common with partnerships in England and Wales and Northern Ireland, the liability of partners will be unlimited in respect of any debts which the firm is unable to satisfy.

Limited liability for the shareholders is therefore a good reason why a large, risky or highly profitable business is more likely to be carried on by a company. If the business carried on by the company goes wrong, it is the company which will be taken to court, and not its shareholders, whereas, if the business of a sole trader or partnership goes wrong, it is the sole trader or partners who will be taken to court.

1.8.2.1 *Personal guarantees*

Of course, the shareholders or directors of a company may have to help the company pay its debts if they have expressly agreed to do so – for example, by giving a personal guarantee that, if the company cannot pay its debts, they will help it out. A bank, for example, may demand a personal guarantee from a shareholder or director if his company borrows money, saying that if the company defaults in repaying a loan, the shareholder or director will repay it. The shareholder or director may be asked to give a mortgage over his home as well.

Unfortunately for the individuals concerned, this is extremely common in the case of small or start-up businesses. The extent of the personal guarantee or mortgage required to be given is often such that the benefit of limited liability is negated for such individuals. However, these obligations are personal, and do not arise from company law.

1.8.2.2   Director's liability

The directors of a company may also be ordered by a court to help the company pay its debts, but only if they have acted fraudulently or in a way defined as improper by company legislation. However, a director who takes regular professional advice and has acted properly and legally should never have to contribute towards the company's debts (see Chapter 12).

1.8.2.3   Publication of its affairs

It is because the shareholders of a company have limited liability that the company is obliged to make certain of its affairs public. A person who is dealing with a company knows he cannot sue the shareholders, but he can sue the company; so he needs to know about the company. Details of certain of the company's affairs are therefore made public by filing information with the relevant registrar of companies. In many instances, the information can be filed electronically. The company must also keep certain of its internal records open to inspection by members of the public. For a person to know that these forms, documents and records are publicly available, he needs to know that he is dealing with a company. As we have seen earlier in this chapter, the name of a private company must include 'Limited' or 'Ltd' and, in the case of a public company, 'public limited company' or 'plc' and the appearance of these words will alert him to this. The person dealing with the company can then make further enquiries, if he wishes, of the registrar of companies, or may inspect such of the company's internal records as are available for inspection.

1.9   OTHER ADVANTAGES OF FORMING A COMPANY

There are other advantages which flow from the company's separate legal personality.

1.9.1   Separation of control and management

A shareholder can control a company which is carrying on a business, and receive a dividend if the company's business makes a profit, without having to become involved in the day-to-day running of the business. The same is not usually true of a sole trader or partners. For example, partners carrying on a business know that they will have to pay the debts of the business if it goes wrong, so they will be reluctant to entrust the management of the business to someone else – 'sleeping' partners who take no active interest in the affairs of the partnership are rare. Even if the size of the business requires the appointment of managers, the partners will probably take an active interest on a day-to-day basis.

Shareholders, on the other hand, have the protection of limited liability. They are therefore more likely to allow their company's business to be managed by someone else without feeling they need to intervene on a day-to-day basis. Company law therefore provides that the shareholders have power to appoint (and remove) special managers, who are called directors, to manage the business of the company. The directors are given stewardship, or custody, of the business of the company.

Since the directors are in a position of trust – looking after the company's business for it – they are subject to all sorts of duties and liabilities. These duties and liabilities are onerous, so that the shareholders and their company are given protection against abuse of their position by the directors.

Of course, a shareholder may also be a director, and often the shareholders and directors are the same people. However, company law deals with directors and shareholders separately. The directors must still observe all of these duties and liabilities when acting as directors, even if they are also the shareholders.

1.9.2   New participants

A consequent advantage of this separation of control of the company (shareholders) and management of its business (directors) is that the introduction of a new shareholder into the company is usually easier than the introduction of a new partner into a partnership.

A new partner is jointly and severally liable for the debts of the business of the partnership, just as much as the most senior or longest-established partner. The new partner will therefore argue that he should have an equal, or substantial, say in how the business is run, and an adequate share in the profits, to recompense him for his risk. The existing partners may disagree. There is much scope for negotiation. A new shareholder in a company, on the other hand, knows that if the company's business is run well, he may receive dividends and the value of his shares in the company should rise but, if the business runs into difficulties, he has limited liability. Consequently, all a new shareholder may be concerned about is whether the business carried on by a company is likely to be profitable, and whether the directors are competent. He will not necessarily be interested in participating in day-to-day management.

1.9.3 Raising capital

Of course, this means that it is often easier for a company to raise new money than it is for a partnership. A person will be far more cautious about putting his money into a partnership by becoming a partner (since he will have joint and several unlimited liability), than he will be about putting his money into a company by buying shares (since he will have the protection of limited liability).

1.9.3.1 Employees and family members

For example, members of a shareholder's family, such as children, may buy shares in the company, or have them bought for them, or given to them. In the case of children under 18 the shares will usually be held on their behalf by trustees under a family trust. If the company is profitable, they (or the trustees on their behalf) may receive dividends. If not, they have limited liability. Limited liability also means that, by gradually increasing the number of shares held by his family a majority shareholder can shift control of the company to his family – leaving it in their hands on his retirement. Introducing family members into a partnership and providing for succession to the partnership business is far more complex.

Employees may also be encouraged to work harder if they and their families are given the opportunity to buy shares in their company. Sole traders and partners are not able to offer incentives to their employees so simply.

The tax laws encourage members of families and employees to buy shares by providing tax incentives if the shares are held in particular ways. For family members there can be advantages in putting shares into special trusts to benefit children. For employees, certain types of share scheme allow employees and their families to buy shares, or the right to buy shares (share options), in their companies, and obtain tax reliefs. Such schemes may be for certain higher-paid employees, or all employees, depending on the sort of scheme the company wishes to operate.

1.9.3.2 Outside investors

Complete outsiders are also encouraged by the tax laws to approach companies and ask to buy their shares. Under the Enterprise Investment Scheme, a person may invest in certain companies by buying their shares and, if certain conditions are met, will obtain tax relief on his investment. Some of the conditions relate to the business carried on by the company (which must be a 'qualifying trade'), the amount invested, and the length of time the shares are held.

1.9.4 Groups of companies

Another benefit of a company's legal personality is the ability to create a group of companies. This can provide benefits, discussed below. There are different rules for determining whether a group of companies exists for accounting purposes (ie in deciding whether 'group accounts' must be prepared) as against determining whether there is a group for general company law purposes. Under the general company law rules, the most common way of creating a group is by ensuring that a majority of the voting shares of a company or companies are owned by another company or companies. At the top of the resulting 'family tree' will be the 'holding' or 'parent' company. Such companies are entitled to include the word 'holdings' or 'group' in their name, although this is not obligatory. All the others will be 'subsidiary' companies.

Examples of groups are:

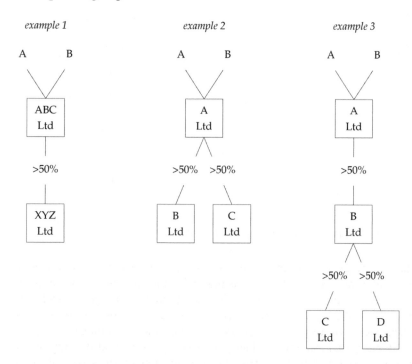

Figure 2 – Examples of groups of companies

It can be seen that one parent company may have many subsidiaries. Similarly, one subsidiary may have more than one parent company. In the third example above, C Ltd and D Ltd both have two parent companies. B Ltd is the *immediate* parent company, and A Ltd is the *ultimate* parent company of both.

If the ultimate parent company is a public company whose shares are 'quoted' or 'listed' on the Stock Exchange or are on the Alternative Investment Market, the value of those shares will appear in the financial press and the shareholder can tell from the value of his shares in the parent company how the group as a whole is doing.

More often, the ultimate parent company is a private company, so that the value of the shares will not be publicly quoted. The value of such shares is often difficult to determine, and will frequently be the subject of negotiation each time a value is needed, such as on a sale of shares, or death of a shareholder.

However, in the absence of any other means whereby A Ltd controls B Ltd (or vice versa), there is *not* a group in the following circumstances:

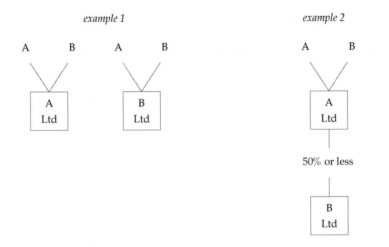

Figure 3 – Examples of non-groups of companies

The advantage of a group of companies is that each subsidiary can carry on a different business. If one business fails, the company carrying it on may become insolvent, but the other companies in the group will not. However, if the businesses are successful, the use of subsidiaries provides a clear means of keeping the results of each business separate, to assess its profitability or productivity. The parent company may also carry on its own business (or provide central and/or management services), but often it acts simply as a central fund, collecting dividends from its subsidiaries, which it can then use to pay dividends to its own shareholders.

Tax laws provide advantages and reliefs to groups of companies. The reliefs vary, usually according to the proportion of shares in a subsidiary which is held by its immediate parent company. To obtain maximum tax benefits, most groups will comprise one ultimate parent company and one or more wholly owned subsidiaries. A subsidiary is 'wholly owned' if all its shares are controlled by another company – it is not necessary for every share to be owned outright by the parent. However, it is not always commercially possible or desirable for a subsidiary to be wholly owned. For example, the subsidiary may have been set up as a joint-venture company, with another organisation holding some of its shares. Alternatively, the long or medium-term intention of the group may be to build a business up and sell it off. 'Parcelling' the business into a separate limited company, and selling the shares in the subsidiary company, either wholly, or in instalments, may be a much more efficient way of doing this than selling the business itself.

Every few years, a group of companies may be reorganised, with the intention of creating a more efficient structure for the group to trade as a whole. Such reorganisations are often complex, and should not be carried out without professional advice. There are always commercial *and* tax implications to be considered.

Companies within a group will often trade with one another – one providing products or services which complement those of another. For example, one may provide raw materials for a manufacturing process of another.

Of course, there are also disadvantages in forming a group of companies. It is not always wise to have a group of companies instead of one single company for the following reasons.

1.9.4.1 Taxation

Corporation tax is charged at two main rates: the 'small companies' rate and the full rate. If a company has no connections with any other companies (it is not in a group or associated with another company in any way), then the rate at which tax is charged depends on the company's taxable profits. For example, if profits are lower than a certain figure, which is reviewed in the budget every year, the small companies' rate will apply.

If the company's profits figure is above the figure for small companies, but below the figure for the standard rate, there are marginal rates for the excess profit over the figure for small companies.

If, on the other hand, there are two related companies, one generating less than the profits figure for small companies and the other generating sufficient profits to be taxed at a marginal rate, the rules become complex because of the relationship between the two companies. Tax planning with groups needs professional advice and great care.

1.9.4.2 Administration

As mentioned already, each company must prepare annual accounts and submit them to the registrar of companies. The accounts of larger companies must be audited (certified as presenting a true and fair view of the company's affairs) by a 'registered auditor'. However, smaller companies are usually exempt from the audit requirement. These rules are dealt with in more detail in Chapter 9. Various other requirements have to be observed each year. Each company will require a separate book-keeping system and the administration generally will be more complicated than having a single company.

It is necessary to take professional advice to determine the benefits and burdens of having more than one company, and make the decision accordingly.

The intention here has been to describe only very generally the concept and principles of groups of companies. Setting up a group is an area where professional advice should be taken at every stage as there are many pitfalls to trap the unwary, especially on the taxation side, which can become very complex.

1.9.5 Status

Another advantage of forming a company relates solely to status. Even though there are many large and reputable businesses carried on by sole traders or partners, the public assume, sometimes wrongly, that a company is more likely to continue in business, and pay its debts, and that a company will be more reputable, than a sole trader or partners.

Often this is true. The benefits of tax and limited liability mean that a company's business is usually of a certain size. It also means that the company is subject to all the formalities and publicity requirements which attach to companies, and this may be indicative of its standing, since such requirements are a disincentive to the frivolous.

1.9.6 Borrowing

For these reasons, banks are often, as a very general rule, more prepared to lend money to companies than sole traders or partners. The bank will also know that a company can create a special sort of mortgage or charge over its property – a floating charge – as a security for money it borrows, which a sole trader, or partners, cannot. (However, do not expect the bank to dispense automatically with the need for personal guarantees from the company's shareholders and directors if a substantial sum is borrowed by their company, even if the company can give a mortgage over its property as security.)

1.10 PRIVATE AND PUBLIC COMPANIES

It is appropriate at this point to define the difference between a private and a public company. Both private and public companies give their shareholders the protection of limited liability – it is not accurate to refer, as many do, to a company which re-registers from private to public as going from limited to public. However, the vast majority of companies are private. So how can one tell if a company is private or public? The Companies Acts say that a company is public if its memorandum of association says that it is. All other companies are private. (This will change from October 2009, when the test will be whether the company's certificate of incorporation says it is a public company.) The Acts then go on to specify a number of benefits and burdens which apply only to public companies.

1.10.1 Company name

The most obvious difference is that the name of a public company must end in 'public limited company' or 'plc' (or their Welsh equivalents). It is a criminal offence for any other company or business name to end in these words or initials.

1.10.2 Offers to the public

Another important difference is that a public company is allowed to offer its shares to the public, but a private company cannot. This means that a public company can send out circulars and advertise in newspapers, etc, offering to sell, or inviting people to buy, its shares, but a private company cannot. The only people to whom a *private* company can normally offer its shares are its existing shareholders and employees and their families, and any debenture-holders (see Chapter 10).

Of course, a person who approaches a private company may buy its shares, but the private company may not itself offer its shares to that person or invite him to apply for them – it cannot take the initiative.

Since the public may find themselves being offered shares by a public company, company law provides them with certain protections. For example, rules made by, and pursuant to, financial services law require that a public company which offers its shares to the public must give the public certain information about itself, in writing, when making such an offer.

1.10.3 Share capital

The Companies Acts also state that a public company must have an issued share capital of at least £50,000 (or, from October 2008, the euro equivalent) with each share paid up by at least one-quarter. For example, if the company has shares of £1, 25p must have been paid by the shareholders, on each issued share. Additionally, if the shareholders have agreed to pay the company more than £1 for those shares (ie they have agreed to pay 'a premium'), the premium must also be paid. Until such requirements have been satisfied, a public company may not trade or borrow money. As proof of satisfaction of these requirements, a public company must have been issued with a trading certificate by the registrar of companies. This contrasts with a private company, which may trade or borrow money immediately it is incorporated, even if it has only one shareholder, holding only one share.

1.10.4 Directors

A public company must have at least two directors, and its secretary must fall within certain categories set out in the Companies Acts. These categories – chartered secretary, accountant, solicitor, etc – are intended to ensure that the secretary of a public company has a certain competence and familiarity with company matters. A private company may have only one director, if its articles allow. A director may, currently, be of any age but, from October 2008, directors must be at least 16. The secretary of a private company need meet no particular criteria – and, from April 2008, private companies will not be required to have a company secretary at all, unless the directors choose to have one.

1.10.5 Technical limitations

There are various other technical limitations on public companies in the Companies Acts – for example, they may not declare dividends as freely as private companies and there are stricter rules regarding the contents of their audited accounts.

1.11 LISTED COMPANIES

However, none of these limitations confers absolute protection on the public, so that a public company may find it difficult to attract new shareholders when offering shares to the public. How can it make its shares more attractive?

The answer lies in the company applying for its shares to be admitted to a 'listing', so that they are bought and sold in a particular 'market'. If the company's shares are 'listed', the public knows that the company has met additional requirements, far and above those set for public companies by the Companies Acts, and will therefore be more inclined to buy the shares of that company if offered to them. In effect, by meeting these requirements, the company is demonstrating that it has good credentials and standing.

There are two main markets in the UK. If a company's shares are to be listed on either market, it must comply with the admission requirements for that market. The junior market is the Alternative Investment Market (known as 'AIM'). The senior market is the Official List of the London Stock Exchange. It is a major task to get a company's shares listed on AIM, and even harder to get them onto the Official List of the London Stock Exchange. However, once a company's shares are dealt with on either of these markets, the public will buy them with greater confidence, because they know that the company will have had to satisfy their respective admission requirements. A company's shares will only be dealt with on one market at a time. Of course, not all public companies' shares are bought and sold on either of these markets. Most public companies' shares are not listed. Many potential investors make the assumption that, if it is public, it is listed. This is not the case.

Indeed, there are many public companies which do not even offer their shares to the public. The articles of such companies may operate much as a private company. Such companies are often public for the simple commercial reason that a customer may feel safer buying from a public company – the words 'public limited company' or letters 'plc' at the end of the name give added confidence. A significant number of companies re-register from private to public every year. The usual reason is to acquire a new kudos or status in their commercial activities, rather than to enable them to offer shares to the public. Still less, in order to apply for a listing on one of the two main markets.

1.12 NAME PROTECTION

Another reason for forming a company is simply for name protection purposes. Of course, a person carrying on a business acquires a certain amount of protection for the name of the business (or the name of a particular product or a brand name), simply by using it. The use of a name in such a way that it is associated by the public with a particular business enables the person carrying on that business to take another person to court if the other has traded off his reputation by using the same or a similar business name. See Chapter 2 for such rights.

Further protection can be obtained for a business name by registering the name on the companies index (see **2.2.1.2** below), as the name of a limited company. If the owner of the business name is a limited company, and the business name is the same as the name of the company then the name is, of course, already registered. However, the business name may be different from the name of the company, or the name may be that of a business carried on by a sole trader or partnership, which is not required to be registered on the companies' index. Consequently, to protect that name, companies are sometimes formed which will not carry on any business whatsoever. They will, however, have the same name as a particular business carried on or to be carried on by a sole trader or partnership, or even a company registered in a different name. The effect of forming a company in that name is to put the name on a public register in circumstances where it would not otherwise appear on any public register. Another person planning to use the name, or a similar name, and making the usual name-checking searches and inquiries is therefore warned off when he sees that the name is registered as a company name. See Chapter 2 for such searches and inquiries.

Such a company will invariably be either a 'dormant' or an 'audit exempt' company. In consequence, all it need lodge at Companies House in each year are unaudited accounts, an annual return, and the annual return fee. No auditors' fees are incurred, although it may be necessary to pay an accountant to prepare the unaudited accounts. See Chapter 9 for a more detailed consideration of accounting matters.

1.13   TAXATION

There can be other taxation considerations in forming a company, notably in relation to the provision of pensions, and of benefits such as cars. The company accountant plays a crucial role in advising on such matters.

1.14   DISADVANTAGES

However, this chapter must end in stressing the disadvantages of running a company.

The formalities of forming the company, and the administrative burden of making its affairs public are obvious, but perhaps the greatest practical disadvantage lies in having continually to remember to draw the distinction between directors and shareholders, and the respective restraints and requirements on their behaviour. A person who is both a director and a shareholder, must always remember in what capacity he is acting at any given moment. The considerations he must have in mind as a director are very onerous, and very different from those he must have in mind as a shareholder.

Additionally, both the shareholders and the directors must remember that the business being carried on is not their business. It belongs to the company, and they must always be aware of this. A classic illustration of this is that ex-partners, who are now directors of a company, often find it difficult to accept that they may not make 'drawings', as they did when they were in partnership, from the company – although private companies can now make loans to their directors in a far wider range of circumstances. They also need to remember that when they spend the company's funds, it is not their money they are spending, but the company's, which is ultimately owned by the shareholders, to whom they are accountable.

CHAPTER 2

THE COMPANY AND ITS CONSTITUTION

2.1 FORMING THE COMPANY

Whilst a natural person is born, artificial persons must be formed procedurally. A company is formed by following a procedure which is set out in the Companies Acts. The procedure requires filing of information with a registrar of companies, and payment of a fee. The information can be filed in paper format, or electronically. There are three registrars in the UK – with registries in Cardiff, Edinburgh and Belfast. There are also branches of these main registries – for example, there is a branch of the Cardiff registry in London (called the 'London Information Centre'), at which documents may be filed, and searches made. For convenience the general term 'Companies House' has been used in this book wherever reference is made to any of the registries.

It is only when the registrar with whom the information is filed issues a certificate of incorporation that the company is in existence. Anyone who makes an agreement on behalf of a company before it is in existence will be personally liable on that agreement, even after the company comes into existence. Such agreements are called 'pre-formation' or 'pre-incorporation' contracts. Legal advice should always be taken before making a pre-incorporation contract. Pre-incorporation contracts need not be in writing, so the absence of a document does not necessarily mean there is no pre-incorporation contract.

When the certificate of incorporation is issued, the company is said to have been created, registered, formed or incorporated. The certificate will state the company's name, date of incorporation and a unique company number. Whilst the name may be changed, the number will stay constant until the company is dissolved. There are no rules as to where the certificate should be kept. Many companies like to display the certificate at the registered office, or a place of business, but this is not a legal requirement. If it is not displayed, it is good practice to keep it with the company's registers, at the registered office.

If the certificate is lost, the registrar will issue a duplicate, upon payment of a fee. The duplicate may be used for all the same purposes as the original.

Ordinarily, the only time when the company will need to produce its certificate is to open a bank account, to deal with overseas authorities or lawyers, or to apply for tax clearance on certain complicated transactions.

Private companies may carry on business immediately upon issue of a certificate of incorporation. A public company must obtain a trading certificate. See Chapter 1 in this respect.

2.2   THE MEMORANDUM OF ASSOCIATION **

Every company, whether private or public, must have a memorandum of association. If the company is private, the current rule is that this document must contain five clauses. These are discussed below. If the company is public, the current rule is that there must also be a statement that the company is to be a public company. The proposed shareholders of the company will decide the contents of the memorandum, although certain matters must be included. The shareholders of the company may change certain parts of the memorandum once the company has been formed, if this becomes necessary, or desirable.

In 2009 the law is going to change. The memorandum of association of a company formed on or after 1 October in that year will merely be one of the official forms submitted when forming a new company. It will state who the intended shareholders of the company are; that they wish to form a company; and that they agree to become shareholders of it. Each shareholder will also have to agree to take at least one share in the company, and either sign it or authorise someone else to sign it on their behalf. Once the company is formed, its job will be done, and it will have no impact on the further operation of the company. New companies formed with the new-style memorandum will no longer need to amend or update their memorandum of association once the company is formed – it simply won't be necessary.

2.2.1   The name

Currently, the memorandum must state the name of the company. The reader is reminded of the distinction between the company name and any business name to be used by the company. It is the company name which must appear in the memorandum.

There are a number of rules which apply to names, which must be observed both when the company is incorporated, and if it subsequently wishes to change its name.

When the function and format of the memorandum changes in 2009, the name of a new company will have to be included in a new application form that will have to be filed with the registrar of companies (with other formation information) when registering a new company.

2.2.1.1 *'Limited' or 'Ltd'*

The name of a private company must either end in the word 'Limited' or 'Ltd' (or their Welsh equivalents) so that the public know that they are dealing with a company. The shareholders of the company must make a choice as to which they want. Incorporation details should not be submitted in which the name appears with one ending in one part, and the other ending in another part. The registrar requires consistency, because he has to be clear as to which version to include on the certificate of incorporation. Once incorporated, it is uncertain whether a company with a certificate of incorporation stating that the name end is 'Limited' can use 'Ltd' as an abbreviation – for example, on its stationery. It is common to do so, but the courts have not been consistent in their attitude to the use of 'Ltd' as an abbreviation of 'Limited', so it is prudent not to use it as such.

There are special rules for companies with a registered office in Wales, which may use Welsh equivalents of 'Limited' and 'Ltd'.

2.2.1.2 *Refusal of registration*

A name will be refused for registration if:

(1) it is the same as a name already appearing on the list of company names at Companies House ('the companies index'); or

(2) its use would constitute a criminal offence; or

(3) it is offensive.

Both (2) and (3) are determined by the registrar of companies (for the Secretary of State for Business, Enterprise and Regulatory Reform) as matters of opinion.

In October 2009, the registrar's powers regarding company names will be extended. He will be able to prevent registration of inappropriate or misleading company names. Regulations will be made governing the letters, characters, signs or symbols (including accents and like marks) and punctuation that can be used, and where they can be used in, a company name. The new rules will enable the registrar to avoid the sort of difficulties he faced in the 1990s, when presented with proposed company names that the existing rules did not cover, for example, names beginning with the @ symbol.

There will also be new rules stating which words, expressions, signs or symbols will be treated as the same (or not) when the registrar is deciding whether a proposed company name is the same as an existing company name.

2.2.1.3 'Sensitive' words

A name will also be refused registration if it contains a 'sensitive' word, unless the written consent of particular bodies have been obtained, or the use is justified by a written assurance from a proposed officer of the company (a director, or the secretary, if it has one), a solicitor, accountant, or company registration agent, that the company meets certain criteria. Current lists of sensitive words for each of Great Britain and Northern Ireland appear in Appendix B – although the lists are amended from time to time, and should be re-checked on each incorporation (or change of name). The rules on sensitive words can be checked at www.companieshouse.gov.uk. Words are usually sensitive if they imply a certain prestige or eminence. For example, if a company wishes to include the word 'international' in its name as a suffix, an assurance must be given that it will trade in at least two overseas countries.

2.2.1.4 Similar names

IS THE PROPOSED COMPANY NAME SIMILAR TO A NAME ALREADY ON THE COMPANIES INDEX? Care must be taken to ensure that the proposed name is not similar to a name already on the companies index. The registrars of companies for Scotland, and England and Wales, amalgamate the companies registered with them into one companies' index for the purpose of determining whether a name is similar to a name already registered. Thus a company may not be registered in Scotland with a name which has already been registered in England and Wales, and vice versa. The proposed name will not be refused registration by Companies House because it is similar to a name already on the index, but a new company registered with a name that is similar to one already on the companies' index may find that it is subsequently ordered to change its name.

First, another company already on the companies index may:

(1) object to the Secretary of State for Business, Enterprise and Regulatory Reform within 12 months of the new name appearing on the index, that the new name is 'too like' its own; or

(2) bring a 'passing-off' action in the courts.

When considering whether names are 'too like', the Secretary of State and the courts apply different criteria. The Secretary of State will simply ask whether the names are in fact similar. His aim is to ensure that, for example, a person seeking to carry out a search against a company is not presented with two very similarly named companies and cannot easily work out which is which. He will ignore the fact they may be in different geographical locations or different trades or businesses.

Second, the Secretary of State may take action against a company on the grounds that its name is 'too like' that of another company on his own initiative, even if he has not received an objection from another company.

To avoid action by the Secretary of State, business people often ask an experienced searcher to check the companies' index for them to ensure their proposed name is not 'too like' that of an existing company. They should do this both on incorporation of a new company and on change of name of an existing company. Professional advisers or a company registration agent will offer such a service. Particularly, they will be aware of special rules – for example, the Secretary of State ignores symbols such as '@' or expressions such as '.com' or 'www' in company names when considering whether they are 'too like'. There are many such rules to take into account (and, from October 2009, there will be new rules that state which words, expressions, signs or symbols will be treated as similar or not for these purposes) so paying for such a service can be a worthwhile investment.

If a passing-off action is brought, the courts will take a wider view and ask not only whether the names are in fact similar but also whether the public have been misled and confused. They will therefore take into account factors such as the nature of the business and the location of each.

Both the Secretary of State, and the courts, may order a company to change its name, with all the attendant expense and inconvenience regarding new stationery, promotional costs, etc, and the courts may award damages against it.

IS THE PROPOSED COMPANY NAME SIMILAR TO A BUSINESS NAME ALREADY IN USE? Inquiries must also be made to ensure that the proposed company name is not similar to a business name already in use. Where the similarity is between a proposed company name and an existing business name, the Secretary of State will not be interested if an objection is made to him. He is only concerned with similar *company* names. However, a passing-off action in the courts is still possible. Once again, professional advice should be sought.

Searches need to be made to check if similar business names are already in use. The companies' index will not reveal business names, so where can a search be made?

- There is no register of business names but a professional adviser might recommend and carry out a search in the trade marks register or other special registers. There are trade mark registries in every country, and it is also possible to register trade marks in registries that offer protection in more than one country – for example, registration at the Community Trade Marks Registry offers protection across the EU and beyond. It may be sensible to search the registries for all the countries in which the company's goods or services will be sold.

- However, there should also be extensive checking in trade journals, *Yellow Pages*, etc, by the directors.

- Many business, product or brand names are registered as domain names on the internet or are mentioned in websites or by visitors to chatrooms. Particular proposed names can be checked against registered domain names under top-level domains such as .com, .net and .org by using the 'whois' facility at www.internic.com and country code top-level domains by using the whois facilities on the relevant registrar's site – for example, .uk domain names can be checked using the 'whois' facility at www.nominet.org.uk. If registering under one of the smaller or more obscure country code top-level domains, it is wise to check with the relevant registry that their whois information is up to date.

- Search engines such as www.google.com can be used to search the web generally.

Of course, if the company is taking over the business name used previously by a sole trader or partnership, and merely adding 'Limited' there is less likely to be a problem.

In all searches and inquiries, the company is looking for names which are similar enough to the company's, so that the public are misled into confusing the two names. For example, Abkem Limited and Abchem Limited are obviously similar and confusing. There may be other less obviously similar names which also cause confusion.

IS THE PROPOSED BUSINESS NAME OF A COMPANY SIMILAR TO AN EXISTING NAME OR EXISTING BUSINESS NAME? If any company is going to use a business name it should carry out the same checks and inquiries as it did for its company name, to ensure that the business name is not similar to company names, and other business names, already in use. If it is, there is the danger of a passing-off action.

PROTECTING A COMPANY NAME OR A BUSINESS NAME. Other ways of protecting both the company name or any business name should also be considered. One effective way to protect a name is simply to use it – the wider and greater the reputation attached to a company or business name, the less likely that another business will be able to use it without confusing or misleading the public into thinking that they are associated with your business, and the more likely you are to win if you bring a passing-off action against it in the courts.

Another way to protect a company or business name is to register it as a trade mark. Registered trade marks can be names, logos, slogans or any combination of them (and can also be shapes, colours, sounds or 3-dimensional forms), and registration can confer substantial protection against their unauthorised use by another. However, if it is intended to register a name as a trade or service mark, the name must be capable of registration at the relevant Trade Marks Registry. As well as the UK trade mark registry (at www.ipo.gov.uk), the company may wish to trade outside the UK, in which case it may consider registering a trade mark in other national registries for the territory in which it wishes to trade.

There are also supra-national registration systems that offer protection in a number of countries. For example, registration of a European Community trade mark at the European Community registry (go to www.oami.europa.eu/CTMOnline/RequestManager) offers protection in every EU country, without the need for individual registrations in national registries. Another option is to register an International Trade Mark with the World Intellectual Property Organisation (www.wipo.int) under a treaty called the Madrid Protocol, that will give protection in every country that has signed up to the treaty.

In each case, the trade mark to be registered must be distinctive, and not merely descriptive of the goods. For more information on trade mark registration, see Chapter 16.

Clearly, choice of a name or a business name is a complicated matter. Legal advice should always be taken.

2.2.1.5   Changing a company name or a business name

A company may change its name by a special resolution of its shareholders. Business names, on the other hand, may be chosen and changed by the directors. The same checks should always be made on a change of name or business name as are made when choosing an initial name.

A special resolution to change the company's name must be filed with the registrar of companies. It is not until the registrar issues a certificate evidencing the change of name that the change of name is effective.

The company should take great care not to order new stationery, etc, in the new name until either the certificate is issued, or the company is quite sure that it will be.

From October 2009, there will be new rules on how to change a company's name. If the name is altered by special resolution of the shareholders, the company will also have to file a notice that it has passed the resolution with the registrar of companies – an extra requirement.

This is because, for the first time, a resolution to change the company's name can be made conditional on some future event, such as a sale of the company. The registrar will not, however, issue a change of name certificate until he is told that the event has occurred. A notice is therefore required, that tells him whether the resolution is conditional, and whether the event has occurred. If the event has not occurred, the company must file a further notice when it does, and the registrar will issue the certificate then.

The purpose of the notice, therefore, is to alert a person looking at the company's public record that a change of name is imminent, even if the registrar has not yet issued the certificate. The company should beware of conditional change of name resolutions, however, because the name is not 'reserved' while this is going on – so it would be possible for another business to register that name for itself at any time prior to the issue of the certificate.

Under the new rules, a company will also be able to change its name by any other means provided for in its articles of association. For example, they could provide that the directors can resolve to change the company's name, without involving the shareholders at all. In that case, the company will have to file notice of the change with the registrar of companies, together with a statement that the change has been made in accordance with the rules in the articles.

2.2.1.6 *Monitoring company and business names (see Figures 4 and 5)*

Once a company has registered and used its name, or started using a business name, it must ensure that it is aware of any new company names or business names which are registered or used, and which are similar to its own, so that it can take action to protect its name or business name.

It might make regular name checks through its advisers or search agents, or subscribe to a name-watching service, as well as using the grapevine. The companies' index, trade mark registrations and the web can all be monitored.

Monitoring is likely to become even more important from 1 October 2008, when new 'company name adjudicators' will be introduced under the Companies Act 2006. When that happens, any individual or person who believes that an existing company name:

- is the same as a name associated with him, and in which he has goodwill; or

- is sufficiently similar to such a name as to be likely to mislead by suggesting a connection between the company and him

can object to a company names adjudicator who will decide whether or not to uphold the objection. The objector does not need to have registered the same, or a similar limited company name himself – objections can be made by a sole trader or a partnership, for example.

These new rights mean that businesses, including unincorporated businesses, are likely to be much more diligent in monitoring the companies' index for new company names that are the same as, or similar to, their own, so they can object to them as early as possible. So promoters of proposed new companies will also need to be more diligent when checking that their proposed names are not already being used by another person.

The new rules set out the circumstances in which the objection will be upheld, and when it will not. In effect, if the name has been registered in good faith, the adjudicator will not order a change of name – for example, if it was registered before the objector started using the same or a similar name for his activities, or the company has incurred substantial start-up costs that tend to show it is a genuine trading company. If, on the other hand, it has been registered in bad faith – for example, to prevent the objector from registering the name, or to damage the objector's business by confusing the public – the adjudicator is likely to uphold the objection.

If the objection is upheld, the company is ordered to change its name before a date set by the adjudicator. In default, the adjudicator can choose a new name for the company.

There will be rules about initiating an objection, procedures, adjudication fees, service of documents by the parties on each other, how evidence is to be given, payment of the winning party's costs by the loser and how and when to appeal.

The adjudicator will have to publicise his decision, and his reasons for it, by publishing them on his website within 90 days of making it, or by 'such other means as appear to him to be appropriate'.

2.2.1.7   Company identity theft

A common scam is for fraudsters to change a company's records at Companies House and then run up credit in its name. First, the rogue checks the company's credit rating. If it's good, the rogue files forms at Companies House notifying appointment of a fictitious new director and a new registered office address for the company.

The registrar of companies (who cannot check that all these documents are genuine, and is not obliged to by law) registers them. The rogue is now able to order high-value goods and services on credit, using false ID to pretend he is a director of the company. To a third party searching at Companies House, all seems in order. The rogue disappears, without paying.

It is medium-sized and smaller businesses that are targeted with this scam. Here are the three protective measures recommended by the police and Companies House:

2.2.1.7.1   Check the company's record at Companies House frequently

To make sure it hasn't been targeted, a company can check its registered office online at any time, free of charge, on the Companies House website (www.companieshouse.gov.uk), using the WebCheck service.

Keying in the company name or number, and clicking 'search', and then clicking on the company's registered number when it appears, gives access to registered office and other details, which can then be checked to ensure they have not been changed without the company's knowledge.

Click 'Order information on this company' to buy a 'directors' appointment report' for £1, which will provide the directors' details, using secure online credit card payment. These details can then be checked to ensure that no fictitious director's details have been filed without the company's knowledge.

2.2.1.7.2   File electronically

A company can pre-empt fraudsters by signing up to the Companies House PROOF service on its website. This online filing scheme for company documents means that certain information (including changes in directors and registered office) can only be filed electronically. Paper forms will be rejected. Each company is given a user name and password, authentication code and recognised email address to use to file documents electronically. The fraudsters do not have access to these, so the public record cannot be tampered with. The service is free.

2.2.1.7.3   Delegate monitoring

Companies that subscribe to the Companies House Direct online search service for £5 per month can monitor their public record (and, if they want, those of competitors, customers or business partners) for 50p per company per year. Companies House will notify the company by email whenever a document is received and filed against it.

If the company filed that document, it can ignore the email and there is no charge. If it did not, it is on alert that a fraudster may be at work, and can download and pay for an image of the document, to see what has been filed.

2.3   TAKING LEGAL ACTION ***

The bringing or defending of any objection or action can involve substantial expense. Professional advice will always be required, and it will be necessary to explore and co-ordinate all possible legal remedies. For example, the objection and/or action may also give rise to possible action for breach of other 'intellectual property rights' such as copyrights, designs or patents, and all remedies pursued should be co-ordinated if they are to be achieved.

2.3.1   Domicile

The second clause in the memorandum states where the registered office of the company is to be located. It should state either England and Wales, Scotland or Northern Ireland and not the actual address of the registered office. This determines which registrar of companies has jurisdiction over the company, and where it sends information about itself. For example, a company which states that its registered office is to be located in England and Wales is said to be domiciled there and will be subject to the rules of the registrar of companies in Cardiff. Once the domicile of a company has been chosen, it cannot be changed. For example, the registered office of a company registered in Scotland must be in Scotland. It cannot be changed to an address in, for example, England and Wales or Northern Ireland. Of course, there are no constraints on a company trading in other jurisdictions, irrespective of where it is registered, provided it complies with applicable laws in those other jurisdictions. Finally, a company domiciled in, for example, England and Wales can move its registered office freely *within* England and Wales.

It is possible for the memorandum to state that the company's registered office is to be located only in Wales, rather than England and Wales. This permits the company to deliver some documents to the registrar of companies in Welsh. This clause in the memorandum cannot be changed.

In 2009, when the function and format of the memorandum of association changes, the company's domicile will instead be included in the new application form that must be filed with the registrar of companies when forming a new company.

2.3.2 The objects and powers

The Companies Acts currently require a company to state its objects – the activities for which it was incorporated. This statement of objects must appear in the memorandum. Whilst the company is recognised as a person in law, it must not carry on any activity which is not specified in this statement. It is the shareholders who decide upon the contents of the memorandum in this respect.

To ensure that companies can do everything an individual can do, shareholders have traditionally allowed their companies to have a very long statement of objects, divided into many paragraphs. These are called 'objects clauses'. It has also been the practice to set out, in the same statement, all of the ancillary and subsidiary transactions which a company may need to carry out in order to achieve its objects. For example, the power for the company to borrow money, sell parts of its business, and buy new businesses. The clauses setting out these transactions are called the company's 'powers'. The maxim has always been 'if in doubt, put it in'. However, company legislation now contains provisions which mean that objects and powers of modern companies may be far shorter. However, professional advice is still required when drafting an object or powers, since the new rules are full of technical traps for the unwary. Whether modern or not, before a company enters into any new or unusual transaction, the objects and powers must be checked and, if necessary, legal advice sought, to ensure that they cover the proposed transaction. In any event, a company should ensure that its objects and powers are reviewed periodically by its professional advisers, to ensure that it continues to cover the company's activities – say every 2 years, and certainly upon the introduction of new legislation affecting companies.

A company may change its objects and powers by special resolution of its shareholders. Any change takes effect immediately upon passing of the resolution.

Within 15 days of the resolution being passed, a copy of it, and a reprint of the memorandum showing the changes must be lodged with the registrar of companies.

When the function and format of the memorandum of association changes in 2009, a new company will no longer have objects and powers in its memorandum. Instead, the new rules will say that a new company's

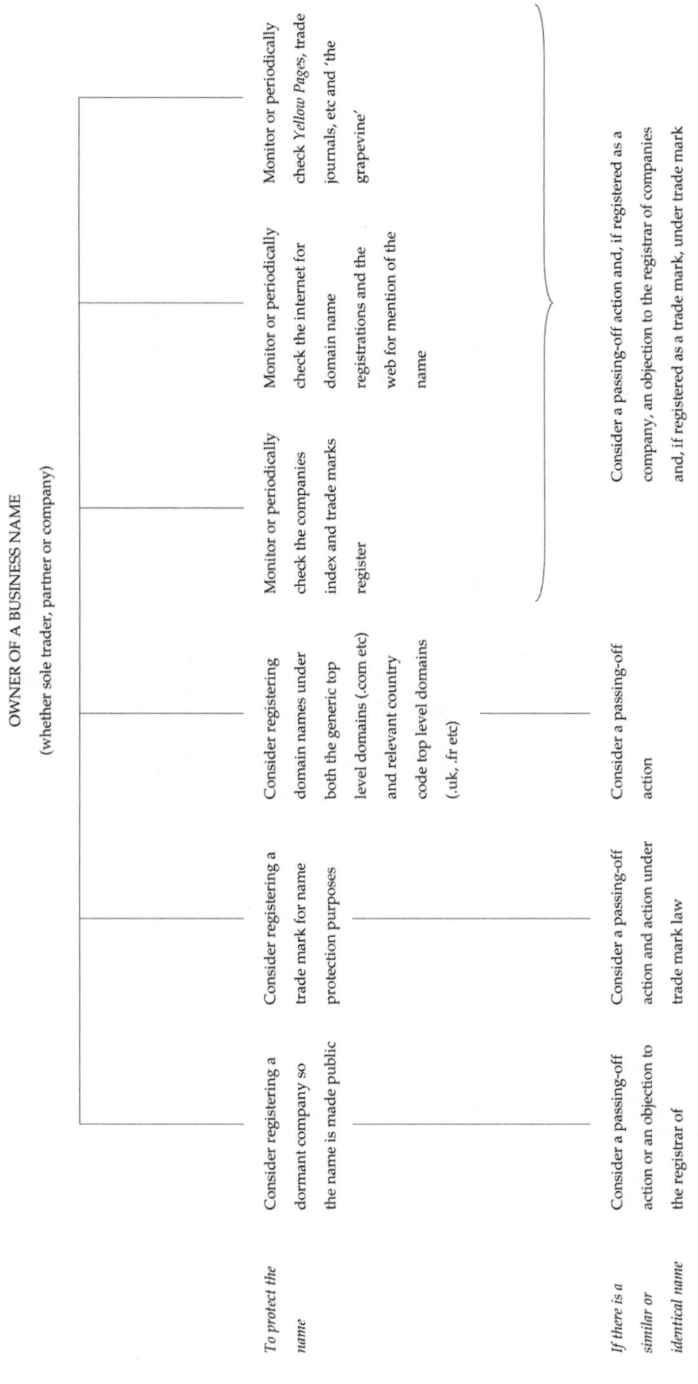

OWNER OF A BUSINESS NAME
(whether sole trader, partner or company)

To protect the name

- Consider registering a dormant company so the name is made public
- Consider registering a trade mark for name protection purposes
- Consider registering domain names under both the generic top level domains (.com etc) and relevant country code top level domains (.uk, .fr etc)
- Monitor or periodically check the companies index and trade marks register
- Monitor or periodically check the internet for domain name registrations and the web for mention of the name
- Monitor or periodically check *Yellow Pages*, trade journals, etc and 'the grapevine'

If there is a similar or identical name

- Consider a passing-off action or an objection to the registrar of companies
- Consider a passing-off action and action under trade mark law
- Consider a passing-off action
- Consider a passing-off action and, if registered as a company, an objection to the registrar of companies and, if registered as a trade mark, under trade mark law

Figure 4 – Business name

COMPANY NAME

To protect the name	Fact of registration on the companies index makes the name public	Consider registering a trade mark for name protection purposes	Consider registering domain names under both the generic top level domains (.com etc) and relevant country code top level domains (.uk, .fr etc)	Monitor or periodically check the companies index and trade marks register	Monitor or periodically check the internet for domain name registrations and the web for mention of the name	Monitor or periodically check *Yellow Pages*, trade journals, etc and 'the grapevine'

| If there is a similar or identical name | Consider a passing-off action or an objection to the registrar of companies | Consider a passing-off action and action under trade mark law | Consider a passing-off action | | Consider a passing-off action, an objection to the registrar of companies and, if registered as a trade mark, under trade mark law | |

Figure 5 – Company name

objects and powers are unrestricted – so it can carry on any activity that is lawful, unless the company's articles of association specifically say that it cannot.

Existing companies, that already have objects clauses and powers in their memorandum of association, will be treated as if these were set out in their articles of association – that is, as if they were provisions included in the articles under the new rules, to restrict the company's activities.

As 2009 approaches, existing companies will need to decide whether they will alter their articles when the changes occur. Many will decide that the objects and powers in their memorandum – drafted to empower the company to do things – will not work as clauses that restrict what the company can do. They will argue that, if a shareholder decides to bring a court case on grounds that the company is carrying on an activity that is not authorised by its objects and powers, it will be very hard to predict how the court will interpret such clauses.

Companies are therefore likely to decide either that they do not want any restrictions at all, or that the provisions need to be redrafted specifically as restrictive clauses, so the shareholders can be as sure as they can be that they will be interpreted in the way they want if there is a dispute over whether the company can carry out a particular activity, or is restricted from doing so.

2.3.3 Statement of liability

The memorandum of every company must state that the liability of the shareholders of the company is limited. A prospective company which does not have such a statement in its memorandum will be refused registration.

This clause cannot be changed unless the company re-registers as an unlimited liability company which is a very unusual type of company.

In 2009, when the function and format of the memorandum of association changes, the company's domicile will instead be included in the new application form that must be filed with the registrar of companies when forming a new company.

2.3.4 Authorised share capital

Every company is required to state in its memorandum the amount of its authorised share capital. Authorised share capital is sometimes called nominal capital. The amount of the company's initial authorised share capital should be sufficient to enable the company to sell shares to raise the money it needs to carry on business in the future. For example, if it is anticipated that a company will need £1,000, after borrowing, in order to carry on business, it should have an authorised share capital of at least £1,000. Of course, it will be easier for the company to sell 1,000 shares of £1 each than say four shares of £250 each, so shares are usually 'denominated' as £1 shares.

A company may be incorporated with an authorised share capital of an amount which is greater than the amount it needs to raise for its initial working capital. After issuing sufficient shares to satisfy that need, it will have a number of unissued shares, which the directors can hold in reserve for some future issue. This means that they will be able to make future issues without going back to the shareholders and asking them to increase the authorised share capital to create more shares.

This may be appropriate if the company knows that it may need to issue more shares in the future – for example, if it has granted options to its directors or employees whereby they are entitled to buy the company's shares in the future, the company may retain sufficient unissued shares in its authorised capital to enable those options to be satisfied when they are exercised.

The statement must also state the number of shares in the authorised share capital, and the nominal (or par) value of each share. Although the nominal value of each share is usually £1, it may be any figure. Some shares may be of one nominal value and others of another, but this is unusual. The importance of the nominal value of a share is that no share may be sold by the company for less than its nominal value.

Payment for a share need not be made immediately. It may be deferred for as long as the company and shareholder agree. However, most private companies require immediate payment when they sell the shares. If the company and the shareholder agree, payment may also be made in any currency in an amount calculated according to the exchange rate at the date of payment.

A company's share capital does not need to be in pounds sterling. It may be denominated in any currency. However, once a share has been issued, it cannot be changed to a nominal value in another currency. The company's annual accounts need not be prepared in the currency of the company's share capital.

The authorised share capital of the company may be sold by the company until it is exhausted. A share sold by a company is said to be issued, or allotted. Directors usually deal with the issue of shares – although they must have a specific authority from the shareholders to do so, that has to be renewed periodically (see Chapter 3). The specific authority is either included in the company's articles of association, or given by ordinary resolution of the shareholders. Any change to the articles must be notified to the registrar of companies in any event. If the authority is given by ordinary resolution, the resolution must be filed with the registrar of companies within 15 days.

If further authorised share capital is required, the directors must ask the company's shareholders to increase the authorised share capital by a further sum, and specify the number and nominal value of the new shares. This is done by ordinary resolution.

A copy of this resolution must be lodged with the registrar of companies, together with an official form, within 15 days after it is passed.

A private company may operate with only one share in issue – the minimum number required by law. There is no need to issue all of the authorised share capital, or even a major proportion of it, provided at least one share has been issued. The same is not true of public companies which must be formed with an issued capital of at least two shares, and may not trade or borrow money unless the registrar of companies has certified that they have a minimum issued share capital of £50,000. See Chapter 1 in this respect. A company may have an authorised share capital divided into classes.

Up to four persons may buy a share jointly. It is the first named in the company's register of shareholders who will be entitled to receive notices, dividends, etc, in respect of the jointly held share, so the secretary of the company must be sure that the register is made up in accordance with the wishes of the joint shareholders.

New rules due in October 2009 will abolish the requirement for companies to have an authorised share capital stated in their memorandum of association. Consequently, the current company law rules for increasing a company's authorised share capital by ordinary resolution, including the requirement to lodge the relevant ordinary resolution, and the official form, notifying the registrar of companies of the increase, will also be abolished.

At the same time, the requirement for directors to go back to the shareholders periodically for an authority to allot new shares will also be abolished, provided all the company's shares have the same rights – that, in the jargon, the company has only one class of shares.

The overall effect will be that directors of a private company with only one class of shares will no longer need to work out how many shares to keep 'in reserve' in the authorised share capital. They will simply be able to issue new shares whenever they like, and without the need for specific authority from the shareholders.

(At the same time, the rules will be changed to allow public companies to be formed with an issued capital of only one share, as a private company can now. The rule saying a public company must not trade or borrow money unless it has an issued share capital of at least £50,000 will remain, but will be extended so that its share capital can be the euro equivalent of £50,000.)

2.4   THE ARTICLES OF ASSOCIATION AND TABLE A ***

The memorandum and articles are two quite separate documents, even though they are usually bound together.

The articles of association of the company are its rules and regulations. The contents of the articles are decided by the shareholders. The articles fix the manner in which the directors and shareholders of the company are to act, both amongst themselves and in relation to each other. Technically, the articles are treated as a contract between each shareholder and the company, so that breach of the articles may be treated as a breach of contract. Of course, matters which are already regulated by the Companies Acts do not need to be dealt with in the articles.

For example, the Companies Acts say that a company may remove a director by ordinary resolution of the shareholders, provided a special procedure is followed (see Chapter 16). Clauses dealing with removal of directors do not therefore need to be regulated by the articles. However, matters not dealt with by the Companies Acts may be regulated by the articles.

If a company does not lodge articles with the registrar of companies, Table A applies as if it were the articles of the company, by default. Table A is a model set of articles. Its contents are decided by the Secretary of State for Trade and Industry. A copy of the current Table A for private companies incorporated in Great Britain appears at Appendix C. The Table A for Northern Ireland is virtually identical.

However, Table A applies, in default, as the articles of any company limited by shares that does not file its own articles of association with the registrar of companies. Consequently, Table A is very widely drafted. Shareholders of most private companies will not want every provision of Table A to apply. They will want to make alterations and additions to Table A, to suit their particular needs and circumstances. The Companies Acts allow shareholders of a company to do this.

One way of doing this is to file with the registrar a set of articles which say that Table A shall not apply to the company at all. A company may then file articles which completely replace Table A with regulations acceptable to its shareholders.

However, most companies will find that Table A is largely satisfactory, and that only a few changes to it are necessary. It is therefore customary to file articles which begin with a clause which says that Table A applies 'except as follows'. There then follows a set of articles which vary or exclude certain provisions of Table A from applying. The rest of Table A continues to apply. The vast majority of companies do this.

Directors and shareholders of companies with articles drafted in this way will need to cross-refer from their articles to Table A. Most companies have a copy of Table A bound into the back of the articles so that it is easy to cross-refer. If not, copies of Table A are available from the Stationery Office for a small fee.

A company's first articles are usually lodged, with the other formation details, with the registrar of companies.

A company may alter its articles, or adopt a whole new set, by special resolution of the shareholders. A copy of the altered or new articles must be filed with the registrar of companies within 15 days after the alteration or adoption. A company need not file a copy of Table A.

Great care should be taken when cross-referring from a company's articles to Table A. This is because there have been around a dozen different versions of Table A; which applies to a particular company will depend upon the circumstances. As a general rule, any Table A which originally applied to the company when it was formed will continue to apply, no matter how old the company is, or how many subsequent versions of Table A have been introduced since, unless the company specifically decides otherwise by a special resolution of the shareholders. If in any doubt, take professional advice.

It is good practice to ensure that articles of association are reviewed by professional advisers periodically – say every two years and certainly upon the introduction of new legislation affecting companies. There may be very good reasons for altering the articles or adopting new articles, to take advantage of powers under new legislation and case law, and to take account of current business practice.

Some of the matters ordinarily dealt with in articles are:

(1) the manner in which shares are to be issued;

(2) the manner in which shares may be transferred;

(3) the manner in which notices are given to and by the company;

(4) directors' powers to vote on matters in which they have a personal interest;

(5) the circumstances in which directors must vacate office, or may be removed;

(6) the extent to which directors and other officers of the company may be indemnified by the company if they make mistakes;

(7) the chairman's casting vote.

The articles provide a balance between the shareholders and the directors. Shareholders could provide in the articles that they must take every decision themselves, but ordinarily they will delegate as much of the day-to-day running of the business of the company to the directors as they can.

For matters which they cannot delegate, see Chapter 16.

From October 2009, new 'default' articles of association will be brought into force. The form they will take has not yet, at the date of publication, been decided. However, it is fairly certain that the name 'Table A' will be dropped, and the new default articles will be called 'model articles of association'. We are also fairly sure that there will be at least two separate model articles of association – one for public companies limited by shares, and another for private companies limited by shares (there are also likely to be separate model form articles of association for companies limited by guarantee). It is also likely that the new model articles will be shorter than Table A and, while they may not exactly be written in plain English, will contain less legal terminology.

The new model articles will apply to all new companies formed on or after 1 October 2009. It is extremely likely, however, that such companies will not want to rely on the model articles in their entirety, just as they do not want to rely on Table A in its entirety under current law. New companies will still therefore want to file articles of association with the registrar of companies which begin with a clause saying that the model articles of association apply 'except as follows', and which then vary or exclude certain provisions of the model articles from applying, just as companies do now with Table A.

As October 2009 approaches, and the contents of the new model articles of association are finalised, many existing companies are also likely to decide to update their articles of association so they are more modern, with effect from 1 October, and apply the new model articles with appropriate variations and exclusions.

2.5 THE FIRST DIRECTORS AND SECRETARY, AND INTENDED SITUATION OF REGISTERED OFFICE

The Companies Acts require that, for a company to be formed, Companies House must be sent details of the proposed directors and secretary, and the intended situation of the registered office. For the rules governing the directors and secretary of a company, see Chapter 5.

The registered office of a company is merely an address for service of legal documents. It may be an accommodation address, although it must not be a post office box number. Often it is the address of the company's accountants or solicitors. The company does not need to carry on any trading activity from its registered office address, but it must keep certain of its registers there for inspection by the public. The address must appear on all business letters and order forms of the company, and on electronic documents such as emails and the company's website.

Whatever the registered office address, the company must be sure that documents delivered to the company at that address will quickly come to the attention of the company's directors. The sort of documents served on the registered office will be writs, summonses, planning notices, and letters from the registrar of companies, threatening to strike the company from his index for failure to file returns.

If the registered office address is to be the home of a director, the secretary or a shareholder of the company, the homeowner must be very careful. There might be legal constraints on using his home for business purposes. These could be as a result of:

(1)   restrictive covenants in his title to the property, prohibiting business use;

(2)   restrictions on business use in his mortgage;

(3)   planning restrictions;

(4)   his capital gains tax position if his home is being used partly for business purposes;

(5)   his liability to local taxation.

Whilst he may argue that there is no business activity being carried on from his home, professional advice should be sought in each case.

Upon issue of the certificate of incorporation of a company, a person who has consented to act as a director in the information submitted to Companies House on the application for incorporation is automatically constituted a director of the company – no appointment or confirmation of his appointment is required after incorporation.

2.6   FORMATION PROCEDURE **

The incorporation procedure in the UK is much simpler and cheaper than in most other European countries. A solicitor, accountant or company registration agent will incorporate a new company within days. Ordinarily, all he requires is:

(1)   the official form duly completed; and

(2)   instructions on the proposed name, objects, authorised share capital, whether the company is to be registered in England and Wales, or in Scotland, and various matters related to the contents of the articles.

The solicitor, accountant or agent, will do the rest, including name-checking and providing subscribers.

If the solicitor, accountant or agent has formation software that has been approved by Companies House, and is registered with Companies House as an approved presenter, the formation details can be filed electronically. Companies House usually form companies filed electronically within 24 hours – usually far quicker than formations filed using paper forms.

From October 2009, the information to be filed with the registrar of companies to form a company will change. Those forming the company will not need to notify the registrar of its objects or its authorised share capital, as the requirement for both will be abolished. However, they will have to file slightly more information about the intended initial issued share capital of the company and the proposed first shareholder(s).

2.7   SAME-DAY INCORPORATION **

In England and Wales or Scotland, it is possible to speed the whole incorporation procedure up, so that a company may be incorporated on the same day as the documents are filed. Additional requirements for a same-day incorporation are payment of an extra fee to Companies House, choice of a name for the company which does not contain a sensitive word, and ensuring that the incorporation documents are lodged before 3pm on the proposed day of incorporation.

Same-day incorporations are not possible in Northern Ireland.

2.8   READY-MADE COMPANIES **

It is also possible to acquire what are called 'ready-made', 'off-the-shelf' or 'off-the-peg' companies, whether private or public. These are companies which have already been incorporated, but have carried on no activity whatsoever. Many solicitors and accountants carry stocks of such companies. Company registration agents certainly do. The companies are incorporated with neutral names, wide objects, standard articles, and, normally, an authorised share capital of £1,000. The subscribers and first director and secretary are employees or nominees of the solicitor, accountant or registration agents, and the registered office will be one of their trading addresses.

Upon signature of official forms by the proposed new directors and secretary in which they consent to act, and notification of new registered office address, and upon payment of a fee, the ready-made company is transferred over. If it is a private company, it is ready to trade immediately. If required, changes will be made to the company before it is transferred, such as changes to the name, authorised share capital, objects and articles – all except the change of name will take effect immediately. However, the change of name only takes effect once the appropriate shareholder resolution has been submitted to the registrar and he has issued a certificate of incorporation on change of name. It is therefore possible to acquire a private company which is ready to start trading in under half an hour, even though the company initially has a 'ready-made' name. However, same-day changes of name are possible, as discussed below. Care must always be taken to ensure that the company has not carried on any activity at all whilst it was a ready-made company. The company papers should include a certificate or declaration that the company has not traded.

Whilst a private company is able to trade with immediate effect from the date of issue of the certificate of incorporation, a public company is required to obtain a further certificate, commonly called a trading certificate, before it may trade or borrow money.

A solicitor, accountant or company registration agent will advise as to the procedure to obtain a trading certificate. The certificate of incorporation is conclusive evidence that all the requirements of the Companies Acts relating to incorporation have been complied with.

2.9   SAME-DAY CHANGES OF NAME **

Whilst the name of a ready-made company cannot be changed immediately, it can be changed on a same-day basis. As with a same-day incorporation, payment of an additional fee to Companies House, choice of a new company name which does not contain a sensitive word and ensuring that the documents to change the name are lodged before 3pm will procure a change of name on the same day.

As with same-day incorporation, same-day changes of name are only possible in England and Wales or Scotland. They are not possible in Northern Ireland.

2.10 WHO WILL NEED A COPY OF THE MEMORANDUM AND ARTICLES?

A company usually has eight copies of its memorandum and articles. All or any of the following may want a copy:

(1)   the auditor or other accountant to the company;

(2)   the solicitor;

(3)   the bank;

(4)   HM Revenue and Customs;

(5)   the company secretary;

(6)   each director;

(7)   each shareholder.

2.11   REGISTERS *

A private company *must* keep the following registers:

(1)   register of directors;

(2)   register of secretaries;

(3)   register of shareholders;

(4)   register of charges (mortgages).

All of these are open to public inspection, although the company may charge a (very small) fee in certain circumstances, for making them available. Invariably, this fee is waived.

It will usually also keep a register of applications for and allotments of shares, a register of share transfers, and a register of dealings, but these are not required under the Companies Acts, and are not open to public inspection.

From October 2009 a private company will also have to keep a register of directors' residential addresses.

2.12 FILING REQUIREMENTS

Many transactions or events generate a requirement to file information (as a hard copy document or statutory form or, in many instances, electronically) at Companies House within a certain time limit. The time limit varies according to the transaction or event. In a few cases, the validity of the transaction or event is dependent on the filing. The filing requirements relating to the transactions and events covered by this book are dealt with in the text.

Whichever document or form is being filed in hard-copy format, the registry will microfilm it for the company's public file, which means that it must be capable of being identified as relevant to the company and capable of being read when the microfilm is magnified. The following registry guidelines should be observed:

(1) use black ink or type;

(2) use bold lettering;

(3) do not file carbon copies;

(4) do not use dot matrix printers to produce documents for filing;

(5) remember that photocopies will result in grey shades which do not transfer well to microfilm records;

(6) always include the company number in a prominent position on the first page, preferably top right-hand corner;

(7) ensure pages are white A4, with a matt finish;

(8) margins should not be less than 10 mm or, if the document is bound, 20 mm;

(9) letters and numbers should not be less than 1.8 mm high, and should have a line width of not less than 0.25 mm.

If information is to be filed electronically rather than on paper forms – new appointments, changes in particulars like addresses, notification of cessation of office, annual returns, dormant company accounts (see Chapter 9) and a number of other filings can be made electronically – this can be done via the Webfiling service at www.companieshouse.gov.uk.

Alternatively, your solicitor, accountant or the company secretary may use company secretarial software that enables him to file information electronically.

Currently, the information that can be filed electronically is fairly limited, but Companies House is committed both to extending the range of information that can be filed electronically, and making electronic filing more accessible.

2.13   FIRST BOARD MEETING *

It is clear that a company need not carry on a business for days, months – even years after its incorporation. Some companies are incorporated solely in order to protect a name, and never carry on a business. See Chapter 1 for the rules as to such dormant companies.

However, before a company starts trading, it will ordinarily want to deal with certain administrative matters. For example, it would be unusual if the company did not wish to open a bank account before trading. The professional adviser or company registration agent should provide an agenda and specimen minutes for a meeting of the board of directors at which these administrative matters may be dealt with.

CHAPTER 3

SHARES AND SHAREHOLDERS IN A PRIVATE COMPANY

3.1 SHARES

As has been seen, the basic structure of a company is that shareholders put money in by buying shares, and then appoint directors who manage the business on behalf of the company.

Shares give shareholders rights which are usually set out in the articles. Lawyers will often describe a share as 'a bundle of rights'.

Most companies have one class of share only. Usually all shares have equal rights. Share rights will usually cover the right to vote at shareholders' meetings, the right to a dividend if there are sufficient profits, the right to divide the company's surplus money (once it has sold all its property, paid its debts and discharged its liabilities) amongst themselves if it is wound up, and equal rights with other shareholders on issue or transfer of all shares.

3.2 SHAREHOLDERS

Any person can be a shareholder, whether an individual or a company, and irrespective of nationality, age or tax status. Persons under 18 years old may be shareholders, although this can have awkward consequences upon sale of the shares. Advice should be taken if this is intended. More usually, shares are held by trustees in trust for the benefit of those aged under 18. However, a company may restrict who is able to own its shares in its articles, so that the articles of each company should always be checked to see if they contain any provision restricting who may be a shareholder. Shareholders of a company are sometimes called 'members' of the company.

A private company may be formed with only one shareholder, or with more. A private company with one shareholder is known as a single member company and is subject to additional rules that do not apply to multi-member companies (see **3.3**).

In contrast, a public company should never have only one shareholder. If it does, and carries on trading for more than 6 months, the sole shareholder will, if he knows he is the sole shareholder, become personally liable, jointly and severally with the company, for payment of the company's debts incurred after that 6-month period. In other words, a sole shareholder loses limited liability. (This rule will change in October 2009, when new law will come into force that allows a public company to have only one shareholder too.)

3.3   SINGLE MEMBER COMPANIES ***

A single member company is subject to special rules.

(1)   It must include a note stating that it is a single member company against the name of the single member in the register of shareholders, and of the date it became a single member company. Upon ceasing to be a single member company, a note of this fact, and the date of ceasing to be a single member company must also be made.

(2)   If the single member is also a director, it must record in writing all contracts entered into between the company and the single member, other than those entered into in the ordinary course of business.

(3)   All informal decisions of the single member not recorded as minutes of a meeting of the single member or as a resolution in writing in lieu of a meeting, must be recorded in writing.

The articles of association of a company which is to operate as a single member company may need to contain special provisions – this is particularly the case if the single member is also to be the sole director of the company. In that instance, the question of how the shareholder's shares will transmit under his will (or his intestacy, if he does not leave a will) must be dealt with if the company is not to grind to a complete halt on the single member's death. If, as will often be the case in a private company:

•   the sole shareholder is also the only director; and

•   the articles say that a deceased shareholder's personal representatives (ie the persons appointed by him as his executors if he has left a will, or his closest relatives who are entitled to deal with his affairs after his death under the intestacy rules if he has not) are unable to transfer his shares to, for example, the beneficiaries under his will without consent of the directors,

then a lacuna occurs because, as a result of the death, the company is without any directors to consent to the transfer. There is no board to appoint a new director, nor the usual powers of the shareholders to appoint a new director because the company has no shareholders. Ordinarily, the personal representatives of a deceased shareholder have no right to vote at general meetings, so they cannot make the appointment.

However, to avoid this lacuna, in the event of the death of a sole shareholder who was also the sole director, but in no other circumstances, it is prudent to have articles which allow the personal representatives to appoint a new director or directors by a written notice of appointment, served on the company at its registered office, but confer upon them no other power to vote. The new board may then deal with any application to transfer shares submitted by the personal representatives in the usual way.

The rule against a sole director also being the secretary continues to apply to single member companies with a sole director – whilst one person may be the single shareholder and the sole director, another person must act as secretary. From April 2008, however, a private company can decide not to have a company secretary. This rule will not be relevant to companies that so decide.

3.4   ISSUING SHARES **

Professional advice will be required in respect of every aspect of issuing shares – the company should involve the adviser at the very outset. The following paragraphs provide an indication of some important considerations. It must be recognised that the duties of directors (for example, to always act to promote the long-term success of the company, and to act within the company's constitution and powers, which includes exercising their powers for a 'proper purpose' – that is, in furtherance of the reason for which they were given those powers by the shareholders – see Chapter 5) are particularly important when the directors propose to issue shares. Issuing new shares is not, for example, a device that a majority shareholder can deploy to ensure that his company remains under his control.

Shares may be issued for cash (see Figure 6), or non-cash payment, including services, but they must never be issued 'at a discount'. This means that they cannot be issued for less than their nominal value. The nominal value of a share is its 'face' value – for example, the nominal value of a share in a company that has issued 1,000 shares of £1 each is £1. The nominal value of the share remains the same, even if the price at which the share could be sold to a new shareholder is more (or less) than £1.

Alternatively, shares may be issued at a premium. A premium is the amount by which the sum that a shareholder is prepared to pay the company for the newly issued share exceeds its nominal value. For example, a company which is about to pay a big dividend might find that someone is willing to buy its £1 shares for more than £1 – say, £1.75. If so, it may decide to issue the share at a premium of 75p. It is up to the company and the shareholder to agree the price for the shares, and when the shares will be paid for. However, it is unusual to find shares in a private company which are not paid for in full (including any premium) immediately on issue. Shares which have been paid for in full are called 'fully-paid shares'. Shares which have not yet been paid for will be either 'nil-paid shares' or 'partly-paid shares'.

Currently, before shares may be issued, the company must have sufficient unissued shares in its authorised share capital. If it does not, it will need to increase its authorised share capital by ordinary resolution of shareholders. A shareholders' meeting may need to be called to deal with this.

This rule will change in October 2009, when the concept of 'authorised share capital' will be abolished. As new companies will no longer have an authorised share capital, the directors will no longer need to check that there are sufficient unissued shares in the company's authorised share capital before they make a fresh share issue.

For existing companies, all of which already have an authorised share capital, transitional arrangements are planned, which say that the authorised share capital of an existing company should continue to act as a restriction on the shares that it can allot, as if such a restriction were included in the company's articles. The transitional arrangements will allow shareholders of such companies to alter their articles to remove this notional restriction by ordinary resolution, rather than by the special resolution that is normally required for a change to a company's articles. As October 2009 approaches, existing companies will need legal advice on whether they should pass such a resolution.

Issuing shares is so important to shareholders that the Companies Acts currently say that the issue of shares must be expressly delegated to directors by the shareholders.

For the directors to issue shares, they must therefore have an express authority to do so from the shareholders. Often the authority is in the articles, but it may also be given by ordinary resolution of the shareholders. Legal advice on an issue of shares should always include confirmation that the directors are authorised by the shareholders to deal with the issue of shares, whether in the articles, or by ordinary resolution. If the directors do not have such an authority, a shareholders' meeting may need to be called to give them this authority.

Again, this rule is due to change in 2009. From 1 October 2009, the directors of a private company that has only one class of shares may allot shares, except to the extent that the articles of the company prohibit them from doing so. Shares are of one class if the rights attached to them are the same in all respects.

For such companies, the current rules saying directors may not allot shares unless authorised to do so by ordinary resolution of the shareholders, or by the company's articles, will no longer apply. Combined with the fact that the requirement for an authorised share capital has been abolished, this means that the directors of a private company with one class of share have greater freedom than previously to allot shares, without going back to the shareholders.

For new companies that are not private, or are private but have more than one class of share, the current rules under which the directors must have an express authority to allot shares will continue to apply.

For existing companies, whose shareholders have already given the directors authority to allot shares, transitional provisions are likely to say that that existing authority will continue but, on its expiry, directors of a private company with only one class of shares will then be able to allot shares freely, subject to any other restriction in the articles. Existing companies will need legal advice on whether to include any such restriction as the date for expiry of the existing authority approaches.

Once the directors of the company are sure that they have authority to issue shares from the shareholders, they must, currently, check to see whether they are required to issue those shares in any special way. For example, the Companies Acts, or the company's articles, or a mixture of both, may state that the directors cannot issue shares to whoever they want. Often they must first offer them to existing shareholders in proportion to the number of shares held by them. Such rights in favour of existing shareholders are called 'pre-emption rights'.

Whatever the case, the provisions of the articles, or the Acts, or a combination of the two, must be strictly observed. Professional advice will always be required.

Shares are usually issued for cash payment. If they are offered to the existing shareholders, in proportion to their existing shares in return for cash, the issue is called a 'rights issue'.

Almost as common is a 'bonus issue'. This is sometimes called a 'scrip issue' or a 'capitalisation'. The last is the most accurate description.

A bonus issue occurs when a company has built up profits and reserves. Instead of paying the profits out as dividend, the shareholders are offered new shares in the company, on the basis that the shareholder need not pay for them. The profits which have built up in the company will be used to pay for the shares instead.

On a bonus issue of 1,000 shares of £1 the company's balance sheet will alter from this:

issued share capital	£1,000
profit and loss account	£1,000

to this:

issued share capital	£2,000
profit and loss account	nil

The company benefits in that it keeps the money, as capital, rather than having to pay it out as dividend, and the shareholders benefit in that they acquire shares without having to find the money to pay for them. In effect, profits have been 'capitalised' into share capital.

In fact, it is not only profits, but also share premium account, capital redemption reserve and revaluation reserve which may be used to pay for a bonus issue.

However, the procedural and tax aspects of a bonus issue mean that professional advice is particularly important.

Whilst not directly relevant to the types of company contemplated by this book, mention needs to be made here of the practice of many Stock Exchange companies of offering 'scrip dividends'. A scrip dividend occurs when shareholders of a company are offered the option to subscribe for further shares in the company, without payment, of a value equivalent to the value of all, or part of a dividend which the company will otherwise pay to them. Whilst there are similarities between a bonus issue and a scrip dividend, the two are, legally, quite different transactions.

It is also quite possible for shares to be issued in return for a non-cash payment. An example of this is the sale to a company of a business formerly carried on by partners in return for shares in the company.

Shares are sometimes offered to existing shareholders on 'renounceable letters of allotment'. This means that a shareholder is given the option of asking the company to issue the shares not to him but to some other person. He does this by completing part of the letter of allotment accordingly, and asking the other person to complete the remainder of it, for return to the company within the time-limit for accepting the offer.

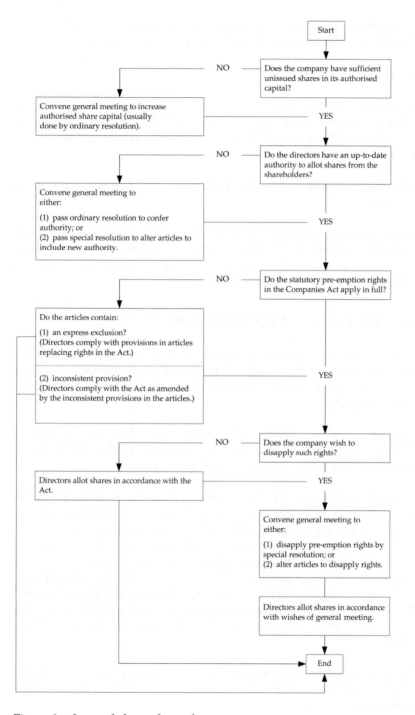

Figure 6 – Issue of shares for cash

A 'renunciation' of shares is treated for some purposes as if it were a transfer of shares by the shareholder to another person, so that for example, the company's transfer articles, or prohibitions on transfer in a shareholders' agreement will apply.

If a shareholder does renounce shares to another person, the name of that other person will go straight into the company's registers, and on the official form (Return of Allotments) filed with Companies House when the shares are issued.

Special rules apply for shares issued under an employee share option scheme.

Every time new shares are issued, the registrar of companies must be told, and, if the payment for the shares is not cash, stamp duty may be payable by the company on the property transferred to it. The company's professional adviser will deal with this aspect.

3.5   REGISTERS AND DISCLOSURE **

Every time a share is issued, it is vital to make the necessary entries in the company's registers. The register of shareholders (or members) is the most important register since it is evidence of the identity of the shareholders of the company.

The register of shareholders of companies that have not yet filed an annual return made up to a date on or after 1 October 2007 with the registrar of companies, is open to public inspection.

However, if a company has filed an annual return made up to a date on or after 1 October 2007, there is no longer an automatic right for a person to inspect its register of shareholders. The intention behind this new rule is that the addresses of a company's shareholders should be protected, to prevent improper use by direct marketing companies, for example, and it should be read in conjunction with the proposal that private companies will, at some stage in the future, no longer file a list of shareholders with their annual return at Companies House, nor disclose details of the new shareholders when notifying Companies House of the allotment of new shares.

The new rule says that a person inspecting the register, or requiring a copy of it, or any part of it, must make a written request to that effect, containing:

- their name and address;

- the purpose for which the information will be used; and

- whether the information will be disclosed to any third party.

If the search is on behalf of a company, they must provide the name and address of the person in the company responsible for making the request on its behalf. If the request says they will disclose the information to a third party, they must give the name of the third party, their address and the purpose for which the information is to be used.

The company must comply within five working days (previously ten) unless it is concerned about the purpose for which the information will be used. If it is, the new law allows it to refer the request to a court within five working days on the ground that the inspection or copies are not sought for a 'proper purpose'. The application must be notified to the person making the request.

There is no statutory definition in the new law of what constitutes a 'proper purpose', but the Institute of Chartered Secretaries and Administrators has produced a useful guide 'ICSA Guidance on Access to the Register of Members', which can be downloaded free at http://www.companiesact.org.uk/icsa-guidance-to-the-act.html.   For example, any purpose that involves communicating with the shareholders in their capacity as shareholders (such as to ask them if they wish to exercise their statutory right to require the directors of the company to call a shareholders' meeting to consider a particular resolution) will almost invariably be a proper purpose, and so will an inspection by a professional adviser such as a lawyer or stockbroker acting for a shareholder client (or his estate, if he has died).

If the application fails, or is discontinued, the company must immediately comply with the request.

If it succeeds, and it appears to the court that the company may receive further similar requests for a purpose that it has already decided is not a proper purpose, whether from the same person, or anyone else, it may order that the company need not comply with those requests either. The order must contain appropriate provisions to identify the requests to which it will apply.

The new law includes a new offence on the part of the person making the request to inspect and/or copy the register, of knowingly or recklessly making a statement that is misleading, false or deceptive in a material particular when requesting access to information.

From the company's perspective, there is also a new offence of disclosing information from the company's register of shareholders to another person when knowing or having reason to suspect that the information will not be used for a proper purpose. It is also possible that disclosing information other than for a proper purpose could breach data protection law – which could, theoretically, lead to an unlimited fine.

Companies that do not already have one should ask their legal advisers to draft a policy or procedure for dealing with requests to inspect their register of shareholders, including guidance on what the company will treat as a proper purpose, and what it will not, and when legal advice should be taken, so as to allow them to fulfil their legal obligations within the five-day time limit.

The new law also requires the company to advise anyone inspecting the register of shareholders:

• whether it is up-to-date and, if not, the date to which it is up-to-date; and

• of any transactions that have yet to be entered into it.

In unusual circumstances, where shares are issued to a director or a person connected with him, and the company is receiving a non-cash payment of a substantial value, the transaction may need to be approved by the shareholders in general meeting before it may go ahead. Such a transaction is called 'a substantial property transaction involving directors'. These rules were introduced to stop rogue directors buying assets from their company at an undervalue or selling assets to their company at an overvalue. However, they sometimes also apply when, for example, two or more partners transfer their business to a company, which they have set up for the purpose. In return the company issues them with shares. If they are directors, and the partnership business is large enough, this may be a substantial property transaction. The company's professional adviser will ensure that the procedural requirements are dealt with.

3.6   SHARE CERTIFICATES *

Every time shares are issued, the company should issue share certificates within 2 months, to the holders of the new issued shares. Share certificates should be properly executed in accordance with the articles and the companies' legislation of each of England and Wales, Scotland or Northern Ireland. Prior to the rules introduced in 1989 and 1990 respectively, share certificates of English and Northern Irish companies always had to be sealed. Now companies do not have to have a seal. If the company has a seal, and decides to use it in respect of the share certificates, English and Northern Irish law requires that the certificates should be sealed and the seal countersigned in accordance with the company's articles. Otherwise the new methods of execution introduced for companies which opt not to have a common seal or, if they have one, opt not to use it, should be followed.

For documents executed before 6 April 2008, the signatures of two officers are always required.

However, from 6 April 2008, new rules provide that documents may be executed by a company either under its common seal (if it has one) or by:

- two authorised signatories; or

- a director of the company in the presence of a witness who attests the signature.

For these purposes, an authorised signatory means a director of the company, the secretary or any joint secretary.

Scottish law has never required share certificates to be sealed, so they may simply be signed by two signatories, each of whom may be either an officer or an authorised person. However, advice should always be sought in relation to execution of documents under Scottish laws as the difficulties inherent in this complex area of law have been compounded by inadequate legislative drafting and consequent repeal and re-enactment of the rules. Not only are the rules complex but the current version of them is hard to find!

3.7   CLASSES OF SHARE **

It is often appropriate to have two or more different classes of share. Each class of share will carry different rights. Such rights are normally set out in the company's articles, but they need not be (unless they are rights to redeem the shares, in which case they must currently appear in the articles – although from October 2009, this will no longer be necessary). Wherever they are set out, they must appear on the company's public record at Companies House. If they are in the articles, they will appear at Companies House in any event. If not, they must be set out on an official form, which is filed instead.

A company will ordinarily start out with only one class of share. These will carry equal rights to vote at shareholders' meetings, and a right to receive a dividend if the company has enough profit to pay one. On a winding up, each share will carry the right to a portion of any money left over after the company has paid off the costs of the winding up and any other debts and liabilities it has. The more shares a shareholder has bought, the more votes, dividend and money in a winding up he will be entitled to. He is being rewarded for having put his money into the company by buying its shares. Often there will be a requirement that, on issue of new shares, or transfer of shares already in issue, such shares must be offered to the existing shareholders, in proportion to their respective shareholdings. These rights on issue and transfer are also rights attaching to shares.

There may come a stage when it is appropriate for the company to create a second or third class of share. For example, the company may wish to raise a great deal of money very quickly, to take advantage of a business opportunity, or to sustain an anticipated growth in its business. In those circumstances, a venture capitalist may agree to provide the money. A venture capitalist is an organisation which makes a business of investing money, usually in companies carrying on a relatively small business but with bright prospects. Of course, the investment is often a risky one, so the venture capitalist will want to negotiate a good return on the investment. The venture capitalist will usually lend money to the company, and also buy its shares. A second, and sometimes a third, class of share is usually created for the venture capitalist. Venture Capital Trusts have also made such investments more attractive for the private investor.

Alternatively, a company may wish to reward its employees for their hard work. However, the existing shareholders will not wish to dilute their voting power – their control of the company. A second class of share for the employees is the answer.

Shareholders of the company will often want members of their family to hold shares in their company so they may enjoy dividends. Often such shares are for younger members of the family – who are too young to have much commercial judgment. In such circumstances, the shares might be held on trust for the youngsters. It would be imprudent to allow such shareholders too much voting power, so a new class of share is created.

The rights, and, indeed, restrictions, which could be attached to the second class of share in each case are set out below. Of course, these rights will not be appropriate in every case, and nor are they exhaustive. Professional advice will always be needed.

3.7.1   Class rights for the venture capitalist

(1)   To block any change in the company's share capital;

(2)   to a dividend in preference to the holders of any other class, up to a specified amount (often a percentage of the nominal value of each share in the class);

(3)   to a further dividend, equally with the other class of share;

(4)   to carry forward the right to a dividend if it is not paid in a particular year (a cumulative dividend);

(5)   to vote, but only if the cumulative dividend is not paid, or the company wishes to do something major, such as alter its objects or wind itself up;

(6) to redeem its shares – to cash them in and get its money back. The terms of issue usually provide for this to happen on a fixed date, or earlier, in certain circumstances;

(7) to preferential rights to surplus money if the company is wound up;

(8) to appoint a director in certain circumstances;

(9) to convert their shares into shares of a different class;

(10) to transfer their shares to other organisations in the same group as the venture capitalist.

3.7.2 Class rights for employees

(1) Not to vote in any circumstances, or to vote, but only in matters relating to employees;

(2) to dividends, equally with other classes of share;

(3) to transfer freely to members of their family, or to trustees of trusts for the benefit of members of their family; otherwise to transfer only in restricted circumstances;

(4) to offer the shares back to other shareholders, employees and their families, on cessation of employment, whether through resignation, bankruptcy or death.

Great care must be taken with employee shares. Tax benefits may be available on purchase and sale of shares, and options to buy shares by employees, if a share scheme is set up which meets the criteria for approval by HM Revenue and Customs. Professional advice is vital if such a scheme is contemplated.

3.7.3 Class rights for the family

(1) Not to vote in any circumstances;

(2) to dividends, equally with other classes of share;

(3) to transfer freely to other members of the family, or to trustees of trusts for the benefit of members of their family, or to members of the family on death. Otherwise to transfer only in restricted circumstances.

Once rights have been attached to shares, they cannot be varied or altered without the consent of the holders of the shares carrying those rights.

Ordinarily the consent of the holders of three-quarters in nominal value of the class shares is sufficient consent.

Subject to this, share rights which appear in the articles may be altered by special resolution of the shareholders of the company.

It is possible to entrench share rights so that they cannot be altered at all. However, this is dangerous, and should only be done after careful thought and professional advice.

3.8   REDEMPTION, REPURCHASE BY A COMPANY OF ITS SHARES AND REDUCTIONS IN SHARE CAPITAL ***

Once a shareholder has paid for his shares, he cannot usually ask the company to repay his money unless the company is wound up. He cannot 'cash his shares in'. However, there are three special circumstances in which he can get his money back.

3.8.1   Redemption of shares

First, the shares might be issued as redeemable shares. On redemption the shareholder gets his money back, and the redeemed shares are cancelled. Currently, the terms of redemption – when it is to occur, how much the shareholder gets back – should be set out in the articles. From October 2009, the rules will change so that the terms of redemption can be set by the directors on issue. Shares cannot be converted into redeemable shares after issue – they must be issued as redeemable shares. The shareholder must know from the outset that his shares may be redeemed and the terms upon which this will happen.

Redemption may occur at a fixed time, or at the option of the company, or of the shareholder, or both. There may be a 'long-stop date' by which redemption must take place in any event. Ordinarily, not all the redeemable shares have to be redeemed at the same time.

Redeemable shares are a useful way of attracting investors who wish to hold shares for a specific time – like a venture capitalist. Once that time has elapsed, the venture capitalist knows it will get its money back, and the company knows, for cash flow purposes, when it will need to make funds available.

A company should not issue or redeem redeemable shares without professional advice.

3.8.2 Repurchase by company of its own shares

Secondly, the company might buy its own shares back. As with a redemption, the shareholder gets his money back and the shares bought back are cancelled. The difference between a purchase and a redemption is that the terms of the purchase are agreed between the shareholder and the company at the time of the purchase, whereas the terms of redemption are fixed at the time of issue of the shares.

A purchase of its own shares can be a very useful way of persuading an awkward shareholder to relinquish his shares, or providing a retiring shareholder with a nest-egg for retirement when he can find no other buyer for his shares.

However, no purchase of own shares should take place without professional advice.

It is important to note that neither a redemption nor a purchase of own shares is carried out as a simple transfer of shares. There are specific procedures to be observed in each case.

3.8.3 Reduction of share capital

Thirdly, a company may reduce its issued share capital by a special resolution, sanctioned by a court order. This is an unusual procedure and, currently, is rarely used by private companies.

However, from October 2008, the procedure will be simplified, and include removal of the need to obtain the sanction of the court, and reductions in capital may be used more frequently then, as an alternative to a repurchase of its own shares by a company.

3.9 FINANCIAL ASSISTANCE ***

A purchase of its own shares by a company should be distinguished from a transaction which lawyers call 'financial assistance'. Financial assistance occurs when a company provides cash or some other help from its own resources to allow someone to buy its shares. A common example is where company A buys shares in company B – an acquisition. Company A borrows money from the bank to do this. Company B creates a mortgage over its property in the bank's favour as security for the borrowing. Company B is clearly giving financial assistance to company A to allow it to buy company B's shares. Of course, there are many other examples.

Public companies are pretty much prohibited from giving any sort of financial assistance, and private companies are not allowed to give financial assistance without going through a special procedure that lawyers call the 'whitewash' procedure. Professional advice will always be required.

From October 2008, however, the requirement for private companies to go through the 'whitewash' procedure is to be abolished, which will greatly reduce the legal complexities involved in the acquisition of one company by another.

One exception from the rules on financial assistance that already applies is a bonus issue. A company which issues new shares to its shareholders, but pays them up itself, from its profits, would be giving financial assistance were it not for the fact that the Companies Acts specifically exclude bonus issues from the rules prohibiting financial assistance.

3.10   TRANSFER OF SHARES **

Transfer of shares which are already in existence should be distinguished from an issue of new shares. Shareholders have a free right to transfer their shares, subject to any restrictions which they might agree to impose on themselves. Such restrictions usually appear in the company's articles, or in a shareholders' agreement. Almost all private companies will have some sort of restriction, although it will vary from company to company.

Most companies simply provide that a shareholder may only transfer a share if the directors of the company approve the transfer. Directors do not usually need to give reasons for any refusal.

Another common restriction is to say that a share may not be transferred unless it is offered to the other shareholders first. In this circumstance it is usual to provide that, if necessary, the shares are to be valued by an independent expert. This can prove costly – it is difficult to value a private company's shares – so that an independent valuation should only be used as a last resort. There may be circumstances in which shareholders want to be free to transfer shares, without the directors' consent, and without having to offer them to the other shareholders. A free transfer of this type is commonly allowed in family companies. Shareholders are given a free right to transfer shares to members of their family, or to trustees of a trust set up for the benefit of members of their family.

Of course, it is possible to combine these options. Shareholders might be given a free right to transfer to family members, family trustees, etc, but are required to precede an offer of their shares to any other person by an offer of those shares to the other shareholders.

These are just some of the most common options – the possibilities are endless. All too often, insufficient thought is given to the transfer of shares at the beginning of the company's life. The shareholders simply assume they will find a ready buyer, at the right price, acceptable to those who will remain in the company, when they want to sell. This is not always so in practice. A good professional adviser will always raise the question of transfer, and it should be given careful consideration (see Figure 7).

It is easy to make mistakes without proper advice. A common problem arises when a majority shareholder, who is obliged to offer his shares to other shareholders under the articles, finds that the other shareholders are permitted to accept only some of his shares. He is then left with a minority holding, of greatly reduced value to a purchaser, which he cannot get rid of. A professional adviser will raise issues of this sort, and advise on a solution, such as requiring the other shareholders to accept all the shares before the vendor shareholder is obliged to sell to them.

3.11   BANKRUPTCY OR DEATH OF A SHAREHOLDER **

So far, reference has been made to the transfer of shares, by a shareholder who is alive and solvent. Shareholders do, of course, die, and go bankrupt. In such circumstances, an event occurs which is called 'transmission'. It is automatic.

3.11.1   Death of a shareholder – law of England and Wales and of Northern Ireland

Dealing first with death of a shareholder under the laws of England and Wales or Northern Ireland, a shareholder who dies may leave a will, or he may die without making a will. If he dies without making a will, he is said to die 'intestate'.

A shareholder who has left a will should have named the person or persons whom he wishes to look after his property, including his shares, after his death. The will may require them either to pass his property to his heirs, sell it and give them the money, or a mixture of both. Such a person is called an 'executor' or, if female, an 'executrix'. The executors of the shareholder will apply to the High Court for a document to prove that they are executors and therefore entitled to deal with the shareholder's property. This document is called a 'grant of probate' or 'probate' for short. When dealing with the shareholders' property, the executors are said to 'administer his estate'.

If the shareholder dies intestate, he will not have said whom he wishes to look after his property, or what is to be done with it. In these circumstances the law allows his nearest relatives to look after his property – to 'administer his estate' – and specifies who is to inherit his estate. Such persons are called 'administrators' and the document which they apply for at the High Court is called 'letters of administration'.

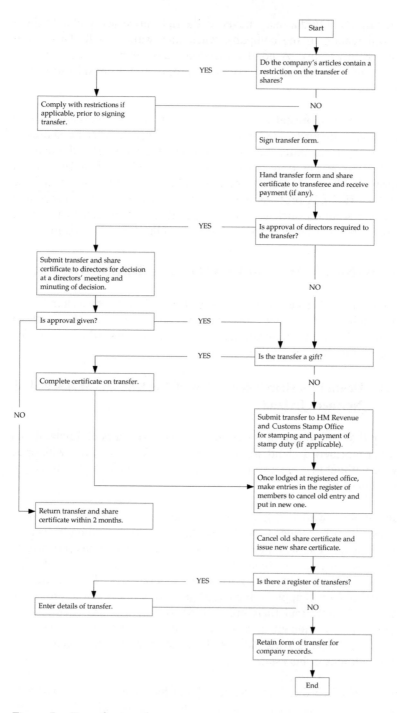

Figure 7 – Transferring shares

The law uses the expression 'personal representatives' or 'transmittees' to cover both executors and administrators – it is these expressions which will often appear in any articles or shareholders' agreement.

The effect of the death of a shareholder is usually that the company recognises his personal representatives as the persons entitled to his shares. This recognition is automatic and is called 'transmission'. Of course, the company will need to see the probate or letters of administration (and the death certificate), stating the names of the personal representatives, before it will recognise them. However, being recognised as entitled to shares does not make the personal representatives full shareholders of the company. The practical consequence is that the name of the deceased shareholder stays in the register of shareholders despite the death, and the secretary merely inserts the names and addresses of the personal representatives as a note in the register, and keeps copies of the death certificate and grant of probate or letters of administration, as the case may be, certified as a true copy of the originals.

The personal representatives do have certain rights. For example, they are entitled to have dividends sent to them, if declared, and to be offered shares on any bonus or rights issue. Dividends or shares received in this way do not belong to the personal representatives. They are added to the deceased shareholder's property and dealt with as if owned by the shareholder when he died.

However, personal representatives are not usually entitled to exercise the voting rights attaching to the shares of the deceased shareholder. For voting purposes, the deceased's shares are held in limbo.

One of two things may then happen. The personal representatives may decide that they want to become full shareholders in respect of the shares themselves. If so, they are often said to 'elect' to become shareholders. Alternatively, they may wish to transfer the shares to someone else, who will become a full shareholder. However, most companies will provide in their articles that any election by personal representatives to become full shareholders, or any transfer by the personal representatives to a new shareholder, is to be treated as if it were a transfer by the shareholder who died. This means that any restrictions on transfer will apply.

For example, if the articles say that no transfer will take place without the shares first being offered to the other shareholders, the personal representatives must offer them to the other shareholders before making an election, or trying to transfer to a new shareholder.

Shareholders often fail to appreciate that the restrictions on transfer will override any provision in their will or in the rules as to who inherits on intestacy. A shareholder who leaves shares to a spouse or children in a will might be surprised to find that the directors of the company refuse to approve a transfer of those shares to the spouse and children by the personal representatives. However, this is quite possible. A shareholder who wishes to ensure that shares end up in the hands of his spouse and children must ensure that the articles of the company contain a free right of transfer of shares to members of the family. The personal representatives are then as free to transfer to the spouse and children as the shareholder himself would have been had he lived. Alternatively, if the directors have power to refuse to register transfers, the personal representatives should check that they will be prepared to approve the proposed new shareholder.

It is not until an election or transfer has been dealt with in accordance with the articles that the deceased shareholder ceases to appear as the owner of shares in the register of shareholders of the company.

3.11.2   Death of a shareholder – Scottish law

In the event of the bankruptcy or death of a Scottish shareholder of a limited company, whether the company is registered in Scotland, or in England and Wales, the provisions of Scottish law will apply to his property – including his shares in the limited company. These provisions are substantially different from those in England and Wales. In the event of bankruptcy or death, advice from a qualified Scottish professional is strongly recommended to anyone not familiar with Scottish law.

In the event of the death of a Scottish shareholder, if the deceased leaves a will which contains the appointment of executors, those appointed will apply to the appropriate Sheriff Court for their appointment as 'executors nominate'. If there is no appointment of executors in the will, or there is no will, the next of kin (or, in some cases, other persons) can petition the Sheriff Court for an order recognising them as 'executors-dative'. Thereafter the executors may obtain confirmation in their name to administer the estate. Although there are differences of procedure prior to such appointment, executors appointed in either circumstances are 'personal representatives' of the deceased to whom the comments above apply.

3.11.3   Bankruptcy of a shareholder – laws of England and Wales and of Northern Ireland

Much the same rules apply on bankruptcy of the shareholder under the laws of England and Wales and of Northern Ireland as on death. Once officially bankrupt, an official called a 'trustee in bankruptcy' becomes recognised as entitled to the bankrupt's shares. The term 'personal representative' also covers a trustee in bankruptcy, so that he can, subject to the articles, elect to become a full shareholder, or may wish to transfer the bankrupt's shares. Until he does one of these, he can receive dividends and shares on behalf of the bankrupt, but cannot vote with the bankrupt's shares.

3.11.4   Bankruptcy of a shareholder – Scottish law

In the case of a bankruptcy under Scottish law, an individual will be recognised as formally bankrupt if he signs a voluntary trust deed or is sequestrated by the court. The person appointed to act as his trustee in either case will be a recognised 'insolvency practitioner' and is generally referred to as the individual's 'trustee in bankruptcy'. Again, he will be treated by the company as the individual shareholder's 'personal representative'.

There are other similar situations in which the court may appoint a 'personal representative' to a shareholder. If he is incapable of managing his own affairs the appointment is of a *curator bonis*. If the estate of a deceased person is insolvent, a judicial factor may be appointed, but a judicial factor may also be appointed in circumstances apart from insolvency, such as where a partnership or even a limited company is unable effectively to manage its affairs as a result of some internal dispute. Generally speaking, all such appointments will be covered by the expression 'personal representative'.

3.12   STAMP DUTY ON TRANSFER OF SHARES *

Stamp duty must be paid on a transfer of shares (but not an election), unless a relief or exemption is available. As with a house purchase, payment of any stamp duty is the buyer's responsibility. Stamp duty is calculated at £5 stamp duty for every £1,000 or part of £1,000, being received by the seller for the shares. Stamp duty calculated in this way is called 'ad valorem' duty.

However, there are circumstances where relief or exemption is available. The most common circumstance is a transfer by way of gift. Such a transfer is completely exempt from stamp duty, provided that the seller fills in an appropriate certificate stating that the exemption applies. Other transfers are not completely exempt but attract a fixed duty of only £5, provided, again, that an appropriate certificate is completed making it clear that only the fixed duty is payable. Circumstances in which those reliefs or exemptions are available, and the certificates which require completion if they are to be claimed, are usually pre-printed on the back of the stock transfer form.

However, there are other, less common, circumstances in which reliefs and exemptions may be available which are not referred to on the stock transfer form. These include reliefs available when, for example, one company 'takes over' another, or transfers of shares of and between companies in the same group take place. These transactions are complex and will always require professional advice and 'adjudication' by HM Revenue and Customs.

3.13   PROCEDURE ON TRANSFER *

The procedure on transfer of shares in a private company by a living, solvent shareholder is as follows.

(1)   The buyer and seller check the articles of the company and any shareholders' agreement to see if any special provisions need to be observed before shares are transferred. For example, do the shares have to be offered to other shareholders before being transferred to the buyer? If so, any such requirement must be observed.

(2)   The seller completes a stock transfer form. The form must be signed by the seller, but if the share is fully paid it need not be signed by the buyer.

(3)   The seller hands the stock transfer form to the buyer, and receives payment, if any. The seller also hands over his share certificates relating to the shares. If he has lost them, the buyer may ask for indemnity for the lost share certificates or insist that the seller obtains duplicates from the company. In the latter case, the company is likely to require an indemnity from the seller. Forms of indemnity are readily available in standard form from legal stationers.

(4)   If the stamp duty is payable, the buyer is responsible for its payment, and should take advice as to the amount payable and whether reliefs or exemptions are available.

(5)   The stock transfer form should be presented to the company. Prior to entering the transfer into the registers of the company, and issuing the new share certificates, the secretary will ensure that:
    (a)   the articles have been complied with. If the directors have power to refuse to register a transfer, they must exercise it within 2 months after the transfer form is presented to the company; and
    (b)   if stamp duty is relevant, that the stock transfer form is:
        (i)   either stamped with ad valorem duty; or
        (ii)   stamped with £5 duty and a stamp showing it has been produced to the Stamp Office, and there is an appropriate certificate of relief; or
        (iii)   the form has not been stamped at all but there is a certificate of exemption; or
        (iv)   marked to indicate it has been 'adjudicated' by HM Revenue and Customs.

It is a criminal offence for the secretary to register a transfer if the stock transfer form has not been properly stamped and/or certified.

The secretary may then alter the registers, cancel or destroy old share certificates, and issue new ones. A shareholder must be given his new share certificate within 2 months after the transfer form is presented to the company. Not only will the register of shareholders require alteration but, if the company has them, the register of transfers, and the register of sealings.

It is not necessary to inform Companies House of a transfer of shares when it occurs.

3.14 SHARES HELD ON TRUST **

It is possible to hold shares on trust. The shareholder may agree with another that he will deal with his shares in accordance with their instructions. The shareholder is then a 'trustee' and the other is a 'beneficiary'. There are many different sorts of trust, each of which gives the beneficiary different rights.

The simplest form of trust is called, colloquially, a bare or, in Scotland sometimes, a simple, trust. It gives the beneficiary the right to direct the trustee as to how to deal with the shares held by the trustee in every respect, and requires the trustee to account to the beneficiary for dividends and other benefits received by the trustee in respect of the shares. The trustee is often called a 'nominee'. The beneficiary is often called a 'beneficial owner'. It is the name of the trustee which will appear in the company's registers, so it is the trustee who is the shareholder. The company is not interested in any arrangement the shareholder has made and, ordinarily, its articles will provide that it will ignore the interests of the beneficiaries, even if the shareholder is merely a nominee under a bare trust. A private company will not ordinarily be able to find out the identity of the beneficial owner of any of its shares although, in certain circumstances, a public company may. In any event, even if the company knows about the beneficial owner, it takes note only of the shareholder. For example, if a beneficial owner of a share tells his nominee to vote for a resolution at a shareholders' meeting, and he votes against it, the company will not be interested in a complaint or objection by the beneficial owner. The beneficial owner's remedy is not to complain to the company, but to take the nominee to court for breach of the terms of the trust.

3.15 WHOLLY OWNED SUBSIDIARIES *

Bare trusts are often used in a group company structure. Often, every company in a group, except the ultimate parent company, will be a wholly owned subsidiary. This does *not* necessarily mean that every share in those companies is held by another company.

Instead, a common arrangement has traditionally been for all but one of the shares to be held by the immediate parent company, and the remaining share to be held by a nominee for the parent company on a bare trust. Under the stamp duty rules, the transfer of a share to such a nominee, or from one nominee to another, is a transfer which, if an appropriate certificate is given, is subject only to a fixed duty of £5. The parent company therefore has control over every share, but, because of the nominee, there are two shareholders in the subsidiary company's registers. The company is still a wholly owned subsidiary, because the Companies Acts define a 'wholly owned subsidiary' as a company whose shares are all held by another company, and that other company's nominees. This was because of a long-established rule that every company, even a wholly owned subsidiary, required two shareholders.

However, since the introduction of the rule that a private company may operate with a single shareholder without that single shareholder losing limited liability, the need for a nominee to hold a share in a private wholly owned subsidiary (so that there are two shareholders) has disappeared. All the shares in the subsidiary may now be registered in the name of the parent. Since most wholly owned subsidiaries are private companies, this applies to most wholly owned subsidiaries. However, in the rare instance of a subsidiary which is a public company, a nominee is still necessary.

The company is also a wholly owned subsidiary if all its shares are owned by another company and that other company is a wholly owned subsidiary.

Under the law of England and Wales and of Northern Ireland, a bare trust over shares need not be declared in writing, although it is sensible if it is. A professional adviser should be consulted in this respect. Under Scottish law, the declaration of trust is required to be in writing in any event.

CHAPTER 4

SHAREHOLDERS' AGREEMENTS ***

4.1 THE BALANCE OF POWER UNDER COMPANY LAW

This book contains many examples of two balances of power under company law. The first is the balance between the freedom of the directors to manage the business of the company profitably, and the need to prevent them from abusing that freedom. The second is the balance to be struck as to the respective powers and rights of the shareholders as against each other.

The Companies Acts and the courts establish a framework within which these two balances are set. It assumes that, subject to certain safeguards against abuse, majority shareholders should have their way.

However, companies are often owned and managed by two or more people who see themselves as having a relationship more akin to a partnership than the relationship envisaged between shareholders under company law – a relationship often referred to as a 'quasi-partnership' by lawyers.

Alternatively, the company may be wrapped around a family hierarchy, or there may be outside investors, or employee shareholders. In all of these instances, there may be good reasons why the usual framework is inappropriate.

4.2 USING THE ARTICLES

Provided sufficient shareholders agree, the articles may be used to vary the framework. The shareholders have the option of either relaxing their usual control over the affairs of their company or, more commonly, of tightening the screw, by provision in the articles.

However, two particular problems arise. The first is that the courts will generally only recognise the articles as being capable of giving rights to any shareholder in his capacity as a shareholder. If the articles confer any other rights, they will not be enforceable either by or against the company.

The second is that the courts will not always allow one shareholder to enforce a right given to him by the articles directly against another shareholder.

4.3   SHAREHOLDERS' AGREEMENTS AS A SOLUTION

As a result of these problems, the use of shareholders' agreements is common. The shareholders' agreement is a contract entered into between shareholders of a company to regulate the manner in which their company is to be run, and certain aspects of their relationship with each other. Commonly, shareholders who wish to deviate from the general principle of majority rule will use both special articles, and also a shareholders' agreement to achieve their aim. The provisions of each will supplement the other and the two will operate in tandem so as to meet the wishes of the shareholders. Provisions which might not be enforceable if included in one are included in the other. By this means, shareholders can achieve virtually any balance of power that they wish.

4.4   THE NATURE OF A SHAREHOLDERS' AGREEMENT

Usually, the shareholders' agreement operates as a private voting agreement as to how the shareholders will behave in relation to the company. The shareholders can agree amongst themselves, for example, that they will only vote to alter the articles if they all agree, and this will be enforceable between them. The company itself will often also be a party to the agreement, although there are technical rules which usually mean that the company should only agree to be bound by some, and not all, of the provisions of the agreement.

This is because of certain complicated case law regulating the extent to which the directors of a company can agree something now on its behalf which will fetter the company's ability to do certain things in the future. This case law means that professional advice on the agreement is even more important if the company is a party to it.

So, first, what are the features of a shareholders' agreement as against articles of association, and, secondly, which matters are commonly and appropriately dealt with in a shareholders' agreement?

4.5   FEATURES OF A SHAREHOLDERS' AGREEMENT

(1)   Shareholders' agreements can confer personal rights on the parties to the agreement, whilst articles generally cannot.

(2)   Shareholders' agreements create a direct right of action by any one party to the agreement against any other.

(3)   Shareholders' agreements, if properly drafted, remain confidential.

(4)   Shareholders' agreements cannot be altered except with the consent of every party to them.

(5)   For a new shareholder to be bound by the shareholders' agreement, he must specifically agree to become a party to it.
       As a result of this, a rule of thumb which is often applied when comparing the benefits of including a provision in articles rather than an agreement, or vice versa, is to ask whether the provisions being introduced are relevant only to the particular shareholders of the company at the time, or are intended to apply also to all persons who might become shareholders in the future. If the former, an agreement is more appropriate. If the latter, the articles are more appropriate.

(6)   The remedies available to a shareholder on breach of the agreement may differ from those available on breach of an identical provision in the articles.

4.6   MATTERS COMMONLY FOUND IN SHAREHOLDERS' AGREEMENTS

The contents of a shareholders' agreement will depend upon the relationship envisaged between the shareholders of that company, but the following checklist will look familiar to an adviser who is used to dealing with agreements of this type.

*   Can the power of the minority shareholder to participate in management be protected? The agreement may give the minority shareholder the right to require appointment of himself, or a person nominated by him, as a director, even though his holding would not usually be sufficient to enable him to do this.

*   Will the minority holder receive sufficient information as to the company's affairs? It is common to require that certain management accounts and documents are made available to the minority shareholder to which he would not normally be entitled.

*   Could the majority shareholder force through changes which the minority holder considers crucial to his interests? A minority shareholder is frequently given the power to veto certain decisions, which he would normally have little or no power to influence.

*   Are there positive obligations which the minority shareholder wishes to be able to enforce, such as for the company to declare a dividend whenever it can?

- Can the minority shareholder 'escape' if he wishes? The agreement invariably deals with the circumstances in which a shareholder may sell his shares and it is always crucial to ensure that any formula for valuing the shares is both fair and fully understood by the parties. If, as is common, the agreement provides for remaining parties to the agreement to acquire the shares of any party who dies, the agreement will usually require each party to take out life cover, in favour of the others, so that they have funds to pay for the shares.

The possible methods of regulating how shareholders deal with their shares are virtually infinite. However, the comments on the possible contents of articles of association in relation to transfer in Chapter 3 are also relevant in this context.

4.7   CONCLUSION

Shareholders' agreements offer enormous scope for tailoring legal rights and liabilities to the needs of a particular company and its shareholders. They should, however, be approached with caution – the amateur shareholders' agreement should be avoided, since, if it is ever relied upon, it is more likely to benefit litigation lawyers than the parties to it. Care must also be exercised in relation to the tax consequences of entering into a shareholders' agreement, both in relation to the shareholders' own position, and in relation to the company concerned. In every respect, professional advice is essential.

CHAPTER 5

DIRECTORS AND OTHER OFFICERS

5.1 OFFICERS

The officers of a company are usually the directors and, currently, the secretary. For some purposes, an auditor (if the company has one – see below) is treated as an officer, in the sense that he has a duty to the company when carrying out certain activities. There may be other officers, but these are unusual.

From 6 April 2008 the company secretary is optional for private companies. New companies formed after that date do not need a secretary at all, and the boards of existing companies can vote their company secretary out of office (unless they have specific provisions in their articles requiring them to have a company secretary or that assume that they have one, in which case they should alter their articles first). Alternatively, existing company secretaries may simply continue in office, in which case they have the same responsibilities (for record-keeping and the like) under company law as they did previously.

There is no definition of 'director' (or 'secretary') in the Companies Acts. However, the Companies Acts do say that the word director 'includes any person occupying the position of a director, by whatever name called'. This means someone may be a director who has not been given that title. For example, directors of a company may be called the council of management, but they are still its directors, and subject to all the rules which apply to directors. A company may be the director or secretary of another company. So may a Scottish partnership or a limited liability partnership, since these are legal entities. However, the same is not true of an ordinary English or Northern Irish partnership.

5.2 DIRECTORS' DUTIES **

Despite the fact that there is no definition of a director in the Companies Acts, it is possible to provide a rough definition of a director by reference to his duties.

It is correct to say that a director is a person appointed by the shareholders to manage the business of the company. This means that the job of director will vary from company to company, depending on the nature, size, etc of its business. A director of a major company will be managing a very different business from a director of a very small company. The way in which a director manages the business of the company will also vary according to whether he is one of a number of directors forming a board of directors, or whether he is a sole director.

5.3   SECRETARY'S DUTIES

The job of the secretary is easier to define. He is responsible for compliance with those provisions of the Companies Acts which require the company to keep registers, and make its affairs open to the public, and he is also recognised by the courts as the chief administrative officer of the company. The secretary's responsibility for compliance with the provisions of the Companies Acts in respect of registers and publicity is shared with the directors.

The secretary may also have additional responsibilities under his contract of employment, but these are not statutory responsibilities and will vary widely from company to company.

When it becomes optional to have a company secretary, from 6 April 2008, boards of existing private companies will have to decide whether to retain their secretary or not. Given that responsibility for the secretary's tasks are shared with the directors, and will still have to be carried out by someone, many boards of private companies are likely to choose to appoint or retain their company secretary.

5.4   CONTROLLING THE DIRECTORS **

In managing the business of the company, the directors are in an extremely powerful position. They look after the affairs of the company, and are in a position of trust. They might abuse their position in order to profit at the expense of their company, and therefore at the expense of the shareholders of the company.

Consequently, the law imposes a number of duties, burdens and responsibilities upon directors, to prevent abuse. Much of company law can be seen as a balance between allowing directors the freedom to manage the company's business so as to make a profit, and preventing them from abusing this freedom.

5.4.1 The Companies Acts

The directors of the company are unable to make certain important decisions. The Companies Acts provide that some decisions must be made by, or with the specific authority of, the shareholders. These are set out in Chapter 16.

5.4.2 The memorandum of association

When managing the business of the company, the directors must only carry on activities which are authorised by the company's objects and powers set out in, or implied as a result of the wording of, the company's memorandum. The Companies Acts provide that it is the shareholders who decide the company's objects and powers. If the directors want the company to carry on a business not authorised by the shareholders, they must call upon the shareholders to alter the memorandum.

From October 2009, the function and format of the memorandum of association will change (see Chapter 2) and it will no longer include objects and powers. Instead, it will be able to do anything lawful, unless the company's articles specifically restrict its activities. Directors of companies will not need to check that their activities are authorised by the memorandum, but should check whether their companies' articles contain restrictions.

Existing companies that already have objects and powers in their memorandum are, from October 2009, treated as if these were set out in their articles of association – that is, as if they were provisions included in the articles, operating as restrictions on the company's activities. The directors of existing companies will therefore either have to continue to check that the activities they want to undertake are permitted, given these 'restrictions', or ask the shareholders to pass a special resolution to remove them from the company's articles.

5.4.3 The articles of association

When managing the business of the company, the directors must act in accordance with the company's articles of association. The contents of the articles are a matter for decision by the shareholders. The shareholders may have included restrictions on the directors in the articles. For example, it was once common to find a provision in articles which said that the directors could borrow money from a lender on behalf of their company, but only up to a certain amount. If the borrowing exceeded a specified figure (usually a sum equivalent to the company's issued share capital) the directors had to seek the consent of the shareholders. Such a provision is rare in modern articles, but it illustrates the type of control which may be exercised by the shareholders if they wish.

A more common provision to be found in modern articles is a direction as to the manner in which directors must exercise their powers to allot new shares. Ordinarily, modern articles provide that, when allotting new shares, directors must offer new shares to the existing shareholders, in proportion to their shareholdings, unless the shareholders waive this requirement by special resolution. This is important to a majority shareholder, who wants to retain control of a company in the event that new shares are issued.

The articles will also contain rules as to how directors meet to make decisions, how they delegate their authority, and how they exercise their powers.

Articles sometimes require a proportion of the directors to retire at the annual general meeting and seek re-election by the shareholders if they wish to continue in office. This is called 'retirement by rotation' and is a classic example of control over directors – a periodic review of their position as directors. However, most modern articles do not require directors to retire by rotation.

As discussed above, from October 2009 the articles may contain restrictions on the activities of the company and therefore, necessarily, the activities of the directors.

5.4.4   Disqualification and wrongful trading

The law on insolvency allows directors to be disqualified from being directors of any company if they have acted improperly. In some circumstances, a director can be required to help pay the debts of his company, even though it is a separate legal person. For example, directors of a company who try to 'trade out of difficulty' and fail may be found guilty of 'wrongful trading' and can be made personally liable.

5.4.5   Directors' general duties under the Companies Act

Certain general duties, owed by directors to their company, that were previously common law duties, are set out in the Companies Act 2006. Directors' common law duties evolved as a result of hundreds of different rulings, comments and decisions made by judges in court cases over two centuries. The problem with the common law duties was that each of them had been stated in many different ways over the years, using different forms of words. So whenever it was alleged that a director had breached a common law duty, the lawyers had to look at all the different ways the duty had been articulated in all the different cases. They would then have to argue about the meaning of the words used, and their relevance to their particular client's case. As a result, disputes based on directors' common law duties were often long, complex and costly. The answer was to set certain of the duties out in the Companies Act 2006, using one specific form of words – to 'codify' them – and for the codified duties to replace the previous common law duties. If a duty has been codified, lawyers now only have to argue about the words used in the Act in relation to that duty.

However, much of the wording in the Act has been taken from the old cases, and the Act specifically provides that the new duties should be interpreted and applied in the same way as the old ones were, so lawyers continue to look at the old cases – but only to see what the words used in the Act mean.

As with the common law duties, the consequences of breach of a statutory duty are that a director may have to:

- pay the company damages or compensation for any loss it suffers;

- restore property to the company;

- account to the company for any profit they may have made out of the breach.

In addition, if a director has failed to disclose an interest in a transaction or arrangement, the company may be able to treat it as never having taken place.

5.4.6 The current codified directors' duties

The four duties that are currently codified are the directors' duties to:

- act within the company's constitution and powers;

- exercise independent judgment;

- exercise reasonable care, skill and diligence;

- promote the success of the company for the benefit of its members as a whole.

The first three duties use almost identical wording to that used in previous court cases on their common law predecessors, so there is plenty of guidance on what that wording means.

5.4.6.1 *To act within the company's constitution and powers*

For example, the duty to act within the company's constitution and powers still means the directors must always exercise their powers for a 'proper purpose' – that is, in furtherance of the reason for which they were given those powers by the shareholders. Directors are, for example, almost always given power to issue shares in order to raise money for the company. If shares are issued for another purpose, such as to increase the number of shares held by a particular director, or to dilute the shares held by a shareholder with whom the directors are in dispute, the board may well be found to have acted other than for a proper purpose. Directors are particularly vulnerable if they have acted in a way that benefits them.

5.4.6.2   *To exercise independent judgment*

It is also still clear that the duty to exercise independent judgment does not stop a director from having a personal interest in a company matter, or from taking into account the views of someone else who is more expert or better informed than he is on an issue, whether another director, an outsider or a professional adviser. What he must do, however, is apply his own mind to every decision, and not slavishly follow advice.

5.4.6.3   *To exercise reasonable skill, care and diligence*

The 2006 Act contains specific guidance on how to interpret the duty to exercise reasonable skill, care and diligence. This follows the approach the courts were taking anyway, when applying the former common law duty. First, whilst the courts will recognise that a director may make mistakes, or even act stupidly, there is a bottom line – a minimum duty of skill and care – below which a director must not fall. The Act says that that bottom line is based on what 'may reasonably be expected of a person carrying out the functions carried out by the director in relation to the company' – so you look at the director's job and work out the threshold of competence required to do it. One threshold requirement is that every director is expected to pay attention to the financial state of the company, whatever his particular job.

Second, if a director has special knowledge or skills – perhaps financial skills gained through accountancy qualifications – the director must apply that knowledge or those skills when acting as a director. The minimum duty of skill or care expected of directors with special skills is therefore higher than the norm when it comes to a matter in which those skills are important. They must apply their skills even if they have no day-to-day responsibilities – for example, if they are non-executive directors.

5.4.6.4   *To promote the success of the company*

However, the duty for directors to promote the success of the company for the benefit of its members as a whole uses markedly different wording from its common law predecessor – the duty to act in what the directors honestly believe to be the best interests of the company. It is therefore worth considering this 'new' duty in a little more detail, and the comments and guidance that have been given in relation to it.

First, the government has said that success, for a trading company, will usually mean 'long-term increase in value'. It has also said that, as with the common law duty to act in the company's best interests, courts should be very reluctant, when considering allegations that directors have breached their duty to promote the long-term success of the company, to substitute their own commercial judgment (applied with the benefit of hindsight) for that of directors involved in the hurly-burly of the day-to-day management of their companies. As previously, they should only intervene if no reasonable director would have acted in the way that the director(s) in this case have.

Second, the new rules set out a (non-exhaustive) list of factors that the directors must take into account in order to show that they are promoting the success of their company, including:

- the likely consequences of any decision in the long term;

- the interests of the company's employees;

- the need to foster the company's business relationships with suppliers, customers and others;

- the impact of the company's operations on the community and the environment;

- the desirability of the company maintaining a reputation for high standards of business conduct; and

- the need to act fairly as between members of the company.

As the list is not exhaustive, directors should consider whether, given their company's circumstances, additional or alternative factors should be taken into account. Apart from health and safety, directors' statutory duties that apply anyway (see Chapter 16) and, possibly, the interests of creditors if the company is in danger of becoming insolvent, it is hard to think of any additional factors that might apply; but directors are nonetheless required to consider whether there are any – and to comply with their statutory duty to exercise due skill and judgment when doing so.

The government has also said that not all the factors will always be relevant, and that one factor may be irreconcilable with another: it has given the example of investing in new technology, which may be better for the environment but cause job losses for employees. Provided the directors have thought about which statutory factors are relevant, and the relative 'weight' to be attached to each when deciding what course will best promote the company's success, they have complied with the duty.

Many commentators have remarked that these are factors good directors have always taken into account. The effect of this duty in practice is therefore more likely to be that directors pay more attention to the processes by which they make decisions (so they can show that they have taken the factors into account) than change the factors they think about.

However, the government and authoritative bodies such as the GC100 (made up of heads of legal departments of major listed companies) have made it clear that they do not think the new duty creates an obligation on directors to create a paper trail – for example, comprehensive minutes showing that they have considered each factor, the weight they gave to it, how they resolved inconsistencies, etc – in order to demonstrate that they have complied with the duty. Minutes can continue to be drafted in much the same form as before the 2006 Act.

What is also clear is that, if there is a dispute, it will help if the directors can show they took independent legal advice and that their act (or failure to act) is supported by a majority of the shareholders – or at least those who have no personal interest in the matters giving rise to it.

5.4.7   Future codification of directors' duties

From 1 October 2008, a further two general duties will be codified. These are:

- to avoid conflicts of interest; and

- not to accept benefits from third parties.

5.4.7.1   *Directors' conflicts*

A director 'must avoid a situation in which he has, or can have, a direct or indirect interest that conflicts, or may conflict, with the interests of the company'. In particular, this stops directors from exploiting any property, information or opportunity of the company, even if the company itself is not in a position to benefit from it. There are two ways out – either the directors can authorise the conflict, or the shareholders can include a general authorisation in the articles that allows the directors to exploit such opportunities. As the introduction date for these further duties approaches, it is likely that boards will be asking their shareholders to alter their articles to provide an authorisation.

5.4.7.2.   *Benefits from third parties*

The duty not to accept benefits from third parties stops directors benefiting from anything they do (or do not do) as directors, and also prohibits them from enjoying any benefit they get by virtue of the fact that they are directors. There is an exception if the benefit 'cannot reasonably be regarded as being likely to give rise to a conflict of interest', but if directors want to rely on this exception, they should take legal advice because it is not certain what it means. For example, certain types of corporate hospitality could certainly be caught, but does it depend on how lavish it is relative to the wealth of the directors? Take legal advice.

5.4.8 Duties of disclosure

Directors are currently required by the Companies Acts to reveal to the board the nature of their interest or involvement in any agreements, transactions or arrangements entered into by their company, whether it is a direct or indirect interest or involvement. The disclosure must be to the full board – disclosure to a committee of the directors is not sufficient. There is case law that suggests that such disclosure must be made and minuted even when the company has a sole director, so he is declaring the nature of his interest or involvement to himself!

From 1 October 2008, this rule will be replaced by two new obligations on directors.

First, a director will have to declare the nature and extent of any personal interest he has in any *proposed* transaction or arrangement to be entered into by the company to the other directors. It must be made either at a board meeting, or by notice, and must be made before the company enters into the transaction or arrangement; and a director will have to make a further declaration if the first declaration 'proves to be, or becomes, inaccurate or incomplete'. This obligation is a new codified statutory duty, like the ones discussed above, breach of which could land a director in court for breach of duty, and subject to the penalties mentioned above.

The obligation will not apply if:

- the director is unaware of the interest (or not aware of the transaction or arrangement) – but he will be treated as aware of matters of which he 'ought reasonably to be aware';

- the interest 'cannot reasonably be regarded as likely to give rise to a conflict of interest', ie it is so minor it is really not important;

- the other directors are already aware of the interest (and they are treated as aware of anything of which they ought reasonably to be aware). This means that a sole director no longer needs to declare his interest to himself; or

- the director is interested because the transaction involves his service contract (so it is self-evident that the director has an interest in it).

Second, a director will have to declare the nature and extent of any interest in an *existing* transaction or arrangement that has already been entered into by the company, to the other directors (unless the interest was declared before, when the transaction or arrangement was still a *proposed* one). The declaration must be made as soon as reasonably practicable, at a board meeting or by notice. Similar exceptions apply to those above.

However, despite the similarity to the rules regarding *proposed* transactions or arrangements, this new obligation is merely a Companies Act requirement, so that failing to comply is merely a breach of the Act, which could result in a penalty. It is not a statutory duty that could result in a court action against directors for breach of their duties.

Whichever rules apply at the time, it is good practice for the chair to remind directors of their obligations as to disclosure at the beginning of every board meeting, to prompt their compliance, if appropriate.

In certain circumstances, a transaction involving a director must be approved by the shareholders before it may be entered into by the company. These circumstances are included in the list of matters requiring a decision of the shareholders in Chapter 16.

5.5   ACTIONS AGAINST DIRECTORS BY SHAREHOLDERS ON BEHALF OF THEIR COMPANY **

Since a breach of duties by a director is a wrong against the company, it is the company that is the proper person to bring a court case against a director for breach of duty. However, it is the directors who manage the day-to-day business of the company, and that usually includes deciding whether the company should bring court cases in particular circumstances. If a majority of the directors are involved in the breach, they are hardly likely to resolve that the company should bring a court case against themselves. There have therefore been circumstances when the courts have allowed a shareholder to bring a court case on their company's behalf against directors who, the shareholder alleges, have breached their duties. These court cases are called 'derivative' actions, and any remedy granted belongs to the company, not the shareholder.

However, the circumstances in which a derivative action has been allowed by the courts have been very limited – there had to be some seriously bad behaviour by the directors – and there have been very few such actions in the courts. If what the directors had done was capable of ratification by the shareholders, a derivative action was very rarely allowed – even if the directors also controlled a majority shareholding in the company.

The Companies Act 2006 has introduced a new, statutory derivative action. The grounds on which such an action may be brought are wider, and some of the stringent limitations on derivative actions have been removed. Further, if shareholders try to ratify the breach, and the directors concerned (and people connected with them, such as family and people they are in a permanent relationship with) are shareholders, they are not allowed to vote.

There was some concern that these new rules could result in a spate of actions against directors, and mean fewer people would be prepared to act as directors. However, the new rules also introduce procedural hurdles that a shareholder must overcome before he can bring a derivative action, so the net effect is likely to be that the number of derivative actions will not increase as predicted.

Always take legal advice if a derivative action is threatened.

5.6 SHADOW DIRECTORS *

In many circumstances, the law applies not only to a director, but to a 'shadow director'. A shadow director is a person in accordance with whose directions or instructions the directors of a company are accustomed to act. Under this definition, it is possible that a director, or the whole board, of a holding company, and the holding company itself, could be treated as a shadow director of a subsidiary. Judicial comments in legal cases suggest that a bank manager could also be treated as a shadow director of a company if he intervenes in its affairs but that this would only occur if circumstances were exceptional. The problem of shadow directorships can become more acute when a company is approaching insolvency, or has become insolvent.

Professional advisers giving advice in their professional capacity are specifically excluded from the definition of a shadow director in the companies legislation.

5.7 DIRECTORS AND EMPLOYEES **

Care should be taken to distinguish between the status of a director and of an employee. A director is not necessarily also an employee, although he may be. This can be important for the purposes of unfair dismissal and redundancy law. Very simply, a director will also be an employee for these purposes if he has a service contract with the company.

5.8   SOLE DIRECTORS **

A private company may, if its articles allow, have only one director, provided that the sole director is not the secretary as well. One company may be a director of another and this is common in groups of companies. For example, company 'B' may be a director of company 'A'. However, if it is the sole director of company 'A' and it has only one director itself, that person may not also be the secretary of company 'A'.

Consequently (assuming A and B are private companies), the following examples illustrate various situations as either permitted or not permitted.

(The prohibition against a sole director also being the secretary is not relevant to private companies that have chosen not to have a company secretary, as they are permitted to do from 6 April 2008. Nor is it relevant to public companies, that must have two directors in any event.)

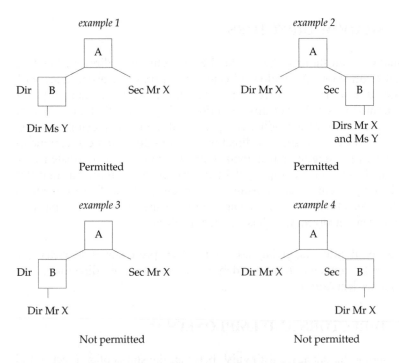

Figure 8 – Examples of sole directors and non-sole directors

5.9   APPOINTMENT OF A DIRECTOR *

Upon issue of the certificate of incorporation of a company, a person who has consented to act as a director when the application for incorporation is made is automatically constituted a director of the company – no appointment or confirmation of his appointment is required.

Subject to the disqualifications and restrictions in the Companies Acts as to who may be a director, the method of appointment of subsequent directors is laid down in the company's articles. The ultimate control as to the composition of the board of directors rests with the shareholders who can always appoint, and – sometimes more importantly – dismiss a director. The shareholders can also fix the minimum and maximum number of directors. However, the board can usually appoint (but not dismiss) a director to his office as well.

Before appointing a director, both the shareholders and the board should check a number of procedural matters, in addition to assessing the competence of the prospective director.

The articles should be checked for any nationality or other restriction on directors. The permitted maximum number of directors should also be checked although there may be no maximum number. If there is, it will have been fixed by the shareholders. If the maximum number needs increasing before a new director may be appointed, the directors will need to ask the shareholders to increase it.

Sometimes directors are required by the articles to also hold shares. This is called a 'share qualification'. The articles will specify the number of shares required to be held. If a share qualification is required, the director must acquire sufficient shares within 2 months of his appointment or such earlier time as is prescribed by the articles. Share qualifications are now relatively rare.

If letterheads and other business stationery, including any electronic documents such as emails and websites, contain details of directors, these should be amended by the addition of the new director's details. Letterheads must include details of either all, or none, of the directors.

The company's bankers should be advised of the appointment. The board may need to alter the instructions as to signatories to the company's bank account if the director is to be authorised to operate the company's bank account.

The company must always obtain the proposed director's particulars and consent to act on the official form. Alternatively, if the appointment is to be notified to Companies House electronically, the director must provide three items of personal information from a list of seven. These items are included in the electronic notification to Companies House as evidence of the director's consent to act.

The form or electronic notification must be lodged at Companies House within 14 days of the date of appointment. There is no fee.

A similar form or electronic notification must also be lodged if the director's particulars alter, within 14 days of the date of the alteration.

Ordinarily, a director must provide his residential address in the details provided to Companies House. Where, however, the director, or a person who lives with him, might otherwise be at serious risk of being subjected to violence or intimidation, application may be made to the Secretary of State for Business, Enterprise and Regulatory Reform for a 'confidentiality order'. If granted, the effect of this is that the director may provide an accommodation address to appear on the public record, with his residential address being kept confidential by the registrar of companies. This is intended to protect directors from being targeted by activist groups, terrorists, etc.

This rule will change from October 2009, when a new director will be able to file a service address, such as his accountant's address (or even 'the company's registered office') instead of his residential address, as of right. However, he will still have to notify a residential address to the registrar of companies and to the company itself (which it must enter in a new register of directors' residential addresses). Both the registrar of companies and the company must keep residential addresses confidential from everyone except a public authority or a credit reference agency (although a director can apply to keep his address confidential even from credit reference agencies in certain circumstances related to their personal safety). There can also be disclosure to third parties in other exceptional circumstances, eg if a court order is made for disclosure on grounds that the service address is ineffective.

An existing director will be able to apply to remove his residential addresses already on file at Companies House if there is a serious risk that he will be subjected to violence or intimidation as a result of the activities of a company of which he is director, secretary or permanent representative, or he has been employed by, or is providing goods or services, to certain organisations, such as MI5 or GCHQ.

Once the new director has been appointed, the secretary must amend the register of directors.

5.10 VACATION OF OFFICE **

Bankruptcy is usually also a ground for vacation of office under the articles. In addition, it is a criminal offence for an undischarged bankrupt to act as director or liquidator of, or directly or indirectly to take part in or be concerned in the promotion, formation or management of, any company except with the leave of the court by which he has been adjudged bankrupt.

A director may always be dismissed from office as a director by a majority vote of the shareholders, provided that a special procedure is followed. The procedure is complex, and legal advice will always be required.

Of course, a director who is removed from office may have rights in respect of his contract of employment. Legal advice should always be taken as to the rights of a director both before he is appointed and in the event of a proposed dismissal. Failure to do so could prove extremely expensive to the company.

In practice, the articles usually also provide for the following circumstances to give rise to vacation of office by a director:

(1)   insanity or mental disorder;

(2)   resignation;

(3)   absence from meetings over a particular period;

(4)   if there is one, failure to acquire a share qualification.

Within 14 days of any vacation of office, a form or electronic notification must be lodged notifying Companies House. There is no fee.

5.11   RESIGNATION ***

A director may resign at any time, even if his fellow board members purport not to accept the resignation. The resignation need not be in writing but without a written resignation a director may find it difficult to prove whether he has resigned or, more commonly, precisely when he did so.

Resignation may constitute a breach of the director's contract of employment, if he is an employee of the company.

A form or electronic notification must be filed, within 14 days of the resignation, notifying Companies House. There is no fee. Technically, the form should be signed by an existing officer of the company. However, the registrar will accept a form signed by the resigned director even though, technically, he is no longer an officer.

5.12   REMUNERATION OF DIRECTORS *

Directors do not have any right to receive remuneration from the company simply because they are directors. A director who wants to keep the remuneration given to him, or in the case of a sole director, that he has given to himself, must be able to show some authority for that payment.

This authority usually appears in the articles – which will say that the shareholders determine the remuneration of the directors. In practice, the shareholders usually exercise this power by delegating it to the directors, who determine their own remuneration. The directors will always have in mind that, if they pay themselves too much, it is possible that they will be dismissed by the shareholders or find themselves defending court proceedings alleging their excessive remuneration is unfairly prejudicial to the shareholders, who would otherwise expect to receive a larger dividend.

5.13   THE SECRETARY

The company must, currently, have a secretary. If the company is a public company there are special rules as to who may act as secretary. Only a person with a professional qualification, or who is sufficiently experienced, may act as secretary of a public company. Any company may have a corporate secretary. There may be joint secretaries, or an assistant or deputy secretary. This can be useful, if the company secretary is not always available – for example, to sign the annual return.

The secretary is appointed, and may be removed, by resolution of the board of directors.

As noted above, from April 2008 private companies will no longer need to have a company secretary.

5.14   SERVICE CONTRACTS ***

Ordinarily, a director will have a written service contract with the company which will define, amongst other things, his executive duties as an employee of the company, and the way in which his remuneration is calculated.

Legal advice will be required on the service agreement, in view of the employment legislation, the possible requirement to obtain approval of the shareholders to the agreement, and the requirements as to disclosure of its contents to the shareholders.

The contract will commonly deal not only with matters such as pay, and holidays, but will also restrict competition from the employee following a resignation, allow the company the right to own patents and inventions created by the director in the course of employment, etc.

Some contracts will have to be approved by the shareholders – primarily, those which will, or may, continue to provide the director with a guaranteed term of employment for more than 2 years – and there are special procedural rules as to how such approval must be given.

Almost all directors' service contracts must be kept at one of certain specified places, such as the registered office, and be open for inspection by shareholders.

5.15   DIRECTORS' AND OFFICERS' LIABILITY INSURANCE ***

It is possible for companies to indemnify their directors, or to pay for and maintain insurance cover, to provide protection for directors against certain risks attached to their office. This insurance cover is known as Directors' and Officers' Liability Insurance ('D & O' insurance) and is increasingly common.

Both the extent of the risk which can be covered, and the tax treatment of premiums and payments, are under constant review, and the trend is towards making D & O insurance more attractive to companies and their directors.

The complexity of the rules, and the fact that they are a 'moving feast' means that professional advice is always required if D & O insurance is to be taken out.

CHAPTER 6

DIRECTORS' MEETINGS

6.1 BUSINESS AT DIRECTORS' MEETINGS

Board meetings (ie meetings of the directors) are necessary to deal with matters of general policy and with other business which must be transacted in a more formal way. Other matters may usually be dealt with by committees of directors, or officers with a particular executive function, on a day-to-day basis. The conduct of board meetings is governed largely by the company's articles. Articles usually empower directors to meet together for the dispatch of business and to conduct the meetings as they see fit.

6.2 CALLING A DIRECTORS' MEETING

When, and how often, board meetings are to be held will depend upon the company and the requirements of its business. In a private company, meetings will be held as and when there is business requiring the board's attention.

However, many companies have a procedure whereby it has been agreed by the directors that board meetings be held regularly at a fixed date and time, which all the directors know about. Consequently, directors' meetings may usually be called as informally or formally as the directors may decide amongst themselves. This is subject to any special procedure in the company's articles. Calling a meeting is sometimes called 'convening' a meeting.

Unless there is something unusual in the articles, the following procedure will apply.

(1) A director or, if the company has one (see Chapter 5), the secretary at the request of a director, may call a directors' meeting. A secretary may not call a meeting unless requested to do so by a director or the directors.

(2) A board meeting may be held anywhere in the world, provided that, given directors' ability to attend, the venue is reasonable. However,

the place at which a board meeting is held may affect the company's tax status so that meetings of a UK company should only be held outside the UK if appropriate advice has been taken.

(3)   In the absence of a standard procedure, agreed by the directors, as to frequency and notice of board meetings each director must be given reasonable notice of the meeting, stating its date, time and place. Commonly, 7 days' notice is given, but what is 'reasonable' depends in the last resort upon the circumstances. Even where it has become the practice to give a certain period of notice, it will often be permissible to give a shorter notice (eg because of very urgent business); but pressure to give shorter notice must sometimes be resisted if an ulterior motive is suspected, such as a desire to prevent a particular director from attending.

(4)   Notice should be given to each director, and even to a director who has indicated that he will not attend a meeting. Usually, articles allow notice to be dispensed with in the case of a director who is not in the UK when the notice is given. The shareholders should be asked to consider whether they wish to alter the articles if all or some of the directors are likely to be outside the UK when board meetings are called. If a director has appointed an alternate, the alternate should be given the same notice as the other directors. Notice should also be given to any person who is to attend for all or part of the meeting and any other person who may have to prepare a statement or provide information for the meeting.

(5)   Since a board meeting may deal with any of the company's affairs which require attention and which lie within the board's competence, there is no need for the notice to specify particular or special business unless the articles require this; routine business will often be described simply as 'general'. Nevertheless, it is good practice to see that notice, even of a routine meeting, contains at least a general indication of the business, with a more precise indication of anything out of the ordinary. The test that the courts have laid down is that the notice must contain sufficient information to enable a director to exercise his judgment as to whether to attend. In practice, a director should always use his utmost endeavours to attend board meetings.

(6)   Unless the articles specifically prohibit this, and provided the directors who receive notice in this way have expressly agreed to it, there is no reason why notice of a directors' meeting could not be faxed or emailed.
It would be prudent for the company to establish written rules governing the giving of notice of board meetings by these electronic means. These would deal with, for example, the circumstances in

which an email is deemed received by a director. Professional advice is recommended if these means of giving notice are to be used – the law in this area is fast moving.

Most articles would permit notice to be given orally, either face to face or by phone, but it would be unwise to adopt this as a general practice.

6.3   QUORUM

If there is not a quorum at a meeting, it may not take place. Articles usually allow the directors to fix the quorum necessary to transact their business. If they do not, the quorum is two. Alternatively, the articles may make other provisions for a quorum, and may even provide for one director to exercise all powers of a meeting of the directors. If the company has a sole director, this power is vital.

A quorum, however fixed, means a quorum competent to transact the particular business. Under most companies' articles, a director may not be counted in the quorum in relation to a resolution on which he is not entitled to vote. A quorum must be maintained throughout the business of the meeting unless the articles provide otherwise. If there is an attendance book, it should be signed by each director who is present, and there should be a quorum of directors competent to vote at all times. The secretary (or a director if the company does not have one – see Chapter 5 – or they are not present) should distinguish clearly between those who are 'present' – directors entitled to be counted in the quorum – and those who are merely 'in attendance' because, for example, they are senior managers or advisers who have been invited to the meeting.

6.4   ALTERNATE DIRECTORS *

Modern articles will allow a director to appoint another director or any other person approved by the rest of the board, to act on his behalf as a substitute, or 'alternate' director. This is useful if the director is abroad, though the power is not limited to this situation. The appointing director may also revoke the appointment. Both appointment and removal of an alternate should be in writing, and signed by the appointing director. The alternate is deemed to be a director 'for all purposes', unless the articles say otherwise, and counts towards the quorum unless the appointing director is also present at the meeting.

Alternatively, articles may not permit the appointment of alternates at all, so each company's articles should always be checked if an alternate is to be appointed.

6.5   THE CHAIRMAN OF THE BOARD *

The articles usually provide for the election of a chairman of the board. They empower the directors to appoint one of their own number as chairman and to determine the period for which he is to hold office. If no chairman is elected, or the elected chairman is not present within 5 minutes of the time fixed for the meeting or is unwilling to preside, those directors in attendance may usually elect one of their number as chairman of the meeting.

The chairman will usually have a second or casting vote in the case of equality of votes. Unless the articles confer such a vote upon him, however, a chairman has no casting vote merely by virtue of his office. He will also have a number of other procedural powers such as the power to adjourn the meeting.

Since the chairman's position is of great importance, it is vital that his election is clearly in accordance with any special procedure laid down by the articles and that it is unambiguously minuted; this is especially important to avoid disputes as to his period of office. Care should also be taken to keep a clear record of his resignation or removal from office. Usually there is no special procedure for resignation. As for removal, articles usually empower the board to remove the chairman from office at any time. Proper and clear minutes are important in order to avoid disputes.

A common problem in disputes as to who is chairman (and therefore entitled to a casting vote) is that different directors have signed, say, a bank mandate form and a copy shareholder resolution, and both have purported to do so as chair without protest from other directors or the secretary. Directors and the secretary should monitor documents signed to ensure that this does not happen.

6.6   PROCEDURAL REQUIREMENTS AT THE MEETINGS

The conduct of the meeting will usually be informal, subject to the overall control of the chairman, and any special rules set out in the articles. Strict rules of debate will usually be inappropriate.

Whilst there may be conventions as to the order of business in a particular company, these are merely rules of practice and not binding. The articles themselves will not usually deal with matters like the order of business, notice of motions, questions, etc.

Ideally, the result of discussion will be unanimity. A division of opinion which cannot be resolved must, however, be put to a vote. Subject to the articles, each director has a single vote and business is transacted by a majority of votes. If there is a tie, the chairman usually has a casting vote. The articles should be checked to see who can vote – sometimes a director is prohibited from voting on a matter in which he has an interest, either himself, or through his family, or his other business associates. However, a director's shareholding, or any other interest in the company's shares, will not usually stop him from voting.

6.7   ADJOURNMENT

Articles usually empower directors to regulate their proceedings as they see fit. This means that the power to adjourn is vested in the meeting as a whole unless expressly placed elsewhere (eg in the chairman), by the articles. Usually the articles allow both the meeting and the chairman to adjourn. Subject therefore to a contrary provision in the articles a motion (or informal suggestion) for adjournment may be put forward at any time and takes priority over the business then in hand. As a matter of practice, notice of the adjourned meeting should be sent to each director.

6.8   SIGNED RESOLUTIONS IN LIEU OF MEETING

Articles invariably provide that a resolution in writing, signed by all the directors for the time being entitled to receive notice of board meetings, is as effective as a resolution passed at a duly convened meeting. This is an exceptional provision to be used only when a genuine need arises. For example, because there is sudden and urgent business and the directors cannot be summoned to a meeting at short notice, or the matter to be decided does not require any discussion at all. The resolution is only effective if signed by all directors entitled to notice.

Where an alternate has been appointed, the signature of either the alternate or the appointor will be sufficient.

6.9   HOLDING DIRECTORS' MEETINGS
ELECTRONICALLY

It is increasingly common for directors' meetings to be held electronically. However, a number of practical issues need to be resolved if this is not to cause problems. It is sensible for decisions on these issues to be included in the company's articles of association. Table A makes no provision for electronic meetings but modern articles of association will do so.

The articles should define the conditions necessary to hold a valid electronic meeting. The overriding requirement will usually be that the means of electronic communication enables each director to hear and be heard by the other participants. This means there can be a debate or exchange leading to a resolution that promotes the long-term success of the company, as there would be at a conventional meeting. Electronic board meetings commonly take the form of a telephone or videoconferencing link.

An important issue is to decide where the electronic board meeting is being held. In a conventional meeting, all the directors are gathered in one place. The meeting is clearly held in that place. However, if directors communicating electronically are in different places, where is the meeting held?

This could cause tax problems if, for example, a director or, more likely, a majority of the directors regularly participate in electronic board meetings from a jurisdiction which taxes companies, wherever incorporated, whose central management and control is located there. If the fiscal authorities learn that directors on their territory participate electronically in board meetings of a UK company, they may investigate further.

Where central management and control is exercised will be a question of fact under the law of the jurisdiction concerned. However, the articles of association may be persuasive under that law. It may, therefore, be important that they prescribe where the company considers the meeting is being held, or the basis upon which that question should be resolved so the local tax authority can be referred to them. For example, it is common for articles to say the meeting is deemed held where the chair is physically present or, alternatively, where the directors agree.

6.10   RECORDS AND MINUTES

Good practice is to prepare a list of directors 'present' at the meeting for signature by each director who attends. The secretary (or one of the directors, if the company does not have one – see Chapter 5) should also record others in attendance, who are not directors. Copies of the memorandum, articles, latest reports and accounts and other important company documents should be made available in case they are required at the meeting.

At the meeting the secretary (or a director) should report any apologies for absence and record subsequent arrivals and departures; these matters should be minuted.

After the meeting draft minutes should be prepared from notes taken at the meeting. The purpose of these minutes is usually to record what was decided and not to report what was said. The board must not allow the minutes in these circumstances to become a report of what directors, especially dissenting directors, actually said; but, upon request, a director may be recorded as having dissented from a decision or voted against a resolution passed by a majority.

However, this usual rule may be displaced in the case of important decisions, or by a company in financial difficulties. In such instances, the chair or the board as a whole, may wish to record in the minutes the reasons for certain decisions, or the basis upon which they were made. The minutes can then be produced if the decisions need to be justified at a later date, for example, to prove to a subsequent liquidator that the directors have acted properly and, particularly, are not guilty of wrongful trading (see Chapter 12). Similarly, the minutes may record reasons for dissent.

Minutes may be kept in a bound book but, in practice, are almost invariably kept in a loose-leaf book. This is permitted by the Companies Acts, subject to 'suitable precautions' being taken, such as numbering of the pages to prevent alteration. However, minutes of board and committee meetings do not have to be made available at the company's offices for inspection by members, unlike minutes of general meetings. They are usually, therefore, kept separately.

Any signed resolution in lieu of a meeting must be entered in the minute book.

6.11   COMMITTEES AND EXECUTIVE OFFICERS

Directors are frequently authorised by articles to delegate some or all of their powers to a committee of members of the board (and such a committee may consist of a single director). The board may also authorise delegation to a managing or other executive director. A managing director is usually given the same powers as the rest of the board put together, so appointment of a managing director should not be made without very careful thought. See Chapter 8 in this respect. In any event, such delegation is revocable and may be made conditional. Accordingly, a committee may be set up ad hoc, or as a permanent institution, for example to execute documents or approve share transfers. In delegating functions the directors may prescribe the committee's procedures as well as its powers; for instance, as to voting and the appointment of a chairman. However, in default, the same rules apply to committees as to the main board.

It is vital for the main board to be sure that they have a proper system of supervision in respect of a committee or executive officer, since otherwise they are in breach of their duty to act in the best interests of the company. Such supervision might include a written specification of the powers of the committee or executive officer and/or a regular requirement to report back to the main board.

The minutes should be signed by the chair of the meeting, or of the next succeeding meeting, since they are not otherwise evidence of the proceedings at the meeting. The minutes are not required to be approved by the board as a whole but it is good practice if they are, especially if the chair of the next meeting was not present at the meeting to which the minutes relate.

CHAPTER 7

SHAREHOLDERS' MEETINGS
(GENERAL MEETINGS)

7.1 GENERAL MEETINGS

A general meeting is a meeting of the shareholders of the company. General meetings are either called by the directors because a specific matter has arisen which requires a decision of the shareholders, or are convened because a proportion of the shareholders have demanded one, to consider one or more resolutions that they want put to a general meeting, in accordance with a procedure in the Companies Acts.

Before October 2007, every company had to hold at least one general meeting every year, called the annual general meeting. There were special rules for such meetings: for example, as to the period of notice to be given, and what had to be included on the notice of the meeting. Under the Companies Act 2006, private companies no longer need to hold an annual general meeting, unless their articles of association specifically require them to do so. Very few private companies' articles will do so unless they are old – for example, they are based on the 1948 Table A.

If the articles do require a private company to hold an annual general meeting, and make specific provision for calling and conducting it, the directors must follow the articles. To the extent that the articles do not make any provision, the 2006 Act will apply. The board will find that there are no special rules for annual general meetings of a private company in the 2006 Act, so the same provisions for calling the meeting, and its conduct, will apply as for any other general meeting.

7.2 MATTERS REQUIRED TO BE REFERRED TO SHAREHOLDERS

The matters which require a decision of the shareholders will vary from company to company. Some matters must be referred to them in every company, such as a decision to alter the company's articles, because the Companies Acts require it. Other decisions may have to be referred to the shareholders of a particular company as a result of specific provision to that effect in the company's articles. The officers of each company need to be aware of the matters that must be referred to their shareholders.

The matters required to be referred to shareholders under the Companies Acts are set out in Chapter 16.

7.3 TYPES OF SHAREHOLDERS' RESOLUTION

Once the company's officers have identified a matter as one that has to be referred to the shareholders, they must identify the type of decision or 'resolution' required to be made or 'passed' by its shareholders.

There are two types of resolution, each of which has differing requirements as to the majority required if it is to be passed. The different majorities required for each resolution reflect the different importance attached to each type of decision by the companies legislation and/or the company's articles.

The types of resolution can be summarised as follows.

Type of resolution	Majority required	Requirements for filing with the Registrar of Companies
Ordinary resolution	Over 50% of the votes cast at the meeting	Not normally required to be filed, except for an increase in authorised share capital, or shareholders' authority to the directors to allot shares
Special resolution	At least 75% of the votes cast at the meeting	All special resolutions must be filed

The 14-day notice period can be extended by a company's articles of association, and many companies' articles provide for a 21-day notice period for special resolutions. If they do, this 21-day period must be observed, or the articles changed.

The articles of some companies may refer to extraordinary resolutions. This type of resolution was abolished by the Companies Act 2006. However, transitional arrangements mean that if an existing company's articles specifically require its shareholders to pass an extraordinary resolution in relation to a particular matter, they must continue to do so, and the old rules regarding extraordinary resolutions are treated as if they still applied. These rules provide that 14 clear days' notice must be given of an extraordinary resolution, and it must be passed by at least 75% of the votes cast at the meeting. The extraordinary resolution must be filed with the registrar of companies within 15 days.

Elective resolutions, which shareholders of a private company could pass under the old law to dispense with the need to hold an annual general meeting every year, the need to present the accounts to shareholders in a general meeting, and to reappoint the auditors at every meeting at which the accounts were presented, have been abolished.

However, elective resolutions are still required to, for example, extend the period for which directors can be given authority to allot shares (see Chapter 5) so it exceeds 5 years.

For companies that still need to take account of extraordinary and elective resolutions, the rules for each can be summarised as follows.

Type of resolution	Notice period	Majority required	Requirements for filing with the Registrar of Companies
Extraordinary resolution	14 clear days	At least 75% of the votes cast at the meeting	All extraordinary resolutions must be filed
Elective resolution	21 clear days	100% of the votes of the shareholders	All elective resolutions must be filed

7.4 CALLING A GENERAL MEETING

If the articles do not provide otherwise, the board may call general meetings at any time. Calling a general meeting is often called 'convening' the meeting. If there are not sufficient directors present in the UK to have a board meeting, any director or any shareholder may call a general meeting. If the company has one – and having a company secretary will be optional for private companies from April 2008 – they can do this, in each case, by instructing the secretary to call the meeting.

In addition, shareholders may always require the board to call a general meeting by depositing a document called a 'request' at the registered office. The request must state the general nature of the business to be dealt with at the meeting and may include the text of a proposed resolution – provided that the resolution is not defamatory of any person, frivolous or vexatious and it would, if passed, be legally effective.

Shareholders who deposit a request must ordinarily represent one-twentieth (5%) or more of the total voting rights of the company at the date of deposit, or it is not effective. However, to discourage shareholders from constantly requesting general meetings, the proportion of shareholders required in order to request a meeting goes up to one-tenth (10%) in certain circumstances, eg if fewer than 12 months has elapsed since the last general meeting (if any) called pursuant to a request.

If the request is effective, the directors must, within 21 days of the deposit of the request at the registered office, resolve to call the general meeting. They must call it for a date within 28 days of the date of the notice convening the meeting (so preventing the directors from calling the meeting for some distant date in the future). If the directors fail to do so, the shareholders making the request may themselves instruct the secretary to call a general meeting as if they were the directors, or do it themselves, and may recover any expenses they have incurred.

If the board calls the general meeting, a board meeting should be held to resolve to call the general meeting. The directors should instruct one of their number or some other person that they authorise in this respect (which will, if the company has one, usually be the secretary) to call the meeting by sending out notices. That person must be instructed by the board to call the meeting and cannot call the meeting himself.

7.4.1 Requiring the board to circulate a statement to shareholders *

Even if shareholders have not requested a general meeting themselves, they still have the right to require the company to circulate a statement to the shareholders, of not more than 1,000 words, with respect to any proposed resolution, or any other business, to be dealt with at a general meeting.

The request must be made by shareholders representing at least 5% of the total voting rights, must identify the statement to be circulated and must be authenticated (see below) by the person or persons making it. The request must be received by the company at least one week before the relevant meeting and the shareholders of a private company will have to pay for it, and deposit 'a reasonably sufficient sum' of money in advance, unless the shareholders resolve otherwise.

If a request is made, the company must circulate the statement in the same way as the notice of meeting and either at the same time, or as soon as reasonably practicable after. Failure to comply is an offence.

7.4.2 The notice *

Notice of a general meeting must be in writing and will normally set out the wording of the resolutions to be proposed in full (and must do so in the case of special resolutions). The notice must contain a statement regarding the right of a shareholder to appoint a proxy.

Consequently, the secretary should prepare the notice to include:

(1) the date, time and place of the meeting;

(2)   details of business to be transacted including ordinary and special resolutions;

(3)   a reminder of the right of a shareholder to appoint proxies – this must tell the shareholder of their statutory right to appoint another person as their proxy to exercise all their rights to attend and to speak and vote at a meeting of the company, and any more extensive rights conferred by the company's articles to appoint more than one proxy.

Failure to observe these requirements may be an offence and, in some circumstances, may mean the notice is invalid.

7.4.2.1   To whom should notice be given?

The notice should be given to the persons entitled to receive it under the articles of association. Usually these are shareholders who hold shares carrying the right to vote, personal representatives (if the shareholder has died), the directors and the auditors (if the company has any).

The way in which notice is given ('the method of service') is dependent on the articles. Articles usually provide that notice is to be served personally or by post to a shareholder's registered address – the address in the register of shareholders.

7.4.2.2   Electronic communications from companies to their shareholders **

Companies have been able to communicate electronically with a shareholder for many years, provided that both the company and the shareholder agreed, but the Companies Act 2006 has widened the circumstances in which they can do so and also extended the rules in other ways. There are two particularly significant changes.

First, before the 2006 Act, companies could only supply notice of general meetings, statutory accounts and summary financial statements (public companies only) electronically. Now, they can send or supply any document or information required to be sent or supplied to shareholders under the Act electronically.

Second, where the company wishes to communicate documents or information to shareholders by 'making it available' on a website, shareholders can, for the first time, be deemed to have agreed to this, provided certain conditions are met.

There is no requirement for a company to include provisions in its articles before it can take advantage of the 2006 Act rules, but it is sensible to do so. For existing companies that have already made provision for electronic communication in their articles under the pre-2006 Act rules, see below.

Under the 2006 Act, it is possible to give notice of a shareholders' meeting (and also any other document or information that can be sent or supplied to a shareholder under the Companies Acts) electronically – for example:

- by fax, email, text, SMS or using any other electronic medium and, in the case of email, either in the email itself, or as an attachment to it;

- by putting it in electronic form, such as on a disk or CDROM, and sending it by conventional means, eg by post; or

- by 'making it available' on a website.

Making a document or information such as a notice 'available on a website' means posting it on a website and notifying the shareholder that it is there.

If the document or information is sent by fax, email, etc, to a shareholder or put into an electronic form and sent by conventional means, the key requirement is that the shareholder must have specifically agreed to receive the document or information electronically, by the means that the company has used. He cannot be deemed to have agreed. If given by fax, email, SMS or other means requiring an electronic address, the shareholder must provide the company with an electronic address, such as a fax or phone number, or an email address, for that purpose.

A shareholder can also specifically agree that documents or information can be sent or supplied to him by making them available on a website. But if he does not, the 2006 Act says he can be deemed to have agreed, provided certain conditions are satisfied.

First, the shareholders must have either altered the company's articles of association, or passed an ordinary resolution, stating that the company may communicate with shareholders through a website. The special resolution to alter the company's articles, or the ordinary resolution, must be filed at Companies House within 15 days.

Second, the company must have asked each shareholder, individually, to agree to receive documents or information by means of a website (either generally or in relation to specific documents or information). The company does this by sending a 'request' to the shareholder. The company cannot send a request to a shareholder if it has already sent one to him in relation to the same or similar documents or information within the last 12 months. The company must therefore keep clear records of which shareholders have had requests, which documents or information the requests related to, and when the requests were sent.

If the shareholder does not respond within 28 days from the date the request is sent, he is deemed to have agreed that the documents or information specified in it can be made available via a website. The request must clearly state the effect of a failure to respond by the shareholder (ie that he is deemed to have consented if he does not reply within 28 days starting with the date on which the request is sent).

The Institute of Chartered Secretaries and Administrators recommends in its *Guidance on Electronic Communications with Shareholders 2007* (reference number 160207) (see below) that the request includes other information to help the shareholder, including details of the software/hardware a shareholder will need to see the documents or information on the website, and a statement that the shareholder can limit the documents or information he is prepared to receive via a website.

If the document or information is posted on a website, the shareholder must be notified that it has been posted, the address of the site it is on, how to find it on that site and how to access it. That notification can be sent electronically, provided a shareholder has specifically agreed that it can be.

Where the document posted on the site is a notice of general meeting, the notification must also state that it concerns a notice of a company meeting, and specify the place, date and time of the meeting.

A document or information is treated as sent or supplied to the shareholder on the date the notification is sent, or the date it first appears on the website, whichever is later.

The company must provide a document or information on a website in a way that it 'reasonably considers' will enable shareholders to read it, and retain a copy of it – eg by printing it off.

The Companies Act may specify a particular period that a document or information must be available on the website. For example, a notice of general meeting must be available throughout the period beginning with the date of the notification and ending with the conclusion of the meeting. If no such period is specified, the document or information must be available for a period of 28 days beginning with the date on which the notification is sent. There is a 'let-out' if the failure to make a document or information available on a website is wholly attributable to circumstances that it would not be reasonable to have expected the company to prevent or avoid, such as an IT failure.

Even if a shareholder has agreed to electronic communications from the company, the company must provide a hard copy of any document or information sent or supplied electronically, within 21 days, if the shareholder requests it. Failure to comply is an offence by the company and every officer.

In addition to the rules in the 2006 Act, companies also need to think about practical issues like the format that an email attachment should take, whether the company wishes to monitor whether an email has been opened, whether shareholders need to acknowledge response, and how, and many similar issues.

The Institute of Chartered Secretaries and Administrators *Guidance on Electronic Communications with Shareholders 2007* (reference number 160207), referred to above, provides an excellent indication of the issues involved, and practical solutions to problems. It can be downloaded, free of charge from http://www.companiesact.org.uk/icsa-guidance-to-the-act.html.

Companies usually make provision for these practical matters in internal policies and procedures, agreed by the board. This means they can be altered simply and easily to take account of, for example, technological advances. If, however, the shareholders want control over these rules, they could instead be included in the articles of association, requiring a resolution of the shareholders both when they are set up and on any proposed amendment.

Existing companies beware. Many have provisions allowing electronic communications in their articles that pre-date the 2006 Act. By definition, such articles will only allow the company to send notices, accounts and summary financial statements electronically. They may also have inadequate articles in relation to making documents or information available via a website. Their articles will therefore act as limitations on their ability to communicate with shareholders electronically, and they should consider altering them to take advantage of the 2006 Act rules.

7.4.2.3   Electronic communications from individual shareholders to their companies **

The 2006 Act also provides that any document or information to be sent or supplied to companies by their shareholders under the Act can be sent or supplied electronically. For electronic communication such as emails, it must supply an electronic address for this purpose. The company must specifically agree that this can happen, save in two circumstances when it is deemed to have agreed.

If the company gives an electronic address in (1) any notice of general meeting sent to shareholders, or (2) any proxy form or invitation to appoint a proxy, it is deemed to have agreed that any document or information relating to proceedings at the meeting or relating to proxies for that meeting, respectively, may be sent by electronic means to that address by its shareholders.

There is an exception if the notice makes this subject to any conditions or limitations. A company that does not wish its shareholders to be able to send it documents or information relating to the meeting, or to proxies, electronically, therefore needs to omit any electronic addresses from these documents, or say that including the address does not constitute deemed agreement to receiving documents or information from shareholders electronically.

7.4.2.4   *How much notice should be given?*

If posted, notice is deemed under modern articles to be given 48 hours after posting. If given electronically, a notice is deemed served 48 hours after despatch. These periods may be varied by the company's articles of association.

The length of notice for calling a general meeting is 14 clear days, unless the company's articles provide for some other, longer, period. They may well do so – for example, many articles provide that 21 days' notice must be given of a meeting to consider a special resolution. Saturdays, Sundays, bank and public holidays are all counted when calculating these notice periods. The day the notice is given and the day of the meeting are not counted in calculating the notice period. This can be very important when the notice is given by post, because, under the current version of Table A (if it applies to the company), it is not deemed given until 48 hours after posting.

7.4.2.5   *Short notice*

If it is agreed by a majority in number of the shareholders who have the right to attend and vote at a meeting and who hold not less than a certain percentage in nominal value of the shares giving that right, the meeting may be held on less than the 14 clear days' notice otherwise necessary. The required percentage will vary according to the company, but it is usually 90%, unless the articles provide for some other percentage. Often, they do – a percentage of 95% is common – so directors should always check their own articles of association. (See Figure 9 below.)

Consent to short notice need not be given in writing, but it invariably is. The written consent should be kept with the company records.

7.4.3   What is the business of the meeting?

Matters dealt with at a general meeting will be those specific matters for which the meeting is called. See Chapter 16 for some of the matters requiring a decision by ordinary or special (or extraordinary – see **7.3**) resolution at a general meeting.

7.4.4   Signed resolutions in lieu of a meeting – written resolutions *

The Companies Act 2006 permits shareholders of a private company to pass resolutions without holding a general meeting by signing a resolution in writing – either the same document, or several documents each of which accurately states the terms of the resolution. Public companies may not pass resolutions in writing.

A written resolution passed pursuant to the 2006 Act can be used to pass every single sort of resolution except two, and it is as good as if a general meeting had been held, and all necessary formalities observed – the only exceptions are resolutions to remove a director, and to remove an auditor before the end of his period of office.

It is no longer possible to pass written resolutions pursuant to a provision in a private company's articles – they must all be passed in accordance with the statutory procedure in the 2006 Act. Provisions in articles that purport to allow passing of written resolutions must be ignored.

Key requirements of the statutory procedure in the 2006 Act are:

- circulation of copies of the proposed resolution to every shareholder who would have been entitled to vote on it if it had been proposed at a general meeting;

- circulation of an accompanying statement;

- that the requisite majority of the shareholders have indicated their agreement to the resolution, within the relevant time limit.

In the vast majority of cases, the board will be the originator of a proposed written resolution. However, the shareholders holding at least 5% (or such lower percentage as is specified in the company's articles) of the total voting rights in the company entitled to vote on the resolution can require the directors to circulate a proposed written resolution. This includes a right to provide a statement of up to 1,000 words to accompany the proposed resolution. The request can be made in hard copy or electronic form. It must identify the resolution and any accompanying statement, and it must be authenticated (see below) by the person(s) making it.

Unless the shareholders resolve otherwise in advance, the requisitionists have to deposit a sum with the requisition that is reasonably sufficient to cover the company's expenses of circulating, etc the written resolution.

Subject to payment of costs and provided that the resolution is not defamatory of any person, is not frivolous or vexatious and would, if passed, be legally effective, the company must circulate the resolution and statement within 21 days of receiving the request.

Whether the board originates the written resolution, or is responding to a shareholders' requisition, the procedure is as follows.

The board must send or submit a copy of the proposed resolution to every eligible member:

- by sending copies at the same time (so far as is reasonably practicable) to them in hard copy form or, with the necessary consents, electronically;

- if it is possible to do so without undue delay, by submitting the same copy to each of them in turn (or different copies to each of a number of eligible members in turn); or

- by a combination of the two.

An 'eligible member' is a shareholder who would have been entitled to vote on the resolution if a general meeting had been held on the date copies are first sent or submitted to a shareholder.

The copy of the resolution must be accompanied by a statement telling the shareholder how to signify agreement to the resolution and stating the date by which it must be passed if it is not to lapse.

The written resolution and statement can be sent in electronic form to each shareholder who has specifically consented to electronic communications and/or, if the written resolution is to be made available via a website, they are deemed to have consented to the document being made available in that way. If they have consented to that too, the company can also send the notification electronically. See **7.4.2.4** above.

The resolution is still valid if these rules are not followed, but failure to comply is a criminal offence.

Subject to any different provision in the company's articles, on a vote on a written resolution:

- In a share company, every shareholder has one vote for each share that he holds.

- In a company without share capital, every shareholder has one vote.

The percentage vote required to pass a written resolution depends on whether the resolution is proposed as an ordinary resolution or a special resolution. For an ordinary resolution a simple majority of the total voting rights of the eligible members is required. For a special resolution not less than 75% of the total voting rights of the eligible members is required. It is no longer necessary for every voting shareholder to agree to the resolution, as it was under the pre-2006 Act rules.

The period allowed for indications of agreement from eligible members can be set out in the individual company's articles of association. If this has been done, the resolution is passed if adequate indications of agreement are received within that period. If no period is specified for this purpose in the company's articles, then adequate indications must be received within a period of 28 days beginning with the circulation date.

A shareholder indicates agreement when the company receives from him (or from someone acting on his behalf) an authenticated document identifying the resolution and indicating his agreement to the resolution. The document must be sent to the company either in hard copy or electronic form.

The accuracy of the register of shareholders is vital to carrying out correctly the procedure for written resolutions of the shareholders. So is the availability of an up-to-date copy of that company's articles of association. The person responsible for the company's administration must be sure they can identify who the 'eligible members' are and be able to demonstrate that they were all properly circulated. They must also be able to calculate correctly whether or not the required majority consent has been received in the required time limit.

Methods that a company might invite shareholders to use to signify their consent to a proposed written resolution, sent out by email, might include:

- Signing and returning (or faxing to a specified number) a hard copy of the resolution.

- Signing, scanning and emailing a pdf of the signed resolution.

- Sending an email to the return email address of the company confirming that it is from (or sent on behalf of) the shareholder and that the shareholder agrees to the resolution.

Where an email consent is from somebody sending it on behalf of the shareholder, or from a shareholder that is itself a corporate body (eg in the case of a wholly owned subsidiary), the company receiving the consent needs to establish that the sender has authority to act on behalf of the shareholder.

If a company circulates a special resolution as a proposed written resolution, the circulated resolution must state that it is being proposed as a special resolution.

A copy of the resolution must be kept, as well as a record of the signatures on it, as if it were minutes of a meeting, and, if the resolution would have had to be lodged if passed at a general meeting, the written resolution must be lodged.

7.4.4.1 Authentication of documents ***

A hard copy document is authenticated if it is signed. A document supplied in electronic form is authenticated if:

- the identity of the sender is confirmed in some way specified by the company; or

- where the company has made no express rule, if the communication contains or is accompanied by a statement of the identity of the sender and the company has no reason to doubt that statement.

A company's articles may provide that, if a document is sent by one person on behalf of another, it can require reasonable evidence of the authority of the former to act on behalf of the latter.

Companies need to decide whether they will make rules for confirming the identity of senders of electronic documents or, if they do not, what might constitute a reason to doubt that a statement is made by whoever is purporting to make it. Take advice.

7.4.5 Generally

7.4.5.1 Who is present?

The secretary or, if the company has opted not to have a company secretary, a person authorised to do so by the directors, should ascertain and list who is present, for the minutes. Provision of an attendance list for signature by all attendees is sensible from the secretary's point of view.

7.4.5.2 Quorum

A quorum must be present. Normally the required quorum is two persons entitled to vote on the business of the meeting. If a quorum is not present

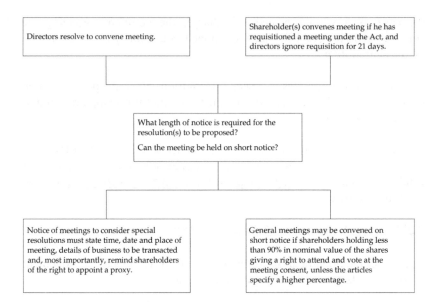

Figure 9 – Calling a general meeting

throughout the meeting, the meeting usually ceases to be effective. The articles should be carefully checked in these respects.

If the company is a single shareholder company, it can hold a general meeting at which only the single shareholder is present, and the single shareholder will constitute a quorum at that meeting, irrespective of any provisions of law, or of the company's articles, to the contrary. However, it is prudent to alter the articles of a proposed single shareholder company in any event, so as to achieve consistency between the articles and the rules. The single shareholder must still be given formal notice of any general meeting and, if it is to be held on short notice, he must consent to the short notice as if he was one of a number of shareholders.

Otherwise, it is only in very exceptional circumstances that one person may constitute an effective meeting, or quorum, at a meeting. Subject to those circumstances, it is still not possible for one shareholder to constitute a meeting, or a quorum at it, where the company in fact has more than one shareholder, but the others choose not to attend at a proposed general meeting.

7.4.5.3   *Chairman*

The chairman of the board (if any) is usually also entitled to be chairman at shareholders' meetings if he is present and willing to act. If not, the directors nominate one of their number to act as chairman of the meeting. If no director is present and willing to act, the shareholders may choose one of their number to be chairman of the meeting.

7.4.5.4   *Voting procedure*

During the meeting, and subject to the articles, any resolution put to the vote will be decided on a show of hands unless before, or on the declaration of the result of the show of hands, a poll is demanded. The chairman, or two shareholders, or a single shareholder holding at least one-tenth of the issued shares has the right to demand a poll. On a poll, each shareholder normally has one vote for each share he holds.

7.5   RECORDS AND REGISTERS *

After the conclusion of the meeting, minutes recording the proceedings and resolutions passed may be prepared, signed by the chairman and kept with the company's records.

Any requirements to file special resolutions or other items with the registrar of companies must be complied with.

7.6   THE ANNUAL RETURN *

Under the Companies Acts, every company must submit an annual return to Companies House every year, with a fee. This can either be submitted as a hard copy form, or filed electronically either by using the Webfiling service at www.companieshouse.gov.uk or by licensing company secretarial software that is approved by Companies House for electronic filing purposes. The fee is less if the annual return is filed electronically.

The annual return contains information as to the share capital, shareholders and officers of the company.

The annual return will be made up as at a date not later than the anniversary of formation of the company, or, if different, the anniversary of the last annual return date, and must be lodged within 28 days of that date.

7.7   PROXIES AND REPRESENTATIVES

A proxy is a person appointed by a shareholder of a company (whether an individual shareholder or a company that is a shareholder of another company – a 'corporate shareholder') to exercise all or any of his rights to attend and to speak and to vote at a general meeting of the company. The 2006 Act provides a statutory right for a shareholder to appoint a proxy. The right applies equally to shareholders in companies that only have a single shareholder, as well as where there are multiple shareholders.

Note the requirement for a notice of meeting to contain a statement about shareholders' rights to appoint proxies, referred to above.

An appointment of a proxy must be in writing and be lodged at the company's registered office before the meeting. The wording of a possible form of proxy is usually set out in the company's articles. There are two versions – either the shareholder may give his proxy a full discretion as to whether and how he exercises all or any of the shareholder's votes, or the shareholder may set out on the form the way he wishes the proxy to vote on particular resolutions.

For a company having share capital, a shareholder may appoint more than one proxy in relation to a meeting, provided that each proxy is appointed to exercise the rights attached to a different share or shares held by that shareholder. This power is designed for the case where the shareholder is holding different shares on behalf of different people, but there is no restriction on its use.

It is common practice to send out a form for appointment of a proxy (or proxies) with the notice of meeting, with instructions on how to complete and return it for an effective proxy appointment. The 2006 Act regulates how this is done – take advice, as failure to comply is an offence.

The 2006 Act also sets out how early any appointment of a proxy must be received by the company. Any provision in a company's articles is void in so far as it would have the effect of requiring the proxy (or document) to be received by the company (or any other person) earlier than:

- in the case of a meeting or adjourned meeting, 48 hours before the time for holding the meeting (or adjourned meeting);

- in the case of a poll taken more than 48 hours after it was demanded, 24 hours before the time appointed for taking the poll;

- in the case of a poll taken not more than 48 hours after it was demanded, the time at which it was demanded.

In calculating these periods, no account is taken of any part of a day that is *not* a working day.

If the shareholder wants to terminate the appointment of his proxy, the termination is only effective if notice of termination is received by the company (or other person specified in the company's articles) before the start of the meeting. The company's articles can specify an earlier time for receipt of the notice of termination, but such provisions are subject to the same restrictions as those stated above for provisions about when proxy appointments must be received.

The appointment of a proxy to vote on a matter at a general meeting authorises the proxy to demand (or join in demanding) a poll on that matter. A proxy can vote on a show of hands and on a poll.

Nothing in the relevant provisions of the 2006 Act prevents a company's articles from conferring more extensive rights on proxies than are conferred by the Act.

If the company provides an electronic 'address' on the form of proxy, or any invitation to appoint a proxy, it is deemed to have agreed that shareholders can return the form of proxy (and any other document relating to proxies at the relevant general meeting) to the company electronically. 'Address' includes an email address or fax number. The rules are complex and companies should not offer shareholders the option of serving proxies electronically without advice.

A corporate shareholder can appoint either a proxy or a representative to attend a general meeting on its behalf. The word 'representative' has a strict legal meaning in this context. A representative has power to speak and vote on a show of hands, a poll and a demand for a poll, as if they were a shareholder in their own right. Corporate shareholders often prefer appointing a representative rather than a proxy, because the representative merely needs to turn up at the meeting with a copy of an appropriate board resolution of the corporate shareholder, certified as a true copy by an officer of the corporate shareholder, whereas appointing a proxy requires the shareholder to lodge the form of proxy at the company's registered office in advance. However, uncertainty about the wording introduced by the Companies Act 2006 in relation to appointment of multiple corporate representatives means corporate shareholders should take advice if they wish to appoint more than one corporate representative to attend a general meeting on their behalf.

7.8 ELECTIVE RESOLUTIONS **

In the past, there were a number of matters which could be dispensed with by an elective resolution of the shareholders of a private company, which would otherwise apply. These included the requirement to hold an annual general meeting, and to present accounts to a general meeting of the members every year. Only shareholders of private companies can pass elective resolutions, and all the shareholders entitled to vote at general meetings had to vote in favour in order for an elective resolution to be passed. An elective resolution, once passed, could be revoked at any time by an ordinary resolution of the shareholders.

Both elective resolutions, and ordinary resolutions revoking them, had to be filed with the registrar of companies.

In most cases, the ability to pass an elective resolution has been abolished under the Companies Act 2006. However, some elective resolutions passed prior to the 2006 Act continue to have effect. There is also one circumstance – extending the period for which directors can be given authority to allot shares by the shareholders – when an elective resolution may still be passed in any event.

Under this power, shareholders can resolve, by elective resolution, to give themselves power to authorise the directors to allot shares for any fixed period, or even for an indefinite period, rather than for the maximum period of 5 years which otherwise applies.

The shareholders of the company can then give such an authority to the directors, by ordinary resolution or in the articles, in any way envisaged by the elective resolution.

The requirement for shareholders to authorise the directors to allot shares is to be abolished from October 2009. At that point, the ability to pass elective resolutions to alter the period for which the authority is to last will be abolished too.

7.9   PASSING THE ELECTIVE RESOLUTION

An elective resolution is not effective unless it is passed at a general meeting at which all shareholders are present, in person or by proxy (or, in the case of a corporate shareholder, its representative), and all agree to the elective resolution being passed. Twenty-one clear days' notice must be given of the meeting and the notice must state the terms of the resolution and the fact that it is an elective resolution. However, if every shareholder entitled to attend and vote at the general meeting consents to the meeting being called upon shorter notice than 21 clear days, the meeting may be held on less than 21 clear days' notice. The elective resolution must be lodged with the registrar of companies within 15 days after it is passed.

An elective resolution may also be passed as a written resolution without the need to hold a general meeting, but this should not be attempted without professional advice.

7.10   REVOCATION OR CESSATION OF AN ELECTIVE RESOLUTION

An elective resolution, whether current, or passed pursuant to the pre-2006 Act rules, can be revoked by an ordinary resolution – such an ordinary resolution must be lodged with the registrar of companies within 15 days after it is passed. It will also cease to have effect if the company ceases to be private, by re-registering as a public company.

CHAPTER 8

CONTRACTS BINDING ON THE COMPANY

8.1   TYPES OF CONTRACT

Individuals enter into contracts or agreements (the two words mean the same thing) every day – by making a purchase in a shop, buying a car park ticket or signing a contract of employment, for example. Most contracts need not be in writing. With a car park ticket some parts of the contract are written and some are not. Some contracts must be in writing.

8.2   THE OBJECTS AND POWERS OF THE COMPANY

Provided it is empowered to do so in its memorandum, a company can also enter into contracts. Again, these need not be in writing, unless the law requires it.

The company may not be empowered to enter into the contract, because of limits in its memorandum. A company which acts outside its memorandum is acting 'ultra vires' – beyond its powers.

Whilst 'outsiders' are not concerned as to whether the company is acting ultra vires or not, it remains the duty of the directors to ensure that it is not.

8.3   DECISION BY THE BOARD

Usually, a decision of the board of directors will bind the company. But it may be the case that the directors cannot bind the company to a particular transaction – there may be limits which the shareholders have put on them, in the memorandum or articles. However, a person dealing with the company in good faith is entitled to assume that the board, or any person authorised by the board, can bind the company. The directors of the company will get into trouble with the shareholders and the company, for exceeding their power to bind the company, but the company is still bound.

8.4   DECISIONS BY SINGLE DIRECTORS, SECRETARIES OR EMPLOYEES

The directors of a company rarely make a decision at a full board meeting, although they should do so where matters of policy are concerned, or other issues considered crucial to the operation of the company, or where a formal written record of particular decisions is required, or where the Companies Act, company's articles of association or a shareholders' agreement requires them to. Instead, it is often single directors, or the secretary (if the company has one – see Chapter 5), or other employees who enter into contracts with outsiders, on behalf of the company.

Can a person entering into an agreement with a single director, or the secretary, or an employee, of a company be sure that the company will be bound to observe the agreement?

8.4.1   Actual authority

It is open to the directors to delegate some of their authority to one or more of their number – to committees of directors. Some of the powers can even be delegated to one director who holds an executive office, such as finance director. Indeed, when a company appoints a managing director, he sometimes has all the powers of the rest of the board. An outsider dealing with a committee, or single director, or managing director, with actual authority to bind the company on a particular matter, is safe.

Similarly, the directors can delegate their powers to the secretary, or any employee. The signature on a document of an ordinary employee with actual authority to sign that document will bind the company – for example, a receptionist who has actual authority to sign for registered post can bind the company in that respect, in the same way as a director could.

The general principle is that any person with actual authority in a particular matter can bind the company.

From the company's point of view it is crucial that every director, secretary and employee knows the limits of his actual authority – it is vital to establish a chain of authority. Contracts of employment, staff regulations and standing orders, and job descriptions can all help set these limits.

8.4.2   Ostensible authority

What if an employee, for example, exceeds his actual authority? 'Holding out' – the principle of ostensible authority – may apply. This means that an outsider is entitled to assume the employee (or director or secretary) is able to bind the company because, for example, his title implies a certain status, or he has regularly entered into agreements of the same nature before, with the knowledge of the board of directors, but without objection from them.

Whenever an employee is given a special title such as manager, or divisional director, consideration should be given as to the effect this will have on outsiders. Has the employee been given an 'ostensible authority' which he did not previously have?

8.4.3   Usual authority

Outsiders who do not know otherwise are entitled to assume that an officer or employee, who usually has power to bind a company to a particular type of contract, in fact has such power, even if he actually does not.

Directors have a wide usual and ostensible authority – the company holds them out as having very wide powers. The secretary has usual and ostensible authority in relation to administrative matters. For example, a bank manager would not accept a senior manager's signature on a loan agreement, but an agreement for the supply of typewriters for their department would be a different matter.

It is a matter of degree in every case whether a particular employee, director or secretary (if the company has one) has ostensible or usual authority. Whilst the company can seek compensation from someone with ostensible authority who exceeds their actual authority, the company is bound, and seeking compensation may be a useless remedy.

8.4.4   No actual, ostensible or usual authority

What if an employee, director or, if it has one, the secretary, has no actual, ostensible or usual authority, but holds himself out as having authority, and the outsider deals with them? The company is not bound, but the employee, director or secretary may be liable to the outsider for damages for breach of warranty of authority.

8.5   EXECUTING DOCUMENTS – THE LAW IN ENGLAND AND WALES AND NORTHERN IRELAND **

There are two ways that a company can be legally bound by a contract or other document in writing.

A person can sign most (but not all) contracts on behalf of the company, and it will be bound. However, there are certain documents, such as deeds, which must be 'executed' by the company itself, and cannot be signed on its behalf. For example, most documents relating to transfers or mortgages of land must be executed as deeds. A company's articles may also say that certain documents such as share certificates must be executed by the company.

A company can either execute a document using its company seal or, if it does not have one, or chooses not to use it, can execute it by following alternative rules set out in the Companies Acts. Of course, it has to act through human agents in each case, so there are special rules in each circumstance.

8.5.1   Contracts signed on behalf of the company

Whenever someone signs a contract, or any other document, on behalf of the company they should always sign 'for and on behalf of XYZ Limited', otherwise they are personally vulnerable. For example, a director who signs or authorises the signature of a cheque which does not have the proper company name on it can be personally liable to meet the cheque in some circumstances, and also liable to a fine.

In this context, company name means just what it says. Abbreviations, such as 'Bros' instead of 'Brothers' are not allowed if it is the latter which appears on the certificate of incorporation (or certificate on change of name) of the company.

Similarly, failure to include the company name on business letters, notices, official publications, invoices, receipts, letter of credit, and other official documents means that officers may have committed an offence, and be liable to a fine.

Contracts in writing signed by a person on the company's behalf should therefore be signed as follows:

SIGNED by . . . .
for and on behalf of XYZ Limited

8.5.2   Contracts and documents executed using the company seal

If a document has to be executed by the company, or the directors decide they want a document to be executed by the company, the company may decide to use its seal.

The seal is the signature of the company, and its imprint on a document usually has to be witnessed by signature of a director and the secretary or two directors. (It is legally also possible for all or any of the signatories to be persons authorised by the board to sign, rather than directors or the secretary, but this may mean third parties want to see the board resolution giving authority before they accept the document is validly sealed.) The signatories are not signing the document themselves – the effect of their signatures is merely to witness the affixing of the seal. Documents under seal should be executed as follows:

THE COMMON SEAL of
the company was affixed
hereto in the presence of:

.............**Director**
.............**Director/Secretary**

8.5.3   Contracts and documents executed without using the company seal

Having a company seal is optional, so many companies do not have a seal. Even if a company does have a seal, it can decide not to use it on any particular document.

If a company does not wish to have, or to use, a seal, which rule applies will depend upon whether the document is intended to be executed as a deed or not.

Documents not intended to be deeds must, until April 2008, be signed by either a director and the secretary, or two directors, and expressed to be executed by the company. Documents executed this way might be executed as follows:

This document is hereby executed by XYZ Limited.

.............**Director**
.............**Director/Secretary**

In April 2008 the rules change slightly. From 6 April, a document will be validly executed by the company if signed on its behalf by two authorised signatories (which, in this context, means a director of the company and, if the company has one – see Chapter 5 – the secretary) or by a director of the company in the presence of a witness, who signs that he has witnessed the signature.

Prior to April 2008, a document intended to be a deed must make it clear on its face that it is intended to be a deed. For example, prior to April 2008 it might be executed as follows:

This document is hereby executed, with the intention that it be a Deed, by XYZ Limited.

. . . . Director
. . . . Director/Secretary

After April 2008 it will be a valid deed if it is executed by the company and 'delivered as a deed'. For simplicity, a document is presumed to be delivered when it is executed, unless someone challenging its validity can prove that it was not intended to be delivered then (eg because of the wording used in it, or because it is clear from some external evidence that the parties to the document did not intend it to take effect until some later date).

If in doubt as to the execution of documents, seek professional advice.

8.6   EXECUTING DOCUMENTS – THE LAW IN SCOTLAND ***

A company, wherever it is registered, may need to enter into a contract which is governed by Scottish law. Advice should, if the circumstances warrant, be sought from a qualified Scottish professional, in relation to creating and enforcing such contracts. However, the rules as to the power of the company to contract, and the position of its board and employees of the company, are the same, irrespective of whether the company is registered in Scotland, or in England and Wales.

However, execution of a document under Scottish law is a complex matter, and advice should always be sought from a qualified Scottish professional. Scottish law will apply to such documents, irrespective of whether the company is registered in Scotland or in England and Wales.

The current situation is that Scots law requires certain contracts and other legal transactions to be in writing. In addition, certain documents are required to be formally authenticated. If certain formalities are observed in the execution of a document, the document is presumed accurate and to have been executed by the granter, so that the burden of proof falls on the person who wishes to rebut the presumption.

Arriving at the current situation has not been plain sailing. Scots law has been reformed by the Companies Act 1989, the Law Reform (Miscellaneous Provisions) (Scotland) Act 1990 and the Requirements of Writing (Scotland) Act 1995. The latter Act introduced substantive reforms.

These reforms provide that only those documents referred to in the Act are required to be in writing, unless writing is specifically required in relation to a document under some other legislation.

If the granter is a company, the document may be signed by a director, the secretary or a duly authorised signatory. There is no requirement for a witness or use of a company seal, if the company has one.

If the document is to be recorded in, for example, the Scottish property register, it must be formally authenticated. This means that it must either:

(1)   bear to have been subscribed by a director, secretary or authorised signatory and bear to have been signed by a witness to that subscription, and include the witness's name and address; or

(2)   bear to have been subscribed by two directors, a director and the secretary or by two duly authorised signatories, without witnesses.

CHAPTER 9

ACCOUNTS

9.1 'ACCOUNTS' AND 'ACCOUNTING RECORDS'

The word 'accounts' is often heard when business matters are being discussed. Correctly used, it describes the set of figures prepared by a company at intervals which summarise the business results for that period. Another common and interchangeable description of these accounts is the term 'financial statements'.

'Accounts' is also used frequently, and rather misleadingly, to describe the books and records which are kept by the company as evidence of the company's transactions.

These are correctly referred to as accounting records. Accounts then are a summary of the results for a period whilst accounting records provide evidence of day-to-day events and transactions. The accounts of a company will be prepared from the information recorded in the accounting records.

The different types of accounts are discussed later in this chapter.

The public has a legal right to certain information on the financial standing of a company with which it deals. Every company must send its statutory accounts to be filed at Companies House and the public may inspect and take copies of these accounts. The public has no access, however, to a company's accounting records. Accounting records are essential to enable the preparation of both the annual statutory accounts and internal management figures and they represent a key element of the information which the company's auditor will inspect during the course of his audit of the company's statutory accounts.

Every business needs to keep some form of record of the transactions which take place. Without this record, it would be impossible to know what had happened in the past, who owed the business money, or indeed how much the business owed to others or holds in the bank account at any point in time.

The need to keep records not only provides the businessman with information to help him run the company more efficiently, but also protects the public who deal with that company, as it ensures that an accurate record of all the company's transactions is maintained.

9.2 THE BASIC ACCOUNTING SYSTEM

Over the years, as business developed, standard methods of recording transactions, or 'keeping books' have emerged. The traditional technique now is to maintain a system of 'double entry' books. The double entry bookkeeping system records every aspect of each transaction the company makes. For example, if a computer retailing company sells a computer, the following entries would be made in that company's books:

On the debit (left) side	*On the credit (right) side*
Reduction in the value of stock at the cost price to the company of the computer.	Increase in the retained profits representing the difference between cost and retail prices.
Increase in cash at the retail price of the computer.	

The debit (left) side of the equation records *assets*, ie property or cash owned by the company or owed to it. This includes trade debtors (people who owe the company money for goods or services it has supplied). The credit (right) side records *liabilities*, ie amounts which the company owes to some other person. This includes trade creditors (to whom the company owes money for goods and services supplied), loans (which the company owes to lenders) and share capital and profit (both of which the company owes to its shareholders).

9.2.1 Setting up an accounting system

The accounting system of a company must be comprehensive enough to provide details of:

(1) sales made by the company;

(2) amounts owed to the company in respect of these sales;

(3) payments and receipts through the bank account;

(4) assets owned by the company;

(5) purchases made by the company;

(6) amounts owed by the company in respect of these purchases;

(7) wages paid, together with tax and other deductions made from employees;

(8) VAT charged to customers, reclaimable from suppliers and paid to HMRC.

These requirements are defined for a company by the Companies Acts, which provide the legislation for the protection of all parties dealing with the company and ensure that the company will be able to prepare accounts at the end of the accounting period.

The majority of accounting record systems are now held on computers, which will still satisfy the requirements of a double entry bookkeeping system as long as the accounting system software contains the following (which all of the major systems do).

9.2.2　Cash book

The cash book records all the transactions through the bank (despite the name 'cash book') and is the single most important part of the records. It has two sides on each page, the left (or debit) showing the amounts received by the company, and the right (credit) showing all payments made by the company. Each side will be divided into columns, with headings for the types of payments or receipts.

9.2.3　Sales ledger

A sales ledger is a collection of 'credit accounts' which customers hold with the company. When a sales invoice is raised and sent to a customer, the amount and details are entered on the debit side of the customer's account. When the customer pays, an entry is made of cash received, on the credit side of the account, which should be the same amount as the outstanding invoice if the customer has paid the full amount. A corresponding entry is then made on the debit side of the cash book for the cash received.

9.2.4　Sales daybook

The sales daybook is a record of all sales invoices issued by the business, in date order, usually grouped into months. The entry on the debit side of the appropriate sales ledger customer's account is a repetition of the sales daybook entry for the invoice.

Also required are a purchase daybook and a purchase ledger, which are similar to their sales equivalent.

9.2.5 Purchase ledger

A purchase ledger is a collection of 'credit accounts' which the company holds with its suppliers. When a purchase invoice is received from a supplier, the amount and details are entered on the credit side of the supplier's account. When the company pays the supplier, an entry is made of the cash paid, on the debit side of the account, which should be the same amount as the outstanding invoice.

A corresponding entry is also made on the credit side of the cash book for the cash paid.

9.2.6 Purchase daybook

The purchase daybook is a record of all purchase invoices received by the company, in date order, and usually grouped into months. The entry on the credit side of the appropriate purchase ledger account is a repetition of the purchase daybook entry for the invoice.

Once the business is expanding, it is advisable to employ a professional bookkeeper, who will keep the accounting system up to date, fill in VAT returns and run the Pay As You Earn (PAYE) wages system. All this may sound daunting, but in practice the records which need to be kept are not complicated.

Without these records, the directors would have little idea of the company's performance.

The availability of immediate, accurate accounting information is an essential element of the success of any company. The leading software packages now available for companies to computerise their accounting system are well proven, efficient and reasonably easy to operate. They can, however, be costly, so research is required, especially in order to ensure that you purchase the correct version of the software. Usually vendors have a number of different versions of the same accounting software, the difference between the versions being added features, such as stock recording or order processing, which not all businesses will need.

9.3 TIME LIMITS *

The accounting records (both physical and computer-based), including all books and invoices relating to the transactions of the company must be kept safe for many years after the period to which they relate.

Current time limit requirements are as follows:

(1) HMRC (VAT) – 6 years

(2)   HMRC (PAYE and tax) – 6 years

(3)   General accounting records – 6 years

(4)   Department for Work and Pensions – 3 years

It is recommended therefore to keep all the company's accounting records safe for 6 years.

9.4   THE DIFFERENT TYPES OF ACCOUNTS

When the company has started to trade, the directors will need to prepare accounts on a regular basis. There are two basic types of accounts: *management accounts* and *statutory accounts*.

These two types of accounts are prepared for different reasons. Management accounts are prepared on a regular basis (usually monthly) as trading continues. They provide the management with information about the performance of the company.

Statutory accounts are required by law and usually prepared each year. A copy of extracts from these accounts or, for larger companies, a full set of accounts, signed in accordance with the Companies Acts by the directors has to be lodged each year at Companies House in Cardiff, Edinburgh or Belfast, depending on where the company is registered, and the public have the right to inspect these accounts and take copies. The public have no access to management accounts. The two types of accounts are now described in more detail.

9.4.1   Management accounts

Once the company starts to grow, it will become more important to know exactly how things are going on a regular basis.

Management accounts are simple accounts, normally prepared in-house, although in the early stages they may be prepared by the company's auditors where the company does not employ an in-house accountant.

The accounts will show sales, cost of sales, overheads and the profit (or loss) for a set period of, for example, a month. Then the next month another set of accounts will be prepared and the results may be compared, providing the management with invaluable information with which they can manage the business more efficiently.

As things become more sophisticated, the management accounts may include:

(1) departmental or divisional analysis of results;

(2) comparison with preset budgets and variance analysis;

(3) accounting ratios and 'benchmarks'.

Typical accounting ratios used would be:

(a) Gross profit margin, ie $\dfrac{\text{gross profit}}{\text{sales}} \times 100$

which is a crucial ratio, indicating the percentage of profit generated from sales after deducting the direct cost of those sales. This 'gross profit' is then used to absorb the company's overheads, any balance of profit still available after overheads being the company's net profit.

(b) Current ratio, ie $\dfrac{\text{current assets}}{\text{current liabilities}} \times 100$

which provides an indication of the short- to medium-term cash flow strength of the company *at the balance sheet date*. It assumes that all current assets are convertible into cash in the short to medium term, ie within 12 months.

(c) Quick ratio, ie $\dfrac{(\text{current assets}) - (\text{stock})}{\text{current liabilities}} \times 100$

This ratio refines the current ratio to assets and liabilities which will produce imminent, rather than short- to medium-term cash flow *at the balance sheet date* and produces a critical and highly realistic indication of the company's ability to meet its immediate liabilities.

There are many more ratios, covering aspects from stock turnover to net profit margin. Indeed, accounting ratio analysis is a complete subject in itself. The director may wish to calculate a set of ratios which are particularly relevant to the individual company and the recommended course of action is to discuss the subject with the company's auditors or accountants, in order to decide exactly which ratios are the most relevant and should be produced on a monthly basis, as an appendix to the management accounts.

This core financial data provided by management accounts may be supplemented by other types of information to give managers a fuller picture of the company's performance. For instance, in a manufacturing company the management would review production reports, statistics, wastage data and efficiency figures.

Management accounts are of no use if they are out of date, and it is therefore very important to have a monthly deadline (for monthly accounts), of for instance the eighth day of the month, by which date the accounts must be completed and can then be reviewed by the management. Any changes which are then considered necessary as a result of the discussions may be implemented straight away. The effects of these changes will then be reflected in the management accounts prepared for the subsequent months.

Logical and efficient computerisation of an accounting system will make the production of management accounts far quicker and simpler, but caution must be exercised in this area. This topic is discussed in greater detail later in this chapter.

9.4.2   Statutory accounts **

Each year, a company is required to produce a set of statutory accounts. These accounts are similar to management accounts, but are normally more accurate, and disclose more information, or a different type of information. They must be filed at Companies House each year and provide the public with regulated access to the affairs of the company.

Some companies' accounts must be audited by a registered auditor (see Figure 10). The auditor must examine the accounts and underlying accounting records, and report as to whether in his opinion the statutory accounts constitute a true and fair view of the state of the company and results for the period.

The auditor often takes the opportunity available during the course of the audit to make some useful suggestions as to how the company may be able to improve profitability or increase efficiency. The directors of a company are under a statutory obligation to provide the auditor with whatever information he may require which is relevant to his audit of the company's accounts.

However, at the smaller end of the scale, a company may be:

(1)   totally exempt from the requirement to appoint auditors because it is a 'dormant' company; or

(2)   totally exempt from the requirement that the accounts be audited because it is a 'small' company.

Many companies will qualify as both dormant and audit exempt companies, and will have a choice as to their route to audit exemption. Since the 'dormant' company rules require the shareholders of the company to pass a special resolution but the 'small' company rules do not, the latter route is usually preferable.

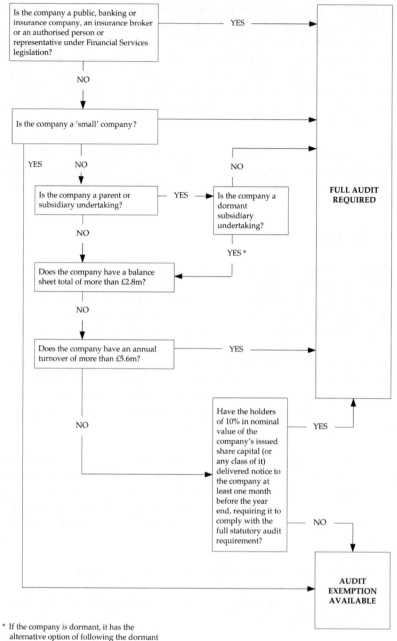

Figure 10 – Audit requirement checklist

9.4.3   Format of statutory accounts

The statutory accounts must present the information in a standard way, as laid out in the most recent Companies Act in force at the time.

The accounts will normally consist of:

(1) balance sheet at the accounting reference date;

(2) profit and loss account for the accounting period;

(3) cash-flow statement;

(4) notes to the accounts,

although smaller companies may only need to file extracts from the above.

9.4.3.1 *Balance sheet*

The balance sheet is a statement setting out all the assets and liabilities of a company at a particular date. A typical format will be:

	£	£
Fixed assets		10,000
Current assets		
Stock	5,000	
Trade debtors	22,500	
Prepayments	3,000	
Cash at bank/in hand	1,500	
	32,000	
Current liabilities		
Trade creditors	23,500	
Corporation tax	1,000	
Other taxes	2,500	
Other creditors and accruals	2,000	
	29,000	
Net current assets		3,000
Total assets less current liabilities		13,000
Creditors due after more than one year		(2,500)
		10,500
Capital and reserves		
Called up share capital		1,000
Profit and loss account		9,500
		10,500

9.4.3.2 *Notes to the balance sheet*

Fixed assets represent the cost (or later valuation) of all fixed asset items – land and buildings, plant and equipment, vehicles, less the depreciation written off the cost up to the date of the balance sheet.

Current assets are defined as all assets due to be collected within 12 months.

Stock is the trading stock the company is holding at the balance sheet date and is normally stated at the lower of cost or net realisable value.

Trade debtors are the amounts (including VAT) which the company is owed in respect of sales invoices raised which have not yet been paid, or to put it another way, the balance on the company's sales ledger at that date.

Cash at bank will be the balance per the company's bank statement at that date, reconciled to include any cheques written or amounts paid in which have not yet been debited or credited to the company's bank account.

Current liabilities are all amounts which the company owes which are due to be settled within the next 12 months.

Trade creditors are the amount the company owes to suppliers and is the opposite of trade debtors, ie the total amount outstanding on the company's purchase ledger at that date (including VAT).

Corporation tax will be any corporation tax the company owes, including that on the current period's profit.

Other taxes represent the total of VAT due and PAYE and National Insurance contributions deducted from employees and not yet paid over to HMRC.

Other creditors are any other items owed by the company which do not fall into any of the above categories.

Creditors due after more than one year are required by the legislation to be shown separately in order to help a reader of the accounts assess the short and longer-term strength of a company in cash-flow terms. Items appearing under this heading will normally be liabilities such as hire purchase balances, or long-term bank loans.

Called up share capital represents the cost of shares issued by the company to its shareholders.

The *profit and loss account* balance will be the total profit generated during the period, net of taxation, as calculated in the detailed profit and loss account statement, together with any balance of profit brought forward from previous periods.

A change in assets of a company from one period end to the next is represented on this side of the balance sheet by a change in the total balance in profit and loss account carried forward. The top half of the balance sheet, however, shows how the profit which has been generated has been retained or used – for example, it may be in the bank as funds in hand, or it may have been spent on renewing fixed assets. It is possible for small companies (see **9.7**) to prepare and file a reduced version of this typical balance sheet.

9.4.4   Profit and loss account

The profit and loss account is a summary of all the transactions taking place during an accounting period. All amounts are shown without VAT, therefore representing the actual cost to the company (as the net of VAT received on sales and VAT incurred on expenditure is paid across to HMRC by the company). A typical profit and loss account for a retail company would be as follows:

	£	£
Sales		100,000
Cost of sales		
Opening stock	5,000	
Purchases for resale	50,000	
	55,000	
Less closing stock	5,000	50,000
Gross profit		50,000
Less overheads		
Wages and national insurance contributions	20,000	
Rent and rates	6,000	
Insurance	1,000	
Telephone	1,000	
Motor expenses	3,000	
Printing and advertising	2,000	
Sundry expenses	2,500	
Depreciation (etc)	5,000	
		40,500
Net profit for the period		9,500

9.4.4.1 *Notes to the profit and loss account*

All figures are net of VAT.

Sales are the sales made during the period, including those unpaid at the end of the period (ie debtors).

Cost of sales is the cost of purchases of goods for resale, adjusted to take account of the opening and closing stocks. The closing stock figure must of course be deducted, because that stock has not been sold during the period and therefore should not form part of the cost of sales figure.

Gross profit is a very important figure, because from it can be deduced the margin the company is achieving on sales. When divided into the figure for sales and converted into a percentage it forms a critical ratio when reviewing the results.

Overheads represent all other purchases made by the company during the period for items which are not directly for resale or involved in the manufacture of goods for resale. The overheads will sometimes be sub-grouped into categories such as finance, factory and marketing overheads.

Net profit is the difference between gross profit earned on sales and the overhead expenses incurred in creating those sales. This figure is then transferred to the balance sheet as above (after deducting corporation tax due on that profit).

9.4.4.2 *Cash-flow statement*

Required to be prepared only by medium-sized and large companies and those companies regulated under financial services legislation. This statement replaces the previous Statement of Source and Application of Funds and sets out the cash generated by the company in the period and how it was distributed or spent.

9.4.4.3 *Notes to the accounts*

Following the above statements in a set of statutory accounts there will be a series of notes giving a breakdown of certain items in the accounts, such as fixed assets, debtors and creditors.

9.5 WHAT IS AN AUDIT? **

An audit is a review of a set of accounts, and examination of the underlying accounting records from which they were prepared.

The auditor will either be presented with a set of accounts to audit, if the company has prepared the accounts itself, or in the case of a smaller company, he will probably prepare them from the accounting records and perform his auditing work as part of the process. The auditor will check all the figures in the accounts, not only to ensure that they are correctly classified (eg incorrect analysis of expenses, or items of a capital nature being written off in the profit and loss account), but also to satisfy himself that the figures are not over or understated.

He will, for example, review the system which produces a figure for total sales made in the period, and should go back through the system to make sure that it is watertight and would not produce an inaccurate sales figure.

He will conduct a similar type of exercise on the different sections of the accounts until he has satisfied himself that the accounts give a fair representation of what has happened during the period.

When the audit is complete, the auditor attaches his certificate to the accounts, which he signs. This certificate is called the audit report and states that the accounts give a true and fair view of the state of the company at the balance sheet date and also that the profit and loss account gives a true and fair view of the events and trading which has been transacted during the accounting period.

If the auditor is unhappy about any area in the accounts, then he is obliged to refer to this in his audit report if he feels that the matter is important enough. In extreme cases, the auditor may not be able to agree that the accounts are correct and will say so in his report. This situation is not common in practice.

There are two types of audit report. The first, where the report refers to any problem or brings attention to a certain point, is called a qualified audit report. The second, the simple report, where the auditor agrees that the accounts are true and fair is generally referred to as a 'clean' audit report.

9.6   DISTRIBUTION AND FILING OF ACCOUNTS **

When the statutory accounts have been prepared and, if required, audited or made the subject of a special auditors report, they are put before a meeting of the company and approved by the shareholders. Once this has been done a copy of the accounts, signed by the directors, in accordance with the Companies Acts, is submitted to Companies House to be filed on record for the public to inspect if they wish. For a private company, the accounts must currently reach Companies House within 10 months of the balance sheet date. From 6 April 2008 the period is shortened to 9 months. For a public company, the time limit is currently 7 months, but this is shortened to 6 months from April 2008.

A copy of the accounts is also distributed to each of the shareholders in the company for their retention.

9.7   EXEMPTIONS FROM FILING FULL ACCOUNTS FOR SMALLER COMPANIES **

Companies with a low turnover figure and a small number of employees are able to send only part of their accounts to Companies House to be filed. These are called 'abbreviated accounts'. The obvious advantage of this is that a limited amount of information is then available to any person inspecting the accounts by way of a company search at Companies House.

Smaller companies are categorised as either small or medium-sized in order to determine which parts of the accounts must be filed at Companies House.

A small company must satisfy two of the following three requirements:

(1)   turnover – not more than £5.6m;

(2)   balance sheet total – not more than £2.8m;

(3)   number of employees – not more than 50.

No profit or loss account, directors' report or cash-flow statement needs to be filed for a small company, and only a simplified balance sheet and a few main notes to the accounts are required to be submitted.

A medium-sized company must satisfy two of the following three requirements:

(1)   turnover – not more than £22.8m;

(2)   balance sheet total – not more than £11.4m;

(3)   number of employees – not more than 250.

A profit and loss account must be filed by a medium-sized company, but this may be modified to omit turnover and cost of sales figures. The rest of the accounts are as normally required with a small exception of the note analysing turnover by geographical area and type of business.

The most likely type of people to carry out a search on a company will be the company's competitors and suppliers, in an attempt to establish the financial standing and credit-worthiness of the company. If the directors wish their suppliers to see the accounts, which is not uncommon when a company applies for credit facilities, then the directors may supply a fuller set of the accounts themselves.

From 31 December 2006, some small financial services providers who were previously not eligible and from 1 April 2007, some small businesses, such as home-finance providers, are now able to claim exemptions as above.

9.8   ACCOUNTING PERIODS

An 'accounting period' is the period of time for which a company prepares accounts, consisting of a balance sheet, profit and loss account, notes to the accounts and, normally, a statement of source and application of funds.

The term 'accounting period' is generally used when describing the statutory accounts of the company rather than other types of accounts such as monthly management accounts. The length of an accounting period must not exceed 18 months or be less than 6 months and will normally be 12 months.

9.8.1   The choice of accounting period end *

Choosing an accounting period end or 'year end date' as it is known, is one of the first tasks to face the new company.

Unless the directors notify the registrar of companies of a different date, the accounting reference date of the company in each year will be fixed automatically by the registrar as the anniversary of the last day of the month in which the company was incorporated.

Logically, the end of the first accounting reference period will be a month end date around one year from the date the company starts to trade, although if the company has a significant gap between the date it was incorporated and starting to trade, care must be taken to ensure that the first accounting period is not longer than 18 months.

Other factors may influence the choice such as a trade which is seasonal, where it would be sensible to end the accounting period at the end of the season. In this way, each set of accounts will show the results of one complete season and allow a meaningful comparison of results from one year to the next.

Administrative considerations can also be important, with many companies arranging for their accounting period end to fall at what is traditionally a quiet time of the year, such as early spring in retailing. This makes it possible for adequate resources to be allocated to the preparation of accounts, stocktaking and other year end procedures.

9.8.2   Changing the accounting period **

It is possible to change (ie shorten or lengthen) the accounting period of a company in certain cases by completion and submission of the appropriate form to the registrar of companies, although rules exist which restrict the ability to extend a current accounting period more than once within a 5-year period or to change an accounting reference date retrospectively.

9.9   COMPUTERS AND ACCOUNTING RECORDS

Standard software packages are available, ranging from simple systems for a few hundred pounds, which will maintain all the accounting records and provide reasonably sophisticated management information, to highly complex packages for a multi-national, multi-currency group of companies.

Hardware is also available at very reasonable cost, with industry standard computers now widespread and supplied with good backup facilities. However, caution is required in selecting computer equipment.

For those who are new to computers, it is essential to learn the basics. One method of achieving this is to attend a course designed for beginners, of which many are available. With an understanding of how a computer works, and how to solve simple problems when they arise (as they almost inevitably will) every director will be able to confidently tackle simple computerisation of his company's accounting system.

9.10   CHOOSING AN ACCOUNTING PACKAGE **

This is an area where it is necessary to seek advice. The majority of practising accountants who deal with the smaller company should be conversant to some extent with the accounting software available on the market. There are a few fundamental questions which should be addressed before either hardware or software is purchased.

(1)   What are the company's accounting system requirements? Is it a specialised trade requiring unusual software?

(2)   What information does the management require from the system? This will be more comprehensive and more quickly produced than was possible with the manual system.

(3)   Do the staff have the knowledge to run the system? If not they should receive training or a computer-literate member of staff should be recruited.

(4)   What is the company's budget for the exercise? It is essential to set a realistic budget and stick to it, otherwise the cost will almost always increase, as refinements are added and additional features are included, which may not be necessary. The cost of small- to medium-sized accounting packages can range from around £1,000 to over £20,000.

(5)   Will the system still be satisfactory in 3 to 5 years' time, considering the company's expansion and diversification plans? Ensure that the system is expandable or can be upgraded to the supplier's larger package.

These are just a few of the points to consider in the implementation of a computer system. Advice should be sought at the earliest possible stage, in order to ensure success.

9.11   SPREADSHEETS AND DATABASES

A computer spreadsheet is a very useful tool for the production of management accounts and reports, as the structure of a report or a set of accounts will, in the majority of cases, be similar or identical each time it is produced. The spreadsheet packages available today are, on the whole, easy to use, powerful and represent good value for money.

Databases will be of use to the majority of businesses. They use the power of a computer to collect, assimilate and sort information in a fraction of the time the task would take manually.

There are many spreadsheet and database packages available on the market, some of which also incorporate word processors. Advice should be sought before committing to a particular package, as it will be very useful in practice to have a package which is well known and tested.

9.12   DATA PROTECTION REGISTRATION

If a company is holding certain types of information about individuals, then it may be obliged to register with the Information Commissioner – see Appendix A for the address and telephone number of the Information Commissioner's Office.

9.13   COMBINED PACKAGES **

As software becomes more sophisticated, combined software packages are more readily available. These use a common database (holding customer, supplier and company information) which serves a number of software packages – typically accounting, CRM (marketing and contact management software), supplier and purchasing software and, increasingly, email.

9.14   APPLICATION SERVICE PROVIDERS (ASP)

The term 'ASP' generally refers to the rental of software or services over the internet. This is a slowly maturing and yet to be widely accepted market, but it is possible for a business to run all (or most) of its software applications, including accounting, over the internet using a remote ASP. This requires a broadband connection, but these are now readily available across most of the UK.

CHAPTER 10

BORROWING AND CHARGES

10.1   TYPES OF BORROWING **

Companies frequently raise money by borrowing. The borrowing can take various forms. For example, 'unsecured loans' are simply contracts between the lender and the company for the loan by the lender and repayment by the company of a sum of money. Here, no mortgage or charge is given to the lender. A company may have a bank overdraft, and a mortgage or charge over the company's property is not usually required. However, borrowing is more likely to be 'secured' – the company will grant the lender a mortgage or charge over the company's property. In this context, property does not only mean land and buildings.

Under the laws of England and Wales and Northern Ireland, a company can usually create a charge over anything it owns, such as plant, machinery, patents etc, and the word 'property' therefore means everything the company owns, which is capable of being charged. The security given by a mortgage or charge is, of course, that the lender has the right to seize and sell charged property if the loan is not repaid. The words 'mortgage' and 'charge' can, generally, be treated as interchangeable. The word 'charge' is used in this chapter.

Since Scottish law of property is based on entirely different principles from those which apply in England and Wales and Northern Ireland, it follows that the law relating to mortgages, charges and other securities over Scottish property is also different.

Scottish law distinguishes between heritable property (ie land and certain interests in land), corporeal movables (goods etc) and incorporeal movable rights (shares, life policies, etc). With the exception of the consideration of the objects and powers of the company and its directors, which are the same in both jurisdictions, this book does not attempt to deal with this specialist area, save to say that advice from a Scottish lawyer should always be sought on any matter relating to secured lending under Scottish law.

Legal and financial advice should always be sought in respect of borrowing and creation of charges.

10.2 THE OBJECTS AND POWERS OF THE COMPANY **

Wherever it is registered, the company must, currently, have power to borrow and create charges in its memorandum. Trading companies have an implied power to borrow, but usually a company's memorandum gives it express power. The memorandum should also contain an express power for the company to create a charge over its property. An appropriate clause should look something like this:

> 'To borrow and raise money in any manner and to secure the repayment of any money borrowed, raised or owing by mortgage, charge, standard security, lien or other security upon the whole or any part of the company's property or assets (whether present or future), including its uncalled capital, and also by a similar mortgage, charge, standard security, lien or security to secure and guarantee the performance by the company of any obligation or liability it may undertake or which may become binding on it.'

From 1 October 2009, the format and function of a company's memorandum of association will change. New companies will no longer have to set out their objects and powers in their memorandum of association. Instead, a company will be able to carry on any lawful activity, including borrowing, and the creation of charges over its property to secure that borrowing, unless the shareholders include restrictions on what the company can do in its articles of association.

Objects and powers set out in the memorandum of association of existing companies will be treated, from that date, as if they were restrictions on its activities, set out in its articles of association. Existing companies will therefore have to decide whether they are happy for those restrictions to apply, or whether to pass a special resolution to remove them from the articles. Take advice.

10.3 THE DIRECTORS AND BORROWING **

Usually, the directors of the company will exercise its powers to borrow and create charges. The articles will provide unlimited powers for the directors to act on the company's behalf in this respect. However, the directors should always check the articles, because the articles may provide that the directors' powers to borrow on behalf of the company are limited, or, alternatively, that they cannot be exercised without a resolution of the shareholders of the company or the consent of a particular class of shareholders. This may be the case with a company which does not have modern articles of association.

10.4   TYPES OF CHARGE **

10.4.1   Debenture

'Debenture' is the word usually used to describe the contract between a company and a lender when money is borrowed. A debenture does not necessarily create a charge at all. It may simply create or acknowledge an unsecured loan from the lender to the company. However, it usually creates at least a floating charge. Consequently, a lender, or a lawyer, may treat the words 'debenture' and 'floating charge' as interchangeable although it is not technically accurate to do so.

10.4.2   Fixed charge

A charge is a fixed charge if certain specific property, such as an office or factory, is subject to it. Such a charge is sometimes also called a 'specific charge'. Whilst property is subject to a fixed charge, the company can only sell, let or charge the property with the consent of the lender.

10.4.3   Floating charge

A floating charge is a charge over the company's property which does not specifically affect the charged property until some event happens which causes it to turn into a fixed charge. Until that happens, it merely hovers or floats over the company's property, like a cloud. Upon the happening of such an event, it attaches to the charged property, as if it had been created as a fixed or specific charge. The cloud drops. A lawyer would say that the floating charge has 'crystallised'. It will crystallise if, for example, the company goes into liquidation or a lender appoints a receiver because the company defaults in repaying a loan.

The advantage of a floating charge to the company is that it may usually buy and sell its property in the ordinary course of its business, even though the property it owns at any particular time is subject to the floating charge, at any time before the charge crystallises, and it may do so without the lender's consent. This is obviously of benefit to the company – it can borrow money without restricting its continued trading activity.

10.5   REGISTER OF CHARGES *

The company must keep:

(1)   A register of charges, to include details of all fixed or specific charges affecting the property of the company and all floating charges on any property of the company.

The register gives, for each charge, a short description of the property charged, the amount borrowed under the charge and the names of the persons entitled to the charge.

(2)   A copy of every instrument creating a charge.

Shareholders and creditors may inspect the register of charges and the copies of documents creating the charges and, if the company refuses to allow inspection, the court may compel immediate inspection. Anyone else can inspect the register on payment of a fee not exceeding 5p.

If a charge is created and no entry is made in the register, the officers of the company who know about and authorise or permit the failure to make the entry are liable to a fine.

The register of charges and copies of charge documents must be open for inspection each day during business hours for at least 2 hours.

10.6   REGISTER OF DEBENTURE HOLDERS

The Companies Acts do not require a register of debenture holders to be kept separately from the register of charges but if there is one, it must be kept at the company's registered office or at any other office of the company where the work of making it up is done. Much of the information in it will merely duplicate the register of charges.

The registrar of companies must be given notice of where the register of debenture holders (if any) is kept unless it has been kept at all times since it came into existence at the company's registered office.

It must be open for inspection by any registered debenture holder, and any shareholders of the company without fee, and by anyone else on payment of a fee not exceeding 5p. Registered debenture holders and shareholders may have copies of all or part of the register.

10.7   REGISTRATION WITH THE REGISTRAR
OF COMPANIES ***

Particulars of certain charges created by companies registered in England and Wales or Northern Ireland must be delivered to the relevant registrar of companies within 21 days after the date of their creation.

If not registered, charges are void in certain circumstances, the money borrowed becomes repayable in certain circumstances, and the officers may be fined.

It is the company's duty to register the particulars of the charge but any interested person, such as the lender, may do so. If the company fails to register it the person taking the charge should register it. A fee is payable on lodgment of particulars of a charge.

Registration is effected by sending prescribed particulars of the charge on an official form, to the registrar of companies within 21 days from the date of creation of the charge.

If the company creates a charge, the directors should check that its professional advisers have not omitted to register the charge.

CHAPTER 11

TAXATION

11.1 TYPES OF TAX

In the UK tax system, there are three main types of tax affecting companies, these being:

(1) corporation tax which is charged on the profits and gains of the company;

(2) value added tax which the company may be obliged to charge on the sales it makes to third parties;

(3) income tax, under the Pay As You Earn system, which is charged on wages and salaries which the company pays to its employees and directors.

Since a change in 2005, all taxation matters (including Value Added Tax) are now handled by the government agency, HM Revenue & Customs ('HMRC'). This was formed by combining the previous agencies of the Inland Revenue and HM Customs & Excise.

11.2 CORPORATION TAX

A limited company is a legal entity, a legal person. Just as an individual's income in any tax year (the tax year currently runs from 6 April in one year to 5 April the next year) is totalled up and then subject to income tax at the rates currently in force, so a company is also subject to tax on its profit and capital gains in an accounting period.

11.2.1 Profit

Profit is defined broadly as the difference between turnover (sales) and all the allowable expenses which the company incurs in order to produce that turnover. This difference also represents the change in total assets of the company from the beginning of an accounting period to the end of the same accounting period.

11.2.2 Which expenses can be deducted? **

In order to arrive at the profit, as outlined above, the expenses of the company are deducted from the sales figure. Some expenses are allowed to be deducted from the sales to arrive at the profit (ie they are allowable deductions) and others are not. In practice, the categories of items which are not allowable deductions are few.

The tax legislation which controls this subject and defines an allowable deduction is complicated and this is an area where professional advice should be sought if there is any doubt as to the allowability of a particular item. There is, however, a fairly reliable 'rule of thumb', which may be applied on a day-to-day basis with respect to expenditure. If the expenditure is relevant to the trade being carried on by the company and is incurred with a view to creating sales, then it is probably allowable. The tax legislation is itself based on this general theory and this rule will be useful in any cases of doubt.

The most obvious allowable expenses of a company will be:

(1)   cost of sales, purchases of goods used in the manufacturing process or in the provision of a service;

(2)   rent, rates, heat, light and insurance for the business premises;

(3)   wages and employer's national insurance contributions for all staff employed and working in the company;

(4)   motor and transport expenses;

(5)   other overheads, advertising, office supplies, training and recruitment costs etc.

Entertainment expenses, directors' personal expenses and legal costs relating to capital expenditure are examples of expenses not allowable as deductions against trading profits.

11.2.3 Tax deduction for assets (capital allowances) **

There is an important distinction to explain at this point relating to assets and their treatment as far as deductibility for tax is concerned. If a company expends funds on overheads, such as rent and rates, or fuel for company vehicles, then that total amount expended is allowable against the profits (when arriving at a taxable profit) in the accounting period in which the overheads occurred.

This is not necessarily the case for assets purchased. An asset is an item of *capital* nature as distinct from an overhead which is a *revenue* expense. This description of expenditure as either capital or revenue is widely used in practice.

Whilst the whole of a revenue expense is allowed against the profits in the period incurred, in some situations, the cost of capital items can only be offset against profit by a portion of the cost of the asset per year.

The accounts term for this deduction is *depreciation* whilst the tax equivalent is *capital allowance*, ie an allowance for a capital item. The first year allowance, ie the percentage deductible in the year of purchase, currently varies and may be up to 100%. The rate at which the remainder of the cost may be offset in the following years varies between types of asset, which may be, for example, vehicles, plant, machinery, or computers.

From April 2008, The Chancellor has announced that a new 'Annual Investment Allowance' will be available (at the time of writing this is subject to the legislation being introduced), with the business able to deduct the first £50,000 of qualifying capital expenditure directly from taxable profits. Certain first year allowances will continue.

Example

A van costs £6,000. How much of this will be allowed against the company's profit in each of the first 3 years?

Year 1	Capital allowance =		£6,000	@ say 40%	=	£2,400
Year 2	Capital allowance =		£6,000			
		less	£2,400			
	unused amount		£3,600	@ 25%	=	£900
Year 3	Capital allowance =		£3,600			
		less	£900			
	unused amount		£2,700	@ 25%	=	£675

and so on until the vehicle is scrapped or sold.

This is only a sample example, outlining the difference between the tax treatment of capital and revenue expenditure.

Capital allowances is a complex area and the amount which can be claimed depends upon a number of factors, including the type of expenditure. In complex cases, expert advice is recommended, as a company may not be aware of available allowances and may therefore not obtain reliefs which are available.

The possible leasing of assets should also be considered when capital items are needed to run the business.

11.2.4   How is the corporation tax calculated?

Once the taxable profits for the period have been established then the corporation tax may be calculated. In straightforward situations the corporation tax due will be the taxable profit, after deducting all allowable items of expenditure and adjusting for depreciation and capital allowances, multiplied by the corporation tax rate.

Example

		£	£
Profit per accounts			10,000
Add:	Depreciation charged	1,500	
	Entertaining expenses included in profit and loss account	400	1,900
			11,900
Less:	Capital allowances		1,200
Taxable profit			10,700

Corporation tax at, for example, 20% = £2,140

11.2.5   The corporation tax rate

There are a range of corporation tax rates, with each rate applying to a band of profits. The rates vary, but typically range from between 20% and 30%.

With the exception of very large companies with high annual profits (eg £1.5m), all corporation tax, for companies formed after 1963, is payable in one instalment, 9 months and one day after the end of the accounting period. So if the company's accounts are made up to 31 March, then the corporation tax due on the profits earned in that period will be payable on 1 January in the following year. Larger companies pay their tax in four quarterly instalments.

11.2.6   Self assessment

Since 1999, a new self assessment method of dealing with payment of corporation tax and submission of accounts has been in force. This replaced the old system of Pay and File, although in many respects it is very similar to that system.

Under self assessment, the company is obliged, within the due date as above, to settle the corporation tax due, based on its own calculation of the liability. No assessment will normally be issued by HMRC at this stage. Accounts in support of this figure must then be submitted to HMRC within 12 months of the end of the accounting period. In addition, a detailed return form is also submitted.

This system of self assessment now applies to both companies and individuals in respect of their taxation affairs and is similar to the system used in respect of VAT, with the onus falling on the taxpayer to recognise and calculate their liability within the time-limits.

Detailed regulations provide for complications such as a change of accounting date, and as would be expected, the taxation authorities have the power to charge interest and penalties on late settlement of taxation liabilities, or failure to submit returns by the due date.

11.2.7   Group taxation **

The taxation of a group of companies can be a very complicated area when the group becomes large and intricate, although in principle the concept is fairly straightforward, and similar to the taxation of a single company. Each company within the group prepares its own tax return, based on the results in its own accounts, and sends this to the company's local tax office as normal.

The differences arise when there is a company in the group which has either made losses in the period or has overpaid corporation tax. The losses or overpayment may then be transferred to another company in the group and used against that company's profit or tax liability, as long as certain conditions have been met between the two companies on share ownership and accounting periods. This use of losses and surplus tax within a group is known as *group relief*.

11.2.8   Distributions ***

A dividend is a distribution of profit to shareholders in a company. Which shareholders receive a dividend will depend on the rights (to dividends) which those shares have. In a simple case, if 100 ordinary fully paid shares are issued in a company, all with the same rights (as defined in the memorandum and articles of association of the company) then all the shareholders will receive the same amount of dividend, which will be one-hundredth of the total dividend to each share issued.

In principle, a dividend is deemed to have been received by the shareholder net of basic rate tax.

The practice of distributing dividends in a small company to both a husband and wife (or partner), which can reduce the overall higher rate taxation charge, assuming the wife has little or no other income, has recently been challenged by HMRC. This has resulted in a lengthy tax case with a ruling in favour of the taxpayer. HMRC are expected, however, to introduce measures from 2008 designed to tackle certain tax saving methods used by such companies, many of which are 'family companies'.

11.2.9   Capital gains tax ****

Tax is charged on a company's capital gains in a slightly different way than for individuals. A limited company's taxable gains are included in the corporation tax computation and taxed at the corporation tax rate. It is important to differentiate between a normal trading profit and a capital gain. A trading profit is generated by trading, ie buying and selling on a regular basis or providing a service to customers, whereas a gain is created by purchasing an asset as an investment, then selling that asset some time later at a higher price.

This distinction between profit and gains is a very important one as it determines the treatment of any income created.

One difference between the way that companies and individuals are chargeable to tax on capital gains is that individuals at present are allowed to make gains of several thousand pounds in each tax year without paying capital gains tax on them, paying tax on the balance. The level of this 'annual exemption' for capital gains tax is announced in the Budget each year. Companies, however, pay tax on the whole of any chargeable gains with the calculations being included with the annual computation of taxable profits.

The more common assets which companies may dispose of to realise a chargeable gain would be:

(1)   land and buildings;

(2)   investments in other companies (shares).

Allowable expenses when calculating the gain will be items such as legal charges on purchase and capital improvement expenditure (but not repairs). In addition, an indexation allowance is added to the original cost of the asset. This is calculated to represent the elements of the gain produced by inflation, which is not taxable.

Subject to certain conditions, tax payable on a capital gain may be deferred if the gain, or part of the gain is reinvested in another asset. Professional advice should be sought.

11.3   VALUE ADDED TAX (VAT)

When a limited company starts to trade, VAT must be considered. Introduced in 1971, and replacing the old purchase tax, VAT is collected and controlled by HMRC.

A company is obliged by law to register for VAT if the supplies made by the company are subject to VAT, and:

(1)   turnover has exceeded a prescribed figure, the VAT threshold, in the preceding 12 months; or alternatively,

(2)   if it is expected that the turnover will exceed the threshold within the forthcoming 30 days.

This means that the company *must* charge VAT on all those sales made which are subject to the tax.

In certain cases, where for instance all sales are zero-rated, as described below, a company may wish to register voluntarily, even if the level of turnover is below the threshold. It would then be able to reclaim all input tax paid on items purchased and would therefore benefit.

Once the company has registered for VAT it will receive a VAT registration number from HMRC and must print this number on all sales invoices.

If a company is registered for VAT then it must charge VAT on all sales which are 'standard-rated' or 'VATable', to use the colloquial term. The sale of goods or provision of service, either or both of which will form turnover, dependent on the type of business involved, are categorised by legislation into three types:

(1)   standard-rated, the rate is currently 17.5% on the selling price;

(2)   zero-rated, where VAT is charged at 0% (ie not at all); but it is very important to distinguish between this and

(3)   exempt, where VAT is not relevant and not *applied*.

If the supplies are all standard-rated, then the company must add VAT (known as output tax) at 17.5% to all the sales invoices and may reclaim VAT on anything purchased which carries VAT (input tax).

If the supplies are zero-rated, then VAT is added to all the sales invoices at 0%, and shown on the invoice, and the company may reclaim VAT on anything purchased to which VAT has been added.

The important distinction to make is if the supplies are exempt rather than zero-rated.

If the supplies are exempt, then VAT must not be charged (at any rate) on any sales made, and the company cannot reclaim any VAT which has been charged on purchases. If all the supplies are exempt, then the company will be unable to register for VAT.

It can get very complicated when some of the sales made are standard or zero-rated and some are exempt – it is necessary to separate the input tax on purchases which relate to the standard or zero-rated items and only reclaim VAT on those expenses.

It is often possible in this situation to agree with HMRC to reclaim a fixed percentage of the input tax, which would usually be based on the percentage split of sales between exempt and the rest.

The excess VAT (output less input) is paid across to HMRC on a VAT return, a pre-printed computer generated form which is completed and sent by post, or submitted electronically to HMRC, usually quarterly, together with a payment for the tax due. Some types of business, ie those who make zero-rated supplies and reclaim all their input tax, will receive refunds on each return, and this can be paid automatically into the company bank account upon submission and acceptance of the return.

It is possible, for smaller companies, to take advantage of 'Flat Rate' schemes, where VAT due is calculated as a percentage of turnover. This eases administration but may not always be beneficial.

11.3.1 Scale charges

If a company provides motor vehicles for use by employees on non-business mileage, additional VAT must be paid each period. The amounts vary, according to the type of vehicle and advice should be sought.

11.3.2 Cash accounting scheme

If a company has to pay over the 'output' tax charged on sales invoices, and it has not actually been paid by the customer, cash flow can suffer, sometimes quite severely. For smaller companies, the cash accounting scheme relaxes the rules, and allows the company to only pay over the output VAT received during the VAT period from its customers. Of course if this scheme is adopted, then the same principle applies to 'input' tax on goods and services purchased.

Advice should be taken on this subject as the adoption of the scheme is not always beneficial and HMRC apply the regulations and limits strictly.

11.3.3   Late returns **

Strict penalties exist regarding late registration, submission of late returns and under declaration. VAT is an area where much care is needed and professional advice will often be required.

11.3.4   VAT inspections

HMRC have a team of inspectors who make regular visits to VAT-registered businesses, to inspect the accounting records and check the information shown on the returns. This is quite routine, and should not be a cause for concern, as long as the VAT returns have been completed correctly.

11.4   INCOME TAX AND PAY AS YOU EARN

Income tax is applied to the earned and unearned income of individuals either in employment or in business as sole traders (ie self-employed). It also applies to a partnership, which is simply a group of more than one sole trader in business together. Each person in the UK is allowed to deduct specified amounts from his total income in each tax year before arriving at a figure for taxable income. The most common deductions would be as follows:

11.4.1   Personal allowance

An amount amended each year in the annual Budget in late autumn. For each tax year, both men and women receive an allowance which may be used against earned income.

11.4.2   Payments into pension schemes **

If payments into a pension scheme are made without tax relief being given at source then, subject to certain limits, which depend on the taxpayer's age and total pensionable income, the total of these pension contributions may be deducted from gross income before arriving at a taxable figure.

Other items are deductible, such as some maintenance payments, professional subscriptions and a few additional allowances in particular circumstances. **

11.4.3   Utilising independent taxation ***

Husbands and wives are taxed separately on all sources of income. Consideration should be given to transferring any income-bearing assets, such as shares or investment accounts, into the name of the spouse who has the least income. This ensures that allowances and the lower rate tax bands available to both parties are fully utilised.

Each spouse may also have to submit a separate tax return and can choose to keep their tax situation completely private from their spouse, if they so wish.

This is outside the intended scope of this book, and is a topic which should be discussed with a taxation adviser in order that tax affairs may be organised as efficiently as possible.

The tax due is then calculated on the balance (taxable income) and a tax liability results. In the case of a person whose only income is from a job, tax will have been deducted from their salary (or wages) each time they receive their pay through the PAYE scheme, and they should have no further tax to pay on that income.

11.4.4   The PAYE scheme

The system of deducting an employee's tax at source each time the salary is paid is called PAYE (or Pay As You Earn). Every employer who pays staff wages is obliged to tax their employees' wages at source.

Each employer operates a separate PAYE scheme, which will have a unique reference number such as: 123/A4567 – where 123 identifies the tax office which controls the PAYE schemes within the particular geographical area, and the A4567 is the reference number of that company's PAYE file in the tax office. 123/A4567 is therefore this company's PAYE reference.

11.4.4.1   Obtaining a PAYE scheme

When the company starts to trade and employ staff, and this includes paid directors who are also employees of the company, the company must obtain a PAYE scheme. This is done by contacting the local HM Revenue & Customs office or visiting the HMRC website (www.hmrc.gov.uk) and requesting that a scheme is set up for that company. The PAYE scheme is then supplied by the relevant district tax office and the employer receives, in addition to the company's PAYE reference number, an electronic pack which calculates the tax and national insurance contributions for each employee, and clear instructions on how to run the PAYE scheme. HMRC also have online calculation systems available for use by employers.

11.4.4.2   How does PAYE work?

Each employee is given a tax code by the relevant HMRC PAYE district. A tax code is a figure representing the annual amount of earnings from this employment that the employee may earn before he pays tax on the balance. Each employee's tax code will have been arrived at generally by adding together all the allowances, pension payments made and adjusting the code for any penalty due for the provision of company cars and other benefits. The resulting figure will comprise the individual's tax-free income for that tax year.

Each pay period, the employer takes the gross pay of the employee and then deducts (for monthly pay periods), one-twelfth of the annual amount of tax-free pay, which will be one-twelfth of the tax code figure. The amount of tax due is then calculated on the balance of income, at lower, basic and higher rate bands (whichever are appropriate), and the resulting tax figure deducted from the gross pay, to arrive at the net pay.

The employee's national insurance contribution for the pay period at the rate currently in force is also deducted from the gross pay.

So the calculation will look like this:

	£
Gross pay for period	1,000
Tax-free pay for period	200
Taxable income	800
Income tax at, say, 20%	160
National insurance contribution at, say, 9%	90
Total deductions	250
Net pay for period	750

The employee receives his net pay of £750 and has paid all his tax and national insurance on that income.

11.4.5   Employer's national insurance contributions

In addition to the employee paying national insurance contributions up to
a certain limit, on his gross income, the employer also has to pay national
insurance contributions. So the cost of employing staff to an employer is
the total of:

gross pay + *employer's national insurance contributions*

An employer's national insurance contributions are calculated as a
percentage of gross pay and must be included by an employer when
calculating overall staff costs.

11.4.6   Paying the tax and national insurance contribution
to HMRC

The employer, at each pay period will be holding an amount of money
representing the tax and national insurance deducted from the employee's
gross pay, together with the employer's national insurance due on that
gross pay. This total sum must be sent in by the company each month, to
the Collector of Taxes, which is the section of HMRC which collects all
tax. It is also possible to settle this liability online.

*11.4.6.1   Late payments and returns ***

It is important to ensure that monthly payments and annual returns arrive
with the Collector of Taxes on time, as interest or penalties may be
charged on any amounts which are paid late.

*11.4.6.2   Part-time and casual workers ****

Great care must be taken when making any payments to part-time or
casual workers as they may have other employment. Even though the
amount of the employee's gross pay from your company may be, taken on
its own, below the tax-free figure for the pay period, they may have other
income against which their total allowances may have been set and
therefore tax may in fact be due on the whole of their earnings from your
company.

*11.4.6.3   Reimbursement of expenses ****

This is another area where the greatest caution is required. Payments
made to employees for reimbursement of expenses may be subject to tax
and national insurance contributions. Any practice whereby a company
makes such payments on a regular basis should be reviewed by the
company's advisers before payments are made.

11.4.6.4 Dispensations **

If the company needs to pay expenses on a regular basis, then it is advisable to approach HMRC and ask for the authority to make these payments. This is called a 'dispensation'. In order to grant this, HMRC will ask to review the company's accounting systems and will look carefully at the amounts the company proposes to pay and the reasons for payment. If it is satisfied, it will grant the dispensation, and as long as the company maintains its accounting systems to the same standard as at the time of the inspection, the dispensation should remain effective.

11.4.6.5 Failure to make deductions ***

If the employer fails to make deductions from any payment to an employee and later it is agreed that these deductions should have been made and then paid over to HMRC, the employer may be liable to pay the deductions (on top of the gross pay already paid to the employee) and could also be liable to penalties for failing to apply the PAYE regulations correctly.

It is also important to be aware of the distinction between 'employment' and 'self-employment' for PAYE and national insurance purposes. A company making payments for services rendered by a person on a regular basis must ensure that the person is registered with HMRC as self-employed. If this is not the case, and HMRC cannot recover the tax from that person, then they may assess the company for tax and national insurance as described above.

CHAPTER 12

INSOLVENCY ***

12.1 INTRODUCTION

Insolvency is an all-encompassing term for what happens to a company when it has been trading at a loss rather than a profit and is now in a position where it is unable to meet its liabilities.

In the early 1980s the law of insolvency was substantially updated and consolidated. The result of this work was the insolvency legislation of 1986. The new law was necessary as it became apparent that the law in effect before the new legislation was not always suitable or able to cope with what was actually happening in the business world.

12.2 SCOTLAND

Insolvency of companies registered in Scotland is the subject of specific legislation, and reference should accordingly be made to the legislation and to works on this subject for detailed information.

The effect of insolvency on a Scottish company and the procedures to be observed are broadly similar in Scotland, in England and Wales and in Northern Ireland.

However, it should be noted that application to the court to order a compulsory winding up is made by petition to the Court of Session (or, in the case of a relatively small company, the Sheriff Court where the registered office of the company is situated) in Scotland. In relation to receiverships, Scottish law provides that a chargeholder may only appoint a receiver if the charge is a floating charge.

The secured creditors of a Scottish company will often agree amongst themselves the order in which their securities are to rank, although there are statutory rules providing for the ranking of securities in the absence of such an agreement.

Although secured creditors can take action to recover their security on their own behalf, it is normal practice for the creditors to leave it to the liquidator, administrator or receiver (as the case may be) to realise the assets in question and pay the proceeds to the secured creditors in accordance with any ranking agreement or the statutory provisions.

12.3   INSOLVENCY PRACTITIONERS

Until 1986, there had been no legal requirement for an accountant, business adviser or other person to have any formal qualification that showed they were competent to deal with the procedures involved when a company became insolvent. The new Act changed this weakness in the law and introduced a new title of insolvency practitioner – professionals who were licensed to act in insolvencies, having proved they were competent to do so. Only licensed insolvency practitioners are now allowed to deal with such matters.

This change was necessary in order to ensure that advisers dealing with insolvency have the required experience, knowledge and professionalism to perform their duties to the highest standard. It is now an offence for anyone to deal with insolvency unless he is a licensed insolvency practitioner.

Insolvency practitioners are governed by the body which issued their licence, the principal bodies being the Institute of Chartered Accountants in England and Wales, the Department of Business, Enterprise and Regulatory Reform (BERR, formerly the Department of Trade and Industry, or 'DTI'), The Law Society and the Insolvency Practitioners Association. Each body oversees the work its members carry out and provides a degree of control which did not previously exist.

12.4   WHAT HAPPENS WHEN A COMPANY IS INSOLVENT?

The different situations which may occur in insolvency are as follows.

12.4.1   Members' voluntary liquidation ***

If a company has finished the task it was set up to do, and the shareholders no longer have any need to keep the company, then they would 'wind up' the company – that is close the company down officially. If any profit is still left in the company at the point the members decide to wind up the company, then this profit would be distributed in the form of a dividend. Any assets would also be distributed or disposed of and the proceeds also distributed. A useful example of this type of winding up is a company formed to mine a coal seam, which has now been emptied of coal, with no prospect of any further seams in the area. The company would then be closed down in accordance with the shareholders' plans. A declaration of solvency is required and advice should be sought.

12.4.2   Creditors' voluntary liquidation ***

This situation would arise when a company has become insolvent, in other words, either it is unable to pay its debts as they fall due or alternatively the liabilities of the company exceed the assets. The company would be under some pressure from creditors in respect of outstanding debts.

The shareholders decide to wind the company up and they would appoint a liquidator (who must be a licensed insolvency practitioner). The creditors are then informed of the shareholders' intentions and the directors convene a meeting.

At this meeting they have the option to appoint another liquidator if the majority of creditors in value – in other words the weight of their vote is in proportion to how much the company owes them – so wish.

The liquidator appointed will then proceed to sell the assets of the company and pay the creditors from the proceeds in strict accordance with the order of payment laid down in the insolvency legislation. This order is set out below.

12.4.3   Compulsory liquidation ***

A compulsory liquidation can arise where either the shareholders or creditors of a company force a reluctant company into liquidation, by making an application to the High Court. Any shareholder, creditor or group of creditors can petition the court for an order to be granted, and if their petition is successful, then the Official Receiver, an officer of BERR, is appointed liquidator.

The proceedings are costly, unpleasant and frequently will end in adverse reports being filed with BERR on some or all of the directors. Sometimes, in a larger case, another liquidator may be appointed by the Official Receiver to deal with the practical aspects of the liquidation, but the reporting and disqualification aspects will always remain with the Official Receiver.

12.4.4   Administration ***

If a company has borrowed money from a bank or other lender, and as a condition of obtaining the borrowing the company has given that lender some type of security over the borrowing, which would usually be a debenture or charge over some of the company's assets, then the party holding the charge has the right to claim back the amount due to him, in certain circumstances.

The commencement of an administration will be activated by the chargeholder (see Chapter 10) giving the appropriate length of notice to the borrower and having done that in the correct manner he will appoint an administrator to handle the matter. The administrator would normally be a licensed insolvency practitioner and will take control of the company with a view to realising assets of the company, the proceeds of which will be primarily for the benefit of the chargeholder. Any surplus funds arising from the disposal of these assets, after repaying the chargeholder and settling the administrator's expenses, will be either paid back to the company or passed across to a liquidator who may have been appointed as a result of the administration of the company.

The administrator is also required, in a similar manner to the liquidator, to submit a report on the conduct of the directors to BERR.

12.4.5　Corporate voluntary arrangements ***

This is a form of administration, which must be approved by a court, designed to allow the company and its creditors or shareholders to formulate an agreed plan and deal with a crisis, without the stigma and hopefully the expense of an administration. They could agree that all creditors be paid say 50p per £1 owed and forgo the remaining balance due, in order to give the company a chance of survival. As long as the required majority agree and the plan is approved by the court, then a licensed insolvency practitioner will be appointed to implement matters. Having proceeded with the plan and achieved its objectives, the insolvency practitioner (described as a Supervisor under this type of arrangement) will step back and leave the company to continue its business.

12.4.6　Order of payment in liquidation **

The order in which the liabilities of a company in liquidation, after settlement of the liquidator's costs, are settled is as follows:

(1)　*Preferential creditors* – the main preferential creditors will be certain amounts due by the company to employees in respect of holiday pay, wages and some pension payments.

(2)　*Secured creditors* – creditors who hold a charge, mortgage or debenture on any or all of the assets of the company. If the charge is fixed, then they rank before preferential creditors. A floating charge, however, ranks after both fixed charges creditors and preferential creditors. A common example of a fixed charge would be a bank which has a charge on the debtors of the company. For a more detailed discussion on charges, see Chapter 10.

(3)　*Unsecured creditors* – the remaining creditors. These will consist of those parties that the company dealt with in the normal course of trade such as the company's trade suppliers, lenders of unsecured loans and so on. From September 2003, amounts due to HM Revenue & Customs in respect of VAT, PAYE and Corporation Tax are no longer treated as preferential creditors (prior to this change, a portion of tax debts were treated as preferential and therefore paid out first). Any amounts due to directors on their loan accounts also falls under the heading of unsecured creditors.

(4)   Any interest payable on debts.

Any remaining balance of funds is then repayable to the shareholders.

12.5   THE ACTIONS OF COMPANY DIRECTORS ***

The liquidator also has a responsibility to submit a report to BERR, not only on every company he deals with but also in respect of the actions of directors, both past and present. This can include the activities of any persons who, although they may not be directors of the company at the time of liquidation, have been directors at any time in the last 3 years of the company's trading.

It is also worth noting that the definition of directors for this purpose includes any person who may have been acting as a 'shadow' director (a person in accordance with whose directions or instructions the directors of a company are accustomed to act) which may be relevant, for example, where a company's sole director may be the spouse of a disqualified director who continues, in fact, to direct operations. This is not permitted, and the disqualified director will also come under the spotlight as a shadow director, in an attempt to avoid this kind of problem.

If an adverse report is filed, then the Disqualification Unit of BERR has the power to prosecute the director on the basis of the report, and may disqualify any persons involved from becoming a director of any other company for a period of up to 15 years.

12.6   WRONGFUL TRADING ***

The liquidator can also bring an action for 'wrongful trading', where the company's trade was continued when the directors were aware, or ought to have been aware, that the company could not avoid insolvency, and a liquidation, and could not meet its forthcoming liabilities. This may lead to the directors being held personally liable to pay all or any of the company's debts. The liquidator can also bring an action for false accounting and other illegal acts, which is an awesome prospect. The responsibility of holding the post of a company director should not be treated lightly.

Ignorance of the company's affairs is no excuse – the law clearly requires the director to keep himself informed as to the company's affairs, so he can judge the state of the company at any time. Directors should take particular care to give proper attention to the company's financial records – and a claim that the company had inadequate financial records, so it wasn't worth looking at them, will compound the director's guilt, not absolve him.

When making a judgment whether a director knew, or ought to have known, that the company was heading for an insolvent liquidation, two tests will be applied to the director. First, he must meet the minimum standard reasonably to be expected of someone carrying out his functions. Simply by virtue of being a director, he will be expected, for example, to have some financial competence. A finance director will, however, be expected to have greater competence in this area than, say, a sales director. Secondly, if he has some additional skill, knowledge or experience over and above the usual standard, he is expected to apply it – he is likely to be judged more harshly because of it.

12.7   CONCLUSION

The law of insolvency has been drafted with great care and with the hindsight of many years of practical experience. It is intended to protect, as far as possible, all parties who may suffer as a result of any company becoming insolvent. It is also designed to eliminate malpractice and illegal acts, and is ruthless on any directors or shadow directors who have behaved improperly.

It is clear that the company director must be acutely aware of his responsibilities, especially in the light of the powers available to insolvency practitioners and BERR.

The law is also designed to assist companies in trouble, by utilising administration on voluntary arrangements, and should any director feel that his company may be in difficulty, then he should seek advice sooner rather than later, as invariably this will be to the company's advantage.

12.8   HOW TO LOCATE AN INSOLVENCY PRACTITIONER

Most accountants in general practice will be able to put you in touch with a licensed insolvency practitioner. Alternatively, many of the larger firms of accountants have separate insolvency departments, staffed by licensed insolvency practitioners.

For further details, also contact the Insolvency Practitioners Association (http://www.insolvency-practitioners.org.uk/).

CHAPTER 13

USING PROFESSIONALS

13.1   IMPORTANCE OF SEEKING ADVICE

No company can realistically expect to succeed without taking some sort of professional advice whenever this becomes necessary. Should the occasion arise when directors feel they are in need of assistance in an area which is unknown to them, then they should seek help and advice from a specialist in that field, just as their own customers will do from them. For example, the solicitor, when he encounters an accounting problem will seek the advice of a suitably qualified accountant as the solicitor's training and knowledge is not in that area. Equally, in another situation the roles of adviser and client will be reversed when the accountant needs some legal advice on a particular topic.

One area where the 'horses for courses' approach is even more important is when dealing with transactions or companies which require consideration of Scottish law. Advice from a qualified Scottish source is a must. A list of Scottish solicitors able to advise on company matters is available from the Law Society of Scotland. For accountants, contact the accountancy bodies whose addresses are given in Appendix A.

13.2   THE ECONOMIES OF USING PROFESSIONALS

Professional advisers such as accountants and solicitors have spent many years studying and training and will have passed professional examinations to enable them to establish their practice and provide a service to the public. In the majority of professions they will also have to be members of their own governing professional body and will probably be unauthorised to practise in their own name unless they have passed the relevant professional exams and undergone the required period of training in a professional environment.

Consequently, in the majority of cases, the professional adviser should be able to perform a task or provide an answer in a fraction of the time in which it would take his client to produce that same result, if indeed the client possessed the knowledge and experience to attempt the task at all.

13.3 FEES

Accountants, solicitors and other professionals are sometimes regarded as being expensive for the service that they provide. There is no doubt that in some cases a client may feel that he has been charged an excessive fee for work which has been carried out, and if this is the case then he should raise this point with his adviser and request a breakdown of the costs incurred in completion of the work involved.

It is of course good practice for a client to agree either a fixed fee, or a ceiling above which the costs cannot rise without prior agreement. Professional fees may also viewed on an 'opportunity cost' basis. If a director is able to produce income for his company of, say, £200 per hour, in doing whatever the company specialises in and the director needs advice on a legal matter, it is unlikely that it would be more cost effective for him to attempt to solve that legal problem himself in, say, 5 hours, when he could have earned £1,000 for the company during that same period of time.

If, instead, a solicitor were to be approached and asked for advice on the matter he would normally be able to solve the problem for the company in a fraction of the time, and his advice would (hopefully) cost substantially less than £1,000.

There is also no guarantee, if the first course of action were to be followed, that the director would have reached the correct conclusion, whereas with a professional adviser this should be the case and the client will, almost certainly, have the right of recourse should poor advice be given and damage result.

13.4 THE TYPES OF PROFESSIONAL ADVISERS

There are many types of professional advisers, surveyors and valuers, architects, actuaries (who deal with pension funds and investments), patent and copyright experts, marketing and advertising specialists, independent financial advisers, computer consultants, and so on, but the three types of advisers which the new company will almost always require either immediately or in the first few months of trading will be an accountant, a solicitor and a bank manager.

13.5 CHOOSING YOUR ADVISERS

13.5.1 Accountants

Accountants operating 'in the high street' and providing advice to the public will be trading either as a sole practitioner, where only one accountant runs a practice with supporting staff (or to put it another way it is a firm with only one partner), or as a larger practice, where several accountants will have got together (ie entered into partnership with one another), and may trade under their collective names – eg Smith, Jones & Co. This of course depends on how many partners there are in the firm. It is advisable when selecting an accountant to consult to ensure that the accountant is qualified. Such a professional should have the training and experience to deal with the company's and directors' affairs competently. There are several different types of qualification in accountancy – chartered accountants, certified accountants, cost and management accountants, etc, but the two qualified accountants most commonly found in public practice are chartered or certified accountants.

13.5.1.1 *What should an accountant do for the company?*

The areas where an accountant will be of assistance to a limited company will be as follows:

(1) discussing the start up, assisting with forecasts and projections;

(2) providing help and advice in the raising of suitable finance for a venture;

(3) organising an accounting and management information system for the company;

(4) advising on taxation matters, both for the company and the directors on an ongoing basis;

(5) advising on VAT;

(6) discussing payroll, PAYE and national insurance systems, and the employment of staff generally;

(7) providing advice on an ongoing basis as the business starts to trade and expand;

(8) providing tax planning advice at periodic intervals;

(9) discussing computerisation, suggesting suitable software and hardware and outlining necessary controls to include in the accounting system;

(10) each accounting period preparing and/or auditing the statutory accounts of the company or providing a compilation report in respect of them (or, alternatively, advising as to exemptions from audit) and then discussing taxation and other matters arising from the accounts;

(11) acting as a 'sounding board' for ideas and potential projects as they arise;

(12) advising on action required when the company is in difficulty and recommending the appropriate course of action, for example, consulting a licensed insolvency practitioner.

13.5.1.2 How should you choose an accountant?

Probably the best way to choose an accountant, if you have no one in mind, is to seek a recommendation.

This may be from someone else in business who is satisfied with the service that he is receiving from his accountant, or failing that from your solicitor or bank manager who will know of a good local firm with the knowledge and experience to be able to provide sound and up-to-date advice.

The choice will have to be an accountant who is qualified to audit the accounts of a limited company, or provide a compilation report, if appropriate, and will normally be either a chartered or certified accountant.

It would make good sense to use the same firm of accountants for all the services required as the overall service the company receives should be improved by the accountant being aware of all the different aspects of the company and directors.

13.5.1.3 Registered auditors and accountants

As mentioned above, one of the services that an accountant will provide to a limited company will be that of auditing or of carrying out the work required in order to provide a compilation report. Many companies are required to have their annual (or otherwise if the accounting reference date has been changed) accounts audited by a suitably qualified accountant who is registered as an auditor by his professional body. This is required under the Companies Act legislation, which governs all legal matters relating to limited companies. The majority of accountancy firms in practice will provide these services; indeed, for many firms it accounts for a substantial percentage of their annual fee income.

Even if your company does not require an audit (see Chapter 9), it is likely that you will ask a qualified accountant to review (or prepare) the company's annual accounts and submit them to the registrar of companies. This will ensure that the accounts are prepared in the required format and should avoid problems (and the possibility of the company being fined).

Some directors may wish to have their annual accounts audited – despite the fact that an audit is not required under the relevant legislation – as it provides an external review of the company's finances and a level of comfort.

13.5.2 Solicitors

Your need for a solicitor will vary depending on what kind of business you are in, but there are several areas where a solicitor would advise a limited company and its directors.

(1) Forming a company, issuing shares, changing the name, etc. (In practice, most firms of accountants will also provide a company formation service.)

(2) Providing help and advice as to the capital structure of the company, such as number and classes of issued shares, and the identity of the shareholders.

(3) Preparing service contracts for the directors, which is an important area, and one which should be addressed in the early stages of appointment.

(4) Providing help and advice in the raising of finance for a venture.

(5) Advising on individual planning for directors and shareholders in relation to possible death – wills, capital gains tax and inheritance tax, and the destination of any shares.

(6) Drafting special articles or a shareholders' agreement to cover special situations such as joint venture, quasi-partnership or deadlock companies.

(7) Advising on protection of 'intellectual property', such as trade or service marks, copyright, patents, designs, etc.

(8) Dealing with matters relating to credit control, debt collection and other litigation.

(9) Dealing with company secretarial matters such as minutes for meetings, company documents and statutory books.

(10) Dealing with the legal aspects of specific transactions, such as the company buying back its own shares.

(11) Dealing with the renting of property and leases, the purchase of property and conveyancing.

(12) Advising on regulatory and compliance requirements as to, for example, the giving of credit, and on requirements relating to obtaining licences to carry on certain businesses. This would include advice on Data Protection Act issues.

(13) Advising on redundancy, unfair or wrongful dismissal, discipline and grievance issues, maternity rights and other employment-related matters, such as health and safety, discrimination.

(14) Drafting standard terms of business.

(15) Drafting contracts for any business/supply or agency agreements the company is to enter into.

(16) Advising on supply contracts, such as contracts to acquire computer systems, and with web designers.

(17) Drafting contracts for the purchase of businesses, and of the shares of other companies.

(18) Advising on action required when the company is in difficulty and recommending the appropriate course of action, for example, contacting a licensed insolvency practitioner.

Once again, choosing a solicitor will very often be the result of a recommendation, although many firms of solicitors will have specialist areas of knowledge. It is therefore important to ensure that the solicitor you select has experience of dealing with the affairs of limited companies. Some solicitors, for instance, deal mainly with non-commercial matters and may not have the necessary experience to provide all-round advice to a limited company. This point is more relevant when selecting a solicitor than when choosing an accountant.

13.5.3   Bank managers

This subject ties in closely with Chapter 10, which discusses the subject of borrowing generally, and the comments in that chapter will apply here also. Your choice of bank manager will depend to a large extent on what it is that you require from the bank. If your borrowing requirements are high, then you will be dealt with by a manager who is at a senior level within the bank and able to sanction that level of borrowing.

On the other hand, if you simply require a corporate (limited company) bank account, and also perhaps a deposit account, then your local manager who may have dealt with your personal banking for some time, will be your obvious choice – assuming that he grants your requests.

Some banks have a policy of not handling corporate accounts within smaller branches, which means you may be passed across or upwards in the bank's structure. If you do not feel happy with this arrangement, then it may be necessary for you to consider moving your business across to another bank, which does handle limited company accounts at local branch level.

The bank manager is normally very experienced in dealing with the affairs of business in general, and should prove to be a useful source of advice on a wide range of matters.

13.5.3.1 *Dealing with a bank* *

In many cases, the first approach to a bank will be in order to obtain funding for the company's activities. It is essential that any request for borrowing is presented in a correct and professional manner, as a bank will be influenced in their decision not only by the commercial sense of any project but also by the people involved in the project and the quality and professionalism of the presentation.

For this reason, if funding of any substance is sought from a bank it is necessary to prepare a business plan, which is a summary of the proposed project together with cash flow forecasts and projected accounts. The company's auditors and advisers should have experience in this field and will be able to assist not only in the preparation of the business plan but also in the presentation of the plan to the bank.

In some cases where funding is required, and depending on the risk and viability of the project, it will not be possible for the borrower to negotiate the most favourable terms between several banks. Indeed, in difficult situations it may be impossible to obtain finance at all.

In recent years, many of the high street banks have rationalised their lending criteria. The halcyon days of the local manager who knew each business in the town well and was able to provide loans and overdraft facilities with no reference to higher authority have disappeared in many banks, although thankfully some of the major clearing banks are now bringing back the tradition of locally based managers who are able to agree loans and overdrafts without having to refer to a higher authority within the bank.

With the current rigorous lending criteria operated by most banks, it is often impossible to obtain funding (particularly for a new venture) without providing security (or collateral).

Bank managers are generally very experienced in assessing situations and appraising the potential success of business projects. They will not normally lend in high-risk situations or without adequate security to support borrowings.

13.6   COMPLAINING ABOUT PROFESSIONALS

Most professionals are subject to rules about the manner in which they deliver their services, and the basis upon which they can calculate their charges.

The Law Societies, in England and Wales, Scotland and Northern Ireland, offer one or more leaflets in respect of such matters, available from those bodies at their respective addresses as shown in Appendix A.

Further information as to the procedures for complaining about particular accountants can be obtained from their relevant professional body. The addresses of those of the main bodies are shown in Appendix A.

13.7   CONCLUSION

Professional advisers can be of invaluable assistance to a company, its directors and future success. Selected with care and used effectively, they will become an integral part of the growing company.

CHAPTER 14

THE INTERNET, WEBSITES AND E-COMMERCE

14.1   INTRODUCTION

The 1990s saw the emergence in the UK of a new and remarkable form of communication – the Internet. With the ability to communicate through this new channel, every business was encouraged to build a website and trade on the Internet. Many vendors were promising that this exciting new medium would transform traditional commerce as they had known it for hundreds of years. But the majority of forecasts were subsequently proved to be overstated and, in the early stages, very few businesses actually gained any significant commercial advantage from use of the technology.

As the years passed, the Internet has gained the acceptance and trust that was lacking in the 1990s and it is now an efficient, reliable way of both promoting your business and actually transacting with customers all around the world. Businesses that simply did not exist in any substance 20 years ago, such as eBay (www.ebay.com) and Amazon (www.amazon-.com), prove just how the Internet can be used effectively to gain the maximum advantage for all. In addition, the number and size of financial transactions that take place across the Internet is staggering, and is set to increase steadily in the future.

Having said this, the Internet is still not an all-encompassing panacea, but neither should it be ignored. It can produce real benefits and every business should consider how it could use the technology and communication abilities to improve efficiency and profitability. This chapter provides an overview of the web-based arena and provides pointers as to where a business should take some action.

14.2   WHAT IS IT ALL ABOUT?

It is useful, first, to distinguish between the Internet, and the World Wide Web (www).

The Internet is the general description for a worldwide network of hundreds and thousands of computers. A useful analogy is the road network in the UK. From one address in a town in one part of the country, it is possible to reach any other address, by using the network of roads, lanes or motorways. The most important factors in locating that destination successfully is to, first, know the exact address you are trying to reach and, secondly, know how to get there in the shortest time. The www is one facet of the Internet network, and the most commonly used by businesses and home users. It uses www as the first part of an address and can therefore be described as one particular set of addresses and links which uses the Internet network as its pathway to connect users.

There are two key elements to using the www as a form of communication. They are:

(1)   the network itself, with its various elements; and

(2)   the interface used to access the www, which is normally the web browser.

14.3   THE NETWORK

Just as the road network consists of connections with different speeds (motorways, trunk roads and suburban links) so does the Internet. Each country is laid out with 'backbone' connections which are very fast, wide cables, and these high speed connections lead into numerous central junctions (Points of Presence or 'POPs') around that country. The countries of the world are also linked with high speed connections, both in the form of underground cables and satellite links. From the junctions in each country, lower speed connections are laid which eventually arrive at a single address. The main telecommunications companies normally provide the high speed connections, and are likely also to supply the link from that network directly to the door of the user. With the introduction of higher speed local networks, it is now possible for households and businesses to experience significantly faster connections, which opens up a wide range of new services, such as streaming of video, accessing software programs situated remotely, bulk backup of data and Virtual Private Networks (VPNs).

14.3.1   Addresses

The analogy of every house having a unique address or postcode works well when applied to the www. Each computer which is connected to the www will have an address, which is normally shown as a series of numbers (eg 193.130.81.82). These numbers identify a location on the network which has been assigned to a particular computer. When a website address is typed into the browser (eg www.jordanpublishing.co.uk), the system converts this into numbers by locating the www address in one of many identical directories across the world and identifying the related numerical address. It then finds the quickest route to that address (and therefore computer) and connects the user's browser to that computer. The speed of the connection will be affected directly by the address look up speed, the 'width' of the cables being used to reach that address and the volume of traffic also trying to use those connections. Driving through a busy motorway junction at the peak of rush hour can be a slow and frustrating experience, and using the www at certain times of the day can be equally irritating.

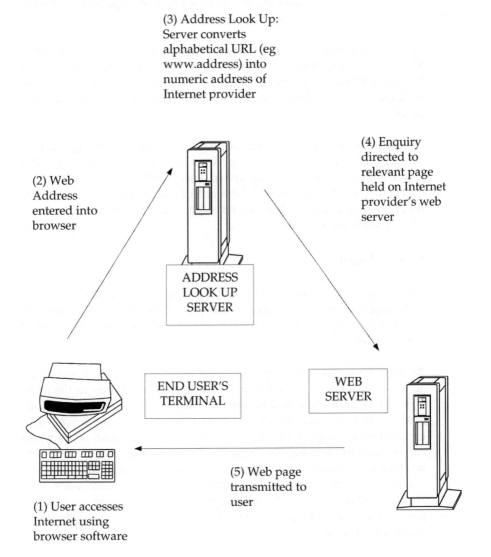

(3) Address Look Up:
Server converts
alphabetical URL (eg
www.address) into
numeric address of
Internet provider

(4) Enquiry
directed to
relevant page
held on Internet
provider's web
server

(2) Web
Address
entered into
browser

ADDRESS
LOOK UP
SERVER

END USER'S
TERMINAL

WEB
SERVER

(5) Web page
transmitted to
user

(1) User accesses
Internet using
browser software

Figure 11 – Basic structure of the Internet

Web servers can be located anywhere on the globe and can hold hundreds of individual websites, each with their own unique numerical Internet provider address (eg http://193.130.81.82 – try it!).

14.3.2   The web browser

The information collected when visiting another address on the www is written in particular computer code which can be translated into graphics by a web browser. The most common form of code used to write traditional web pages is HTML, and there are also many other more sophisticated software languages which can display moving images, produce sound and video images. A complex web page will be written using a number of different techniques and languages.

There are a number of web browsers available, but the most common is Microsoft Internet Explorer, which is supplied as a standard element of Microsoft Windows. Firefox/Mozilla and Netscape are other commonly available browsers. These products are used to surf the web by over 95% of users.

The majority of websites (ie the code written to create the images) can be interpreted by all these browser products, although a minority of sites may not work with one or the other. This is either because the site is deliberately written not to work with one of the products or, more likely, the developers of the site have not considered the usability by all browsers when developing the code.

14.3.3   Email

Email has revolutionised the way people communicate since its widespread adoption in the mid to late 1990s. This chapter does not deal with email in any detail, but it is useful to provide an overview of how a typical email system works.

As with the world wide web, it is based around addresses. Every email address will convert to a numerical address, in a similar way to the www. This numerical address will be that of a mail server, a computer which holds many email accounts (or postboxes). When a message is sent to an email address, the system forwards that message to the email server which corresponds to the numerical equivalent of the email address. The mail will then be collected, either by the email account holder dialling into that mailbox from their personal computer (as with the commonly used Hotmail, AOL or Yahoo! mail accounts) or, in the case of a larger company, by the mail server automatically distributing the mail directly to the user's computer.

Mail is created using email software, which converts the mail into a specific language, recognised by the majority of other email software packages. In this way, mail created using one email package (eg Microsoft Outlook Express) can be read using another email package such as Eudora.

Individuals and smaller businesses are likely to use a dial up mail system, where their computer will dial into a centrally hosted mail server (or postal sorting office) and collect the mail. If the business has more than one mail user, the mail system at the user's end may then pass the mail through the business's internal computer network to the appropriate user's computer.

Larger organisations may have their own mail server on the company premises, which has its own mail address on the world wide network. The mail is then sent directly to that address (and therefore directly to the company premises) and again will be forwarded onto the individual user's computer.

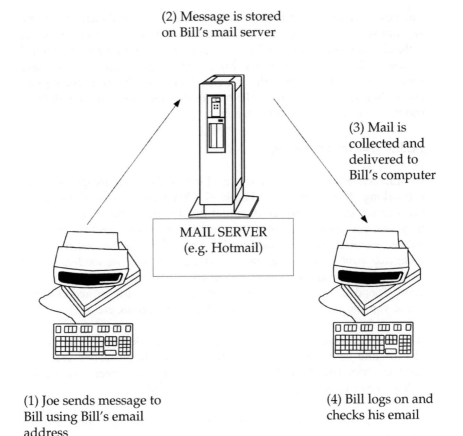

(2) Message is stored
on Bill's mail server

(3) Mail is
collected and
delivered to
Bill's computer

MAIL SERVER
(e.g. Hotmail)

(1) Joe sends message to
Bill using Bill's email
address

(4) Bill logs on and
checks his email

Figure 12 – How email works

This diagram shows how a simple email system works, as used by thousands of individuals who 'dial up' and collect their mail.

In larger companies, the mail server is actually managed by the company and will automatically deliver the mail to the relevant user's mailbox. When he logs on to the system, the mail will be waiting for him.

14.3.4   Blogs

Web logs, or 'blogs', are online discussion forums, where a person can post his opinions on a website – often presented as sporadic thoughts or, more regularly, as an online diary. Readers can post responses to the blogger and to each other's postings, to create discussion 'threads' on the different topics. Software to create a blog can be downloaded free from the web, and is easy to use, so anyone with web access can create a blog.

The potential number of blogs is as numerous as peoples' interests – there are already many hundreds of thousands of them, from blogs on technological issues, where IT workers swap ideas and post technological problems they have had in the hope that a fellow blogger will have encountered and overcome the same problem, and blogs discussing the latest TV reality show or what the manager of the England football team should do, to blogs on garden design.

14.3.5   Social networking

Another development that has transformed the e-landscape is social networking. Sites like Bebo, Facebook, Myspace and YouTube allow users to set up their own confidential online space, free of charge, that they can customise with their own messages, music, photos, graphics, videos, resources, blogs, games, diaries, news of events they are planning, going to, want to promote, etc – anything that can be loaded onto a website. The networking aspect comes from the fact that they can then invite 'friends', by email, to access their space in return for access to the friend's space, and they can swap music, photos, games, etc.

All users can search for other users they know (or don't know but would like to), and invite them to become their friends. In particular, users can see their own friends' friends and, if they want to 'meet' that person online, they can do so through their mutual friend.

It is also possible to set up 'groups' on any subject – as popular or as obscure as the user wishes – that others can then join.

The growth of social networking has been phenomenal. Facebook, the most popular social networking site, has over 16m users worldwide at the time of writing.

14.4 USING THE TECHNOLOGY TO BENEFIT YOUR BUSINESS

Effective use of the available technology can assist a business in a variety of ways. For many businesses, the expectation of increased revenues has not been fulfilled, and the opportunity to reduce costs is now seen by many observers as a more realistic benefit to be gained from correct implementation of the technology. It is important to approach this whole area with care and planning. A clear plan, which is compatible with the overall business strategy, developed and implemented in a logical and measured process, is likely to produce real, lasting benefits for most businesses.

Many businesses are finding that blogs can be an excellent source of market research – rich sources of information about the market's view of your brand and your products or services. Many larger businesses view critical comments on blogs very seriously when planning improvements to their business.

Blogs can also be used by businesses to create and spread the online equivalent of 'word of mouth' awareness of their products or service ('viral marketing'), or put the case for the defence, if they have been criticised. However, it is very easy to make mistakes if you misjudge the audience – many bloggers consider themselves maverick and subversive and any attempt by a conventional business to engage with them online can backfire badly. Finally, you should not post information on a blog on behalf of the business, promoting it or putting your point of view, without declaring your interest.

As with blogs, businesses can quickly find out if they, or their products or services, are being discussed on a social networking site – an even richer source of information about the market's perception of the business, and its products and services, than blogs. But the dangers of trying to engage with users on a social networking site are even greater than on a blog.

14.5 THE VARYING DEGREES OF INTERACTION

The most common areas where use of the technology will benefit a business are as follows – in order of cost and complexity:

(1) simply creating a presence;

(2) as a marketing tool – an electronic brochure;

(3) providing information and assisting customers and prospects;

(4) improving the sales process and saving costs;

(5)   communicating with suppliers and saving costs.

14.5.1   Creating a presence

The website will provide a simple point of contact through a web address, with brief details of the business, an overview of the operations and how to get in touch. It will probably contain a simple email link which will automatically create an email message from the web page and deliver it to the company email postbox. A large percentage of the smaller company websites created in the late 1990s went no further than this. This basic 'starter website' adds very little to the business but, in some cases, the strategy will determine that nothing more is needed.

14.5.2   As a marketing tool

The site will be rich in design and impact. It will contain product or service information, details of satisfied customers with case studies, some history and information about the business and key locations and individuals, contact information and maps. It may contain a marketing survey which users can enter.

14.5.3   An information point

One of the most effective uses of the technology is to provide information to customers and prospects – used often by businesses which sell more complex products or services. The site may contain detailed data and information about products and services and it may be possible to download technical specifications, price lists and images of particular offerings. It may be necessary to pass through a 'Chinese wall', by entering a username and password to access some of this information which the company may not wish to be available to the public.

Many organisations are now experiencing real cost savings from the delivery of information and dealing with enquiries through a structured process within their websites. They find that customers and new enquirers are often very happy to do the work themselves, browsing through catalogues and information, completing an online form to request information and downloading product details and images. For more information on online catalogues, go to www.actinic.com.

14.5.4   Improving the sales process

The ability for customers to order goods and services online was forecast to revolutionise trading practices as we knew them. With a few exceptions, mostly in the B2C (business to consumer) market, most notably books and CDs (eg www.amazon.co.uk), this has not been the case. The reasons are complex, but the willingness of businesses in the early days to trade online was overestimated, the ease of completing a transaction was not dealt with adequately and, most importantly, the fact that business is in many cases a 'one to one' people transaction was ignored.

Huge investment also went into online exchanges, public (sometimes within an industry) locations where a business can visit and transact with other businesses in a similar market or requiring common goods. The majority of these early exchanges struggled to operate at a profit and many closed down. New exchanges have emerged, with better design and functionality and some are succeeding. What has become clear is that online trading is suitable for some goods and services but not for others. Each business must decide if their processes and products would suit this method of transacting.

14.5.4.1   Online selling

14.5.4.1.1   STAGE 1

The first step on the ladder of online selling is to display a catalogue or list of products on the website. These may be organised into sections, to assist the user in finding what he needs, and there may be a search facility on the catalogue. Once the user has chosen a product, he may order this using a simple form (which creates an email message delivered to the business), which means that the business will have to respond manually and deal with the financial side of the transaction in the normal way. Alternatively, it is possible to link the catalogue system on the site into a system which will take the user's credit card details and carry out the transaction automatically. The third party 'transaction enabler' will then collect the funds from the online purchaser and remit them to the vendor, after deducting its fee, which will vary. Online selling in this way is simple but has disadvantages. Unless the business has invested in a sophisticated, integrated system, the transaction may not automatically be entered into the company accounting system, which means that it will have to be rekeyed internally. Again, in a simpler system, the product information on the website is static and will have to be amended manually every time a change is required.

Moving from this stage of online selling (which probably represents over 80% of the online selling currently taking place on the www) into a more sophisticated, integrated model is a major step and requires significant planning and investment.

14.5.4.1.2   STAGE 2

There are a number of elements in the online selling process which can be linked into 'real live' information. Facilitating each of these may require significant investment in time and resource and the relative benefits of each should be carefully considered.

14.5.4.2 Customer details, price structures and habits

If a customer visits a website and the site recognises that customer (see personalisation and cookies in rule (6) of 'the eight golden rules of the web', below), then it can also offer that customer a bespoke set of products or process. The likelihood of that customer ordering goods online will increase if the ordering process is streamlined to fit in with that customer's requirements and past habits. If the site avoids the need for the customer to trawl through the same steps in locating the products he requires, then he is more likely to purchase. Many of the B2C supermarket sites attempt to do this by storing a list of favourites – goods which the customer purchases on a regular basis.

14.5.4.3 Product information

If the product details on a site are delivered in real time from a live database, this not only ensures that the customer is viewing accurate information about the latest products, but also eliminates the need to update the website information and therefore saves ongoing costs. More sophisticated systems will not only generate live product details but may also interrogate stock systems and generate purchase orders online. They may also interrogate the credit account of a customer whilst the customer is viewing the website to determine whether that customer is able to order further product within the predefined credit limits.

*14.5.4.4 Systems integration ****

Integrating product and customer details as described above may require complex database integration and can involve the business systems being accessible online, which creates security and technical issues. In many cases, the long-term commercial benefits of this integration are likely to outweigh the required investment and cultural shift, but moving beyond a simple online ordering 'catalogue' processes will require detailed planning and must form an integral part of the overall business strategy.

Specialist help will almost always be required. For more information on online transaction processors go to one of the leaders in this field, www.worldpay.com.

14.5.5 Communication with suppliers

If a business has made the investment to integrate internal systems with online selling or ordering processes, then it is likely that the integration of suppliers' transactions will be a less costly and painful step. In some cases (where the benefits can be seen more clearly on the purchasing side of the business), it may be beneficial to improve the supplier communication using web technology in advance of the customer areas.

14.6   ONE MAJOR CHANGE – REPLACING EDI

Just as customers may come onto a site and view products for sale, and then place an order, so a business may improve its purchasing function. For decades, many larger businesses used Electronic Data Interchange (EDI) to place orders with smaller suppliers. This is often found in situations where one large purchaser, such as a major supermarket chain, would purchase from numerous smaller suppliers. The purchasing company would implement a bespoke EDI system and make it mandatory for all its suppliers to install the corresponding system and receive orders down the line. Many EDI systems are not web-based and a significant number of smaller suppliers would not generally integrate the ordering system into their internal system, but simply receive an order through the EDI system and then process it in the traditional way. Many EDI systems have gradually been replaced with web-based systems, which make it far easier for a large customer to reach suppliers using a common format and process. It is still likely that the recipient of the orders (the smaller supplier) may not integrate the orders received into its systems, as discussed above in relation to customer and product details, but a web-based ordering system enables the purchasing company to reach almost all the suppliers without the need for the suppliers to implement expensive EDI systems.

14.7   ONLINE ORDERING FOR ALL

Outside the scope of the EDI arena, which only usually relates to a specific relationship between customer and supplier, is the concept of online tendering. A purchasing company can display details of the goods it requires, inducing the packaging requirements, delivery date and time, and detailed technical information about the products it requires. Suppliers can then visit the site, or receive automatic notification of a requirement being posted, and then submit their quotation to fulfil an order. The system can be open to all potential suppliers, or can be restricted, again through the process of usernames and passwords, to preferred suppliers. Most systems will have the facility for a new supplier to apply for registration, and these new suppliers would be vetted by the purchasing company before being issued with a username and password which enables them to access the site and submit quotations. Again, this system can become more and more sophisticated, with further systems integration enabling the production of delivery notes, purchase orders and, ultimately, transmitting the order instruction directly and seamlessly into the sales and delivery system of the supplying business.

14.8   THE EIGHT GOLDEN RULES OF THE WEB

There are eight golden rules that need to be borne in mind when investing in web-based technology:

(1) *Focus on your customers* – they are the lifeblood of the business.

(2) *Avoid endless (and sometimes pointless) internal data.* Pictures and CVs of key management are interesting and useful, but should be deep into the website, not on the first page a user finds.

(3) *Capture your users' details.* Whenever your website receives a visit, try to capture details of that visitor. Demanding pages of information about users will only cause irritation, but requesting an email address and some information, especially when the user has been on the site for some time and is clearly interested will probably not cause offence and will provide you with valuable prospect information.

(4) *Ensure that the navigation is effective.* Plan the pathway through your site carefully. Make sure that the homepage is accessible from every other page. Construct the navigation in a way that makes any place on the site accessible in three clicks or less. Ask third parties to test the site before you launch it and take note of their comments.

(5) *Keep load times down.* Your audience will be accessing the site with differing download speeds. Work on the lowest common denominator. Make sure that images are compressed effectively. Aim for a maximum page load time of less than 10 seconds at the slowest access rate on every page. Make any plug-ins or complex offerings optional.

(6) *Consider personalisation and cookies.* The aim of every site is to increase the number of visits, the length of each visit and the commercial benefit gained from each visit. Requiring a user to 'log in' to all or selected areas of a site enables the site to recognise the user by downloading a small file (a cookie) onto the user's computer. The next time that user visits the site, it will recognise them and may greet them with a 'Hello John' message. This small piece of personalisation is thought to increase the user loyalty to the site and the likelihood of them using the site facilities and returning more often. More sophisticated sites will display differently constructed pages for each user, and may remember their habits from previous visits. Developments such as these can increase the cost of building a website substantially and, once again, the business benefits must be considered in comparison to the cost of implementation.

(7) *Do not give your users unwelcome surprises.* It is very frustrating for a user, for example, to complete a registration form which may involve 5 or 10 minutes' worth of work, and then at the very last screen be asked for something which they may not have access to immediately – or even worse advise the user that they will have to make a

payment for the service. It is bad etiquette to use these techniques on websites and you will probably lose a potential customer permanently if you do so.

(8) *Keep Flash and other web software used to create animation to a minimum.* Unless your site is pure marketing, or you wish to convey your skills at creating complex and 'glitzy' websites, avoid the use of excessive animation. The majority of business users simply wish to access information and to do this quickly. The novelty of moving graphics and clever gizmos on a website is now generally considered passé and probably rather irritating for most.

14.9 LEGAL CONSIDERATIONS

As we have seen, e-commerce – email and the web, including blogs and social networking sites – can benefit your business enormously. Email means you can communicate with customers, suppliers, creditors, the general public and other employees more easily and quickly. The web makes your business visible worldwide so you can create better trading relations with existing customers, attract customers in new markets, compete more effectively with your competitors and attract potential business partners. Blogs and social networking sites give you another means of monitoring the market's perception of your business and perhaps, with enormous care, promoting your business.

Yet these also create dangers. Email creates a new way for you (or, more likely, an employee) to create contractual relations without meaning to, defame third parties, sexually harass or bully colleagues or make trade secrets available to competitors.

Taking orders or communicating with suppliers or other business partners over the web – indeed, by any electronic means – constitutes 'distance selling', to which a specific set of laws apply (see below), and can create other legal issues that you need to address.

A legal issue for businesses, arising from the growth of blogs, is that employee bloggers can denigrate their employer on a blog – or their co-workers, customers or suppliers. They could mention confidential issues relating to the company's products or services, or its trade secrets, such as its processes or pricing plans. If the blog is less than complimentary, or is giving away confidential information, what rights does the employer have to object? Particularly if, as is usually the case, the blog is being maintained in the employee's spare time, or the blogger is now an ex-employee. What can the business do?

Customers can also create blogs designed to praise or, more likely, to denigrate a business, or its products or services, if they are not happy with you. Can the business stop them?

You may find that your terms of business are inadequate – even unlawful – in the context of new customers you attract in other parts of the world, or that those of your suppliers leave you exposed now that parts of your relationship are electronic. You may also need to consider settlement implications because you are being paid in a foreign currency for the first time.

Businesses selling similar goods or services under a similar trading style may become aware of your existence because of your website and take action against you. In many cases, existing law provides a framework for addressing these issues. It is simply a matter of applying familiar legal principles or rules to new circumstances. In other areas, new rules are needed because the law lags behind technological advances. It is in these areas that the greatest difficulties occur. The following points highlight the main areas to think about, but these are all areas where professional advice is strongly recommended.

14.10   HOSTING

If your website is going to be stored ('hosted') on the server of an Internet Service Provider (ISP) rather than on your own server, you need to negotiate a service level agreement that commits the ISP to key performance standards in areas such as website 'availability' or 'uptime' and is clear on how problems will be dealt with. Make sure you are happy with the host's security – firewalls, anti-virus software, etc.

14.11   INTELLECTUAL PROPERTY ISSUES

14.11.1   Trade marks ***

One form of intellectual property is the trade mark. Use of a word, logo, slogan, colour, sound, shape, smell or 3-dimensional form or any combination of them in relation to particular goods or services creates trade mark rights. The courts will allow the owner of a trade mark to sue another business in the courts for 'passing off' if that business is using the same or a similar mark in relation to similar goods or services in a way that is likely to damage the owner's business or goodwill.

If the owner has also registered the mark in a national trade mark Registry or under an international system, such as the European Community or Madrid Protocol system, the owner's rights are even easier to enforce.

However, some businesses may have used and registered a trade mark legitimately in the territories in which they have traditionally operated. If such a business establishes a website, the fact it is using a particular mark is instantly visible to potential customers in territories where the same mark may be legitimately owned and registered by another business. Unsurprisingly, the web has led to a rise in trade mark disputes.

Such disputes cannot always be resolved easily if they arise. When setting up a website, businesses therefore need current, expert advice on how to avoid or minimise the possibility of such disputes.

14.11.2   Domain names ***

Registration of a domain name gives a business surprisingly few rights and/or protections over and above those already conferred by trade mark law.

Domain names are administered by registries that operate under the auspices of the Internet Corporation for Assigned Names and Numbers (ICANN). Around 250 national registries offer registration under 'country code' domains like .fr (France) and .de (Germany). Others are international and offer registration under generic domains. These include the most popular domain, .com and more recently .eu.

Some national registries offer registration under 'second level' domains. The UK registry, Nominet, is one of these. Applicants must register under one of the second level domains such as .co.uk or .ltd.uk, rather than directly under the .uk domain.

Traditionally, ICANN has allowed registries to set their own rules about who can register. A number do have rules that limit registrations to, for example, applicants with a local presence or a pre-existing registered trade mark. For example, widgets.ltd.uk could only be registered by a UK limited company called Widgets Limited.

However, these restrictions are few and far between. For example, while the .ltd.uk domain is restricted, anyone can apply to register under the .co.uk domain. The same is true of the .com domain. These 'first come, first served' domains became a real problem for businesses who found their trade marks were being registered as domain names by cybersquatters – folk with no legitimate interest in a trade mark or other name who registered it and then tried to sell it back to those who did at exorbitant prices. It did not help that the unrestricted domains included the most popular ones.

This has meant that, generally, registering a name under one domain will prevent registration of an identical name under that domain but it does not often prevent either:

- registration of an identical name under a different domain; or

- registration of a similar name under the same domain.

For example, the fact that Widgets Limited has registered widgets.com would not prevent someone else registering widgets.co.uk, or even widgetsuk.com.

However, the tide is now turning in favour of owners of existing rights. First, ICANN has introduced a Uniform Dispute Resolution Procedure (UDRP) that has been adopted by the international registries and a number of the national registries. A trade mark owner (or anyone with a legitimate interest in a name) who is clearly a victim of cybersquatters can apply to have the domain name removed. The UDRP provides quick, easy resolution in clear-cut cases. Application fees are low and the procedure is written, so legal fees can be kept to a minimum.

Other registries have also developed, or are introducing, their own versions of the UDRP. These include the UK's own Nominet.

These procedures do not provide a solution in circumstances where two businesses are legitimately using the same or a similar name but only become aware of each other because of the web. In such circumstances the legal remedy is a passing-off action in the courts, based on usual principles. In practice, the court is the last resort.

As well as the UDRP, there have been some moves towards protecting owners of existing rights against cybersquatters and other infringers at the registration stage. For example, when new generic domains such as .biz and .info were introduced in 2001, ICANN required the new registries to establish rules to protect businesses with existing rights in a name against abusers and/or infringers.

When considering domain name registration strategy – which domains to register under, which variations of names to register, what to do if cybersquatters have already registered your names, what to do if there are other legitimate users of your name already registered – professional, expert advice is vital both to provide as much protection as possible and to ensure that money is not wasted on unnecessary registrations.

14.11.3   Copyright and other intellectual property issues ***

A business commissioning the design of a website from a third party should ensure that the copyright in the website design will belong to it, irrespective of the stage reached in that design. This should take the form of a written agreement between the business and the web designers whereby the designers grant copyright in its work to the business. Practically, the designers should also be asked to provide a digital copy of the design on completion, and at pre-determined stages during the development in case the work needs to be assigned to a different designer for any reason.

If you want to use third party content, obtain a licence to do so from the copyright owner, which applies to its use on the web.

If linking to third party websites, make sure the links do not infringe their intellectual property rights, eg by making it appear that their material is part of your website. Include a disclaimer on your website stating that you are not liable for the contents of third party websites.

14.12   COMPLIANCE WITH DATA PROTECTION REQUIREMENTS ***

The Data Protection Act 1998 requires businesses that collect and use personal information about customers or other individuals to observe eight principles. The data must be:

(1)   fairly and lawfully processed;

(2)   processed for limited purposes;

(3)   adequate, relevant and not excessive;

(4)   accurate;

(5)   not kept longer than necessary;

(6)   processed in accordance with the individual's rights;

(7)   secure;

(8)   not transferred to countries without adequate protection.

Partners in a business partnership are treated as individuals for the purposes of protection under the Act.

The principles mean, for example, that data about an individual cannot be collected on your website or used by you unless the individual consents, or it is necessary under a contract with the individual to fulfil a legal obligation or there is some other necessity. Clearly, websites that capture visitors' details must take this into account.

It also means that businesses must allow individuals access to that information and they can require correction or deletion of that information. The information does not have to be collected or stored electronically for the Act to apply.

One requirement of the Act that exercises businesses is that data collected for one purpose cannot be used for another without permission. For example, if a customer provides an address for the purpose of enabling an order to be processed, it cannot be used, for example, for an unrelated promotion by post unless the customer has consented to the data being used for other purposes. Websites should therefore include a privacy policy saying how you will use information collected, and your order forms should ask customers for permission to use data for other purposes when taking orders online.

Particularly, if you want to send marketing emails, or otherwise communicate electronically with customers, you must either have their specific 'opt-in' or already have a relationship with them. You must always give targets the option to opt-out, both on your website and in any emails you send them.

The Data Protection Act 1998 is a complex and far-reaching piece of legislation that affects businesses far beyond their e-commerce activities. For more information, go to www.dataprotection.gov.uk.

14.13 TERMS OF BUSINESS

14.13.1 Contractual issues ***

The web provides a new means for customers to place orders, who may never have dealt with the business before. It therefore becomes important that they are specifically made aware of its terms of business before placing orders. This is because knowledge of, for example, limitations on the business's liability if something goes wrong will not be implied by a court without a course of dealing.

A simple precaution is to make sure that all customers ordering over the web see the terms of business. Many websites present customers placing an order with their terms of business and require the customer to click 'I agree' before confirming the order.

The web also opens businesses to markets beyond their national boundaries. Terms of business that are perfectly adequate for domestic markets may need revisiting for these wider markets.

For example, terms may need to provide specifically that it is the business's domestic courts that have jurisdiction in the event of a dispute, that payment must be made in sterling and that there are special credit terms for overseas orders.

The business may benefit if the terms tailor the rules of offer and acceptance for web orders. Offer and acceptance is necessary before a contract is concluded and the terms of business can dictate when this happens. For example, retailers usually provide in their terms of business that they are not making an offer to sell by putting priced goods on the shelves. If they were, a shopper could insist on the retailer selling incorrectly priced goods. Instead, the shopper makes an offer to buy at the checkout, and it is up to the retailer whether to accept the offer or not.

A business taking orders over the web may wish to provide that those orders are offers to buy (that the business can decide whether to accept or not when the order is received), rather than offers to sell that the customer can accept by placing the order.

Businesses may wish to provide in their terms that they will not accept orders from customers in certain countries (this should also be clearly and prominently stated in other appropriate parts of the website). This can be one way to help avoid a trade mark dispute with a business in another country. Or it may be because that country has laws that protect customers – that provide cooling-off periods, or override clauses in the terms of business that show liability – which are not acceptable to the business.

Particularly, EU businesses are affected by the EC Directive designed to protect consumers buying at a distance rather than face to face. In the UK, this has resulted in the Distance Selling Regulations, that affect online purchases (other than purchases of financial products, which are separately regulated). For example, you must provide written confirmation of orders, and tell consumers about their cancellation rights (if any) if they can buy or place orders on your site. More information about the Regulations is available at www.berr.gov.uk.

Businesses communicating electronically with suppliers and other business partners would also be well advised to review their trading contracts. For example, the possibility of security breaches that give outsiders access to confidential information may mean that your business will wish to reconsider the confidentiality clause in its contracts.

Your website must contain certain information generally, including your business name and address. If your website includes prices, you must state whether these include VAT and delivery charges.

These are just examples of the issues that can arise. Businesses should get expert professional help in reviewing their terms of business for use online and keep them reviewed as the law develops in this fast-changing area.

14.13.2   Other matters for your terms of business ***

If visitors can download, for example, documents or software from your website, include a disclaimer on the site, limiting your liability for any damage a visitor suffers by downloading from your site, e g because the download includes a virus.

If you offer a chat room/discussion forum, ensure you disclaim liability for visitors' postings in your terms and conditions of use, and that you monitor and remove inappropriate comment.

Make sure other websites aren't diverting visitors to their sites using similar domain names and websites. Consider subscribing to a domain name monitoring service.

If you provide instructions or advice on, eg how to use your products, always include a disclaimer in your terms and conditions of use, to help limit your liability for any damage a user might suffer through relying on your advice.

Finally, if you are in a regulated industry, there may be special legal issues for your website.

14.14   EMPLOYMENT ISSUES – EMAIL AND WEB USE BY EMPLOYEES ***

In the past, businesses have been greatly exercised by the potential for misuse inherent in giving employees access to email and the web. This includes wasting time surfing or emailing, looking at pornographic or other offensive sites, defamation and harassment.

Such misuse can have serious implications for a business that has failed to consider how to prevent it. For example, employers can be taken to court for failing to take sufficient care to stop one employee defaming another by email.

For employers, blogs and social networking presents particular threats and opportunities. The threats include:

*   time wasting;

*   bullying;

*   security; and

*   recruitment.

Employees are spending many hours on social networking sites when they should be working, and there have been dismissals, usually for gross misconduct, as a result. For example, in 2007:

- A major retailer sacked an employee for (vehemently) criticising the company on Facebook. He was asked to remove the criticisms, suspended and, after a disciplinary hearing, sacked for gross misconduct.

- Employees in a national company set up a group on Facebook where they could exchange insults about their employer's customers.

Some employers have responded by banning use of social networking sites during working hours. The majority, however, are drawing up policies, with staff involvement, that permit a small amount of access during breaks, on the understanding that such access may be withdrawn in the event of abuse of the arrangement.

Cyber-bullying of co-workers on social networking sites, where users criticise and abuse fellow workers in online groups, can create liabilities for an employer who lets this happen, or continue, just as much as if it happened on the shop floor or in the office.

Other dangers for employers include workers breaching commercial confidentiality, or damaging the employer's reputation by defaming the employer itself, or colleagues, customers or suppliers on social networking sites or blogs.

There are dangers for employers when recruiting. Some employers have been looking up applicants for jobs on social networking sites to research their backgrounds. This can lay employers open to discrimination claims, on the grounds that not all candidates will have profiles, and personal details that are not required to be disclosed on an application form may be disclosed on, or deduced from, a profile.

Apart from being a distraction for employees, social networking sites look set to become a rich source of research information at some stage – and places where customer dissatisfaction with your products can spread like wildfire. Be prepared to make specific provision in your policies allowing employees onto such sites to research new products or to monitor for and/or respond to comments and opinions about your business posted on them. And ensure that none of your activities breach the Data Protection Act, distance selling or other legislation.

As both law and practice are fast moving in these respects, most businesses have not amended employment contracts to deal with them but have chosen to introduce email and web policies, usually as part of the staff handbook. Business lawyers now routinely draft such policies, tailored to the needs of particular businesses and their cultures. Alternatively, precedents are available on the web for businesses to download and tailor to their own needs.

Employers should consider:

- including a prohibition on employees identifying their business in a personal blog, even if maintained in their own time, or maintained by another person;

- specifying in their email and Internet policy that maintaining or contributing to another person's blog could amount to gross misconduct justifying dismissal in certain circumstances, eg if there is a risk that they may upset co-workers, customers or other third parties, and complaints are received; and

- making specific provision for employees that the business does want to spend time on social networking sites, for business benefits.

Businesses wishing to take more draconian steps can take advantage of the Regulation of Investigatory Powers Act 2000, which allows employers to monitor email received and sent by employees. This is a thorny issue and legal advice is strongly recommended before taking this step.

CHAPTER 15

STRATEGY AND PLANNING **

15.1   INTRODUCTION

One of the key determining factors in the success of most businesses is whether or not there is an overall strategy in place which sets out the objectives and pathway for the business. This strategy will then be achieved by developing a number of plans for each of the key areas in the business.

It is a surprising fact that a very large percentage of smaller businesses have never taken the time to consider and determine their overall strategy, and this is probably one of the main contributory factors to the high failure rate of new starts in their early years.

This chapter provides an overview of the development of strategy and competitive advantage.

15.2   WHAT IS STRATEGY?

There are many different opinions of what exactly strategy is. Some commentators describe it as a plan to reach a goal, others take a more holistic view and see it as a statement of direction for the business. There is no universally agreed definition (although they are all broadly similar), which does tend to confuse.

A satisfactory definition of what strategy is for a business would be:

> 'an overall high level statement of where the business wants to be, the route it needs to take to get there, what the key factors are in measuring that achievement and what the timescales are for reaching the agreed objectives.'

Just as a military general will develop a strategy for achieving his objectives, so an astute businessperson will do the same. The strategy will take into account numerous factors – including market conditions, the competition, expected lifespan of the products or services, and the skills and resources available to the business.

15.2.1   Each strategy will be different and unique to each business

So, for example, a new start business which aims to sell high volumes of low complexity products in an already busy market, such as an internet retailer, may decide that its strategy in the early stages is to reach a point where it has:

- developed systems which are totally reliable;

- achieved consistent and acceptable margins on its products;

- established a solid customer base;

- reached a consistently good level of service.

Once these initial objectives have been reached, a new strategy would be developed for the next phase of the business.

In contrast, an established business which has achieved all of the above may decide that its strategy for the next 2 years is to:

- develop a series of innovative products which it can offer to its existing customer base, alongside its already established offerings;

- increase its customer service levels with further investment as required;

- widen its market reach by, for example, opening new outlets.

15.3   COMPETITIVE ADVANTAGE

The advantage which your business has over its competitors will make a significant difference to the strategy you are likely to adopt as the business moves forward. It is recommended, therefore, that time is spent in discussing and identifying this very important element before moving on to discuss and determine strategy for the business as a whole.

One important point to note is that your business may not currently have any apparent competitive advantage, but as part of the overall strategic planning process it is vital that a policy for gaining a competitive advantage is discussed and agreed upon, even though it may take some time to create such an advantage in practice.

15.3.1 What is competitive advantage?

A business's competitive advantage is that factor (or factors) about the business which make it more attractive to customers when compared to its competitors.

Some examples:

- A low-cost supermarket – lower price of goods.

- A high-class hairdressing salon – expertise and experience of its staff.

- A niche consultancy – unique knowledge of a particular product or market.

- A large courier company – delivering the parcel on time, every time.

As many experienced business operators will know, a competitive advantage for one business will not work for another. Price is not as important an issue to most customers as one may think, with levels of customer service often ranking higher.

Most developed businesses will have carefully considered their competitive advantage and will then assemble almost their whole business strategy around delivering that advantage. So a low-cost supermarket will cut costs wherever it can (eg by stacking the products in the delivery boxes rather than placing them on the shelves individually). Equally, an expensive boutique will spend significant amounts on the premises, fittings and customer service.

The different hotel chains clearly demonstrate various approaches to competitive advantage, ranging from cheap and cheerful right through to very expensive and sumptuous, where every desire is catered for.

15.4 HOW TO DETERMINE WHAT YOUR COMPETITIVE ADVANTAGE SHOULD BE

15.4.1 Step 1 – Market research

A vital and often omitted step in most business planning processes is to actually ask your prospective (or existing) customers for their views. This market research will provide a wealth of important and often surprising information which you can use to determine your competitive advantage and therefore your business strategy.

You may find that the factor which you thought was top of the list (eg price) is in fact much lower in terms of importance for your customers, and what they actually want is consistent, reliable service.

15.4.2   Step 2 – Competitor analysis

Take time to review the competition. What are they communicating as their competitive advantage? What are their marketing messages?

15.4.3   Step 3 – Consider your resources

It may not be possible for you to compete, for example, on price. This is particularly true in FMCG (Fast Moving Consumer Goods) such as food, where the major supermarkets have such huge buying power that a small business simply cannot compete. So the smaller business needs to offer something which the mega retailer cannot do (such as a personalised service).

15.4.4   Step 4 – Make a decision

Procrastination will get you nowhere and a decision needs to be made and the energy of the business directed to achieving that competitive advantage.

15.4.5   Sustainability

Finally, the competitive advantage needs to be sustainable. In other words it must be able to survive trends, cycles and changes in the economy. One mistake which many new businesses make is to try and be too innovative. Ground-breaking technology, products or style of service will be a major hit occasionally (eg the Apple iPod), but many more will fail. Don't try to be revolutionary when starting out.

15.5   LINKING THE COMPETITIVE ADVANTAGE TO THE STRATEGY

Having established your desired competitive advantage, take this back into the strategic planning process. Once the strategy has been determined and plans are then put in place to achieve that strategy and its objectives, the competitive advantage will have a noticeable influence in most areas of the business upon exactly how the strategy is achieved.

15.6   HOW TO DEVELOP YOUR STRATEGIC PLAN

15.6.1   Step 1 – Where do we want to be? And by when?

The first stage of developing a strategic plan is to decide where the business owners want it to be at an agreed time in the future. A date in the future should be set (eg 1 or 2 years away) and then decisions made about where the business needs to be in numerous areas. This discussion will cover the key elements of the business as follows:

- financial performance;

- management and staffing structure and required skills;

- products and services;

- customers;

- market share and geographical coverage;

- innovation;

- sales and marketing;

- funding and investment.

So the strategic plan may say that the business will, in 2 years time, have entered a particular marketplace with two new products. It will require funding of £0.5m to achieve this, have five staff and three senior management, will be achieving a 60% gross margin and net profit break even and will have 150 regular customers ordering product.

It will achieve these objectives with competitive advantage of outstanding customer service and the management will detail this further by analysing the customer service of competitors and ensuring that the business differentiates itself in several key areas. These decisions may influence a number of sub-strategies, eg training, investment in systems, and quality of staff employed.

15.6.2   Step 2 – Carry out SWOT analysis

SWOT analysis is a thorough review of the strengths, weaknesses, opportunities and threats which do or will affect your business.

Examples of SWOT

Strengths	–	Strong skills, sector knowledge, existing contacts, strategic alliances, market trends.
Weaknesses	–	Lack of skills, weak patent position, lack of funding or resources.
Opportunities	–	Emerging markets, government support, future legal or regulatory requirements for your products, strategic alliances.
Threats	–	Competition, legal or regulatory changes, market trends.

15.6.3   Step 3 – How are we going to get there?

The next stage is to develop a mini plan for each area of the business, all of which will be totally focused on delivering the objectives of the main strategic plan. As an example, these may cover the main areas in the business as follows:

Sales & marketing

- Pricing of products.

- Target customers.

- How to communicate the marketing messages to those customers.

- What the messages will say.

- Packaging and image of products.

- Overall image and feel of the business itself – branding.

Finance

- Development of 3-year financial forecasts.

- Cash flow requirements.

- Identifying overheads, salary and all other costs.

- How to manage working capital.

- Determine how much investment/funding the business will need.

- Identifying where this investment/funding will come from.

People

- Creating the required structure of staff and management.

- Preparing specifications for each of the posts, with roles, responsibility and accountability.

- Developing a training plan.

Products/services

- Identification of first products.

- Development of products.

- Consideration of patents and trademarks.

- Costing of products and gross margin.

Each of these will be documented and planned, and assigned to an individual who will be responsible and accountable for that section of the business going forward. In a small business it is likely that one or two individuals may have to manage the whole business.

15.6.4 Step 4 – Implementation

Implement the separate plans for each area of the business, and ensure that milestones and measurement are a key part of this process (see below).

15.7 THE STRATEGIC PLAN IS A LIVING DOCUMENT

Once the overall strategy has been agreed, as far as possible it should remain as is and not be changed. The strategic plan, which delivers this agreed strategy, however, is very much a living document and will constantly be updated as progress is made against targets and milestones. It may need to be amended if obstacles are encountered which simply cannot be overcome. This may require a re-think of the overall strategy in extreme cases. One example of this may be when a business is developing a product but finds some way along the line that there are legal reasons (e g it may be infringing a patent) why it cannot offer that product for sale. This is an unusual situation and this risk should in fact have been identified in the early stages when the SWOT analysis was carried out.

15.8   AND FINALLY, MEASUREMENT

It is vitally important that milestones (ie 'we will achieve this target by that date') are put in place along the pathway. These will be time and activity linked.

So typical milestones could be:

Marketing	–	A database of prospective customers will be developed and ready for use by the end of quarter 1.
Financial	–	Annualised sales (turnover/revenue) of £500,000 will be achieved by the end of year 2.
People	–	A training schedule for all staff will be in place and implemented by the end of quarter 2.

The milestones will be different in each situation but are very important, not only to measure the progress of the business overall against the plan, but also to monitor an individual's performance in their own area. Often, an individual's remuneration will be linked directly into their performance against agreed milestones.

15.9   CONCLUSION

This chapter provides a brief summary of a typical strategic planning process and its constituent parts and it is highly recommended that every business develops and maintains a strategic plan.

CHAPTER 16

FURTHER CONSIDERATIONS

16.1 EMPLOYEES ***

The relationship between the company and its employees is governed by a substantial body of employment and other law. Questions of employment law should always be referred to the company's professional advisers. The law is complex and changes constantly.

The aim of this chapter is therefore to provide an aide-mémoire or check-list, rather than deal with detailed rules relating to any particular matter.

In order to establish the relationship of employer and employee there must be an agreement between the company and the employee, whereby the employee agrees to give services to the employer. It can be difficult to distinguish between the status of an employee and that of an independent contractor. A lawyer will say that the employee enters into a contract *of* service, and an independent contractor enters into a contract *for* services. The distinction can be very important. For example, under a legal rule called 'vicarious liability', an employer may be liable for loss or damage to others which is caused by his employee if in the course of his employment, but not an independent contractor, and an employee may make an employment tribunal claim for, for example, unfair dismissal, whereas an independent contractor has only very limited rights against the business.

The contract between the company and employee does not have to be written. Sometimes, the law will impose additional terms on the employer and employee, which apply whether or not they want them to. For example, in relation to certain types of work or certain types of employee, or as a result of rules established by official bodies such as wages councils. The rules and customs of a particular industry may also apply automatically.

Other terms will be implied in relation to matters which the employer and employee may not have even considered. For example, there is a rule that an employer must pay the employee in cash. This prevents one practice of the nineteenth century, whereby employees were paid in tokens, which could only be spent in the employers' shops.

Whilst the contract need not be in writing, it is sensible to have a written contract for senior or important employees. The contents of the written contract should be very carefully considered, especially those clauses dealing with matters such as benefits in kind for the employee, and the company's right to stop the employee leaving the company and setting up in competition.

If there is no written contract, most employees must be given written information about the main terms of their contract with the employer. This is not a contract, but merely 'for information only'.

The written statement must be given within 2 months of the start of the employment. Some items which must be included are:

(1) the names of the employer and employee;

(2) the date employment commenced, and whether any period of employment with a previous employer counts for the purpose of determining 'continuous employment' (eg for redundancy calculations);

(3) the rate of pay and whether pay is hourly, weekly, monthly, etc;

(4) details of pension schemes, disciplinary rules, grievance procedures, etc.

It is possible to cross-refer to other documents, handbooks or manuals which are made available to the employee by the employer. Forms of written statement are available from legal stationers.

Not all employees are entitled to a written statement. Employees working less than 8 hours a week, spouses of the employer, civil servants, dockers and seamen do not have to be given a statement. Of course, the spouse exemption will never apply if the employer is a company, irrespective of the relationship of the employee and any director or shareholder of the company, with whom the employee deals.

If any change is made in the matters referred to in the written statement, there is a special procedure for notifying the change to an employee. Legal advice should always be taken.

Most employees will also be entitled to an itemised statement of pay, containing necessary information as to, for example, the gross and net pay, and the amount and nature of any deductions made.

The employer does not automatically have to provide the employee with work, provided that the employee is being given the benefits which the employer agreed to give in the contract of employment. An employee may therefore be given work as and when the employer wishes. However, there may be tax problems if the benefits being given to the employee are out of proportion to work being done.

Health and safety at work are important matters, and the employer must be sure that the legal and other requirements are observed at work premises. There are a number of Acts of Parliament which may apply, dealing with matters as diverse as cleanliness of machinery, and use of lifting tackle. However, the basic duty behind all the legislation and rules is the duty requiring the employer to take reasonable care for the safety of employees. This duty is commonly divided into three limbs, whereby the employer must provide:

(1)   competent staff;

(2)   adequate machinery, plant, premises and materials;

(3)   proper systems of work and supervision.

What this entails will depend upon the nature of the business carried on by the employer, and the particular job of the employee. The employer should ensure that proper advice is taken in respect of its own particular business.

Discrimination is also proscribed by legislation. Discrimination may occur because of sex, race, nationality, colour, ethnic or national origins, sexual orientation, religious or other philosophical beliefs, age, marital status, previous criminal offences committed by the employee, trade union membership, or through unfair selection for dismissal or redundancy. Quite apart from existing employees, the question of possible discrimination should be carefully considered when advertising for new employees, or for employees to fill new positions. Discriminatory advertising is unlawful for both the employer and the publication where the advertisement appears.

The employer is responsible for paying contributions to social security, both on its own account, and on behalf of the employee. The employer must also insure all employees against liability for bodily injury and disease suffered in the course of, or because of, their employment. Other types of insurance which the employer should consider include the following:

(1)   public and product liability insurance;

(2)   fire and special perils;

(3) theft cover;

(4) business interruption insurance;

(5) glass insurance;

(6) money insurance and credit insurance;

(7) documents and goods in transit;

(8) motor insurance;

(9) business travel insurance;

(10) professional indemnity;

(11) engineering insurance;

(12) personal accident insurance;

(13) personal health insurance;

(14) directors' and officers' liability insurance.

It is possible to get single policy insurance for particular trades, so that only one premium need be paid to cover an amalgamation of appropriate policies.

There is a complex body of law governing the rights of employees in relation to sickness, pregnancy, dismissal and redundancy. The employer must have a proper understanding of the principles behind this body of law. Legal advice should always be sought in specific cases. However, a further consideration of the detailed rules is beyond the scope of this book.

16.2 LIST OF MINORITY RIGHTS OF SHAREHOLDERS

There follows below a list of the rights of minority shareholders.

Description of right	Description of the type and minimum size of group required to exercise right
Any shareholder can petition the court and show that the company's affairs are being or have been conducted in a manner which is unfairly prejudicial to the interests of some part of the shareholders (including himself) or to all of them or that an act or proposed act or omission of the company is or would be prejudicial. The court has very wide discretion to make whatever order it thinks fit.	*Any* shareholder of the company.
To apply to the court for the company to be wound up on the grounds that it is 'just and equitable' that the company should be wound up. Note that the application should show that the person applying has an interest in the winding up, ie there will be some surplus assets to be distributed. Because a successful application 'kills' the company it will usually be in a shareholder's interests to use another right if one is available.	*Any* shareholder of the company.
To apply to the court for an order restraining the company from carrying out a future 'ultra vires' act, ie an act which it has no legal power to do because it is not authorised by its memorandum.	A minority shareholder.
To apply to the court on behalf of all innocent shareholders for compensation in respect of an act which is not authorised by the company's memorandum of association but which has already been committed. Note there are very strict legal rules which must be satisfied before such an action can succeed, for example there must have been a fraud on the minority and the wrongdoers must be in control of the company.	A minority shareholder.

Description of right	*Description of the type and minimum size of group required to exercise right*
To apply to the court for relief where his personal rights as a shareholder have been infringed. Note it is very difficult to provide any useful guidance as to when the courts will allow such an application to succeed. There must have been a very fundamental type of wrong done to the applicant which cannot be ratified by the majority of shareholders – for example, an attempt to remove the applicant's right to vote. It is therefore not advisable to rely on this right unless no other remedies are available. It is only likely to be successful in *extreme* circumstances.	*Any* shareholder of the company.
To request the holding of a general meeting, notwithstanding anything in the articles of the company.	Holders of one-twentieth of the paid-up capital carrying voting rights at the date of the deposit of the request or, if a meeting has already been called pursuant to a request within the last 12 months, one-tenth.
To apply to the court for cancellation of an alteration to conditions in memorandum which could have been contained in articles. The court has wide powers to make such an order as it thinks fit.	Holders of 15% of the issued capital of the company or of any class.
To apply to the court for cancellation of variation of class rights: (i) where the memorandum or articles provide for such variations to be subject to the consent of a specified proportion of that class or a resolution of that class; (ii) where class rights not contained in the memorandum and the articles do not contain provisions for the variation of class rights.	Holders of 15% of the issued shares of the relevant class, being persons who did not consent to or vote in favour of the variation.

Description of right	Description of the type and minimum size of group required to exercise right
To require the circulation of resolutions and notices.	(i) Shareholders representing one-twentieth of the total voting rights of all the shareholders having a right to vote at the meeting to which the requisition relates; or (ii) not less than 100 shareholders holding shares on which there has been paid up an average sum of at least £100 per shareholder.
To demand a poll at a general meeting on any question other than the election of the chairman of the meeting or the adjournment of the meeting. Any provision in the articles preventing this is void.	(i) Five shareholders having the right to vote at the relevant meeting; or (ii) a shareholder or shareholders representing one-tenth of the total voting rights of all shareholders having the right to vote at that meeting; or (iii) a shareholder or shareholders holding shares in the company conferring a right to vote at the meeting and upon which has been paid up at least one-tenth of the total sum paid up on all shares carrying that right.
To apply to the court for cancellation of a special resolution approving any payment out of capital for the redemption or purchase by a private company of its shares. Application must be made within 5 weeks of the date on which the resolution was passed.	Any member of the company other than one who consented to or voted in favour of the resolution (any creditor of the company may also apply).

16.3   LIST OF MATTERS TO BE DEALT WITH BY SHAREHOLDERS UNDER THE COMPANIES ACTS – BRIEF INFORMATION

16.3.1   Alteration of objects

A company may alter its memorandum with regard to its objects by passing a special resolution. This power will be abolished from October 2009, when the format and function of the memorandum of association will change. New companies will no longer include objects in their memorandum of association, and the objects of existing companies will be treated as restrictions on their activities, set out in their articles.

16.3.2   Alteration of articles

Subject to the provisions of the Companies Acts and to the conditions contained in its memorandum, a company may alter its articles by passing a special resolution. From October 2009, this will also apply to objects treated as included in the articles – see 'Alteration of objects' above.

16.3.3   Change of name

Currently, a company may change its name by passing a special resolution. Note the change does not take effect until the registrar of companies issues a certificate of incorporation on change of name.

From October 2009, a company will be able to change its name by any other procedure included in its articles of association. See Chapter 2.

16.3.4   Alterations to capital

If authorised by its articles a company may, by ordinary resolution passed in general meeting:

(1)   increase its authorised share capital by creating new shares (from October 2009, the concept of authorised share capital will be abolished, so it will no longer be possible to pass a resolution to increase it);

(2)   consolidate and divide all or any of its share capital into shares of larger amount than its existing shares;

(3)   convert all or any of its paid-up shares into stock and reconvert that stock into paid-up shares of any denomination;

(4)   subdivide any of its shares into shares of a smaller amount;

(5) cancel shares not issued at the date of the passing of the resolution to cancel them and thereby diminish its share capital by that amount (again, this will no longer be appropriate once the concept of authorised share capital is abolished in 2009).

Shares are subdivided if, for example, one share of £1 is turned into ten shares of 10p. Shares are consolidated if, for example, five shares of £1 each are turned into one share of £5. When consolidating shares in this way, care must be taken to ensure that each shareholder will end up with a whole number of shares.

16.3.5 Reduction of capital

A company may pass a special resolution to reduce its capital – currently an application to the court for an order to confirm the reduction must then be made, but the procedure is due to be simplified, including abolition of the requirement to obtain a court order, from October 2008.

16.3.6 Declaration of dividends

Subject to the provisions of its own articles, a company usually declares dividends after the end of an accounting reference period by passing a resolution in general meeting. However, the articles often allow the directors of the company to pay an 'interim' dividend during the course of an accounting reference period without referring the matter to the shareholders.

16.3.7 Giving authority to the directors to allot shares

The directors of a company cannot currently allot any shares unless they have been given authority to do so either by the company's articles or by ordinary resolution passed in general meeting. This requirement is, however, due to be abolished from October 2009 for private companies having only one class of share capital.

16.3.8 Removal of a director

A company may, by ordinary resolution of which special notice has been given, remove a director at any time regardless of anything in its articles or in any agreement between it and the director.

At least 28 days before the meeting at which such a resolution is to be proposed, special notice of the resolution must be given to the company by the shareholder(s) proposing it and the company must then give at least 21 days' notice of the meeting to all its shareholders.

A director should not be removed unless professional advice has been taken.

16.3.9   Authorising the giving of financial assistance

Generally, a company is prohibited from giving financial assistance to a third party for the purpose of an acquisition of the company's shares but in some circumstances it may do so. If the proposed financial assistance is authorised by the Act the giving of it must be approved in advance by special resolution of the company. Note that there are other essential detailed procedural requirements which must be observed to make the giving of the financial assistance lawful.

A private company will, from October 2008, be able to provide financial assistance without having to go through those procedures. This is likely to reduce the legal work required in many takeovers, when one company acquires the shares in another, to make that company its subsidiary.

16.3.10   Authorising a purchase by the company of its own shares

In certain circumstances, a company can purchase its own shares.

If a private or public company is proposing to do so and the purchase money is to come from its distributable profits then the contract for the purchase must be given prior approval by a special resolution of the company.

If a private company is proposing to do so and the purchase money is to come from capital that payment out of capital must be approved by a special resolution of the company. (Note that if the proposed payment is to be made from capital the company's creditors or any dissenting shareholder can apply to the court for cancellation of the special resolution. Note also that there are complex procedural requirements in respect of a purchase of a company's own shares which must be observed – the requirements are particularly stringent in the case of a purchase from capital.)

16.3.11   Removal of auditors

A company may remove its auditor before the expiration of the auditor's term of office, regardless of anything in any agreement between the auditor and the company, by passing an ordinary resolution of which special notice has been given.

16.3.12 Director's contract of employment for more than 2 years

Where it is proposed that a provision should be included in an agreement whereby a director's employment is to continue (or may continue) for a period of more than 2 years and during that time the employment:

(1) cannot be terminated by the company by notice; or

(2) can be terminated only in specified circumstances,

then that provision must have the prior approval of the company given by a resolution passed in general meeting.

16.3.13 Substantial property transactions involving directors

The prior approval of the shareholders must be given by a resolution in general meeting before a company enters an agreement:

(1) whereby a director or a person connected with a director, acquires or is to acquire one or more non-cash assets of a specified value; or

(2) whereby the company acquires or is to acquire one or more non-cash assets of a specified value from a director or a person connected with a director.

Professional advice will be required with regard to the 'specified value' and note that there are some exceptions to this rule.

16.3.14 Shareholders' voluntary winding up

If a company is solvent, its shareholders can pass a special resolution that the company should be wound up. During the course of the winding-up there will be periodic meetings of the company's shareholders and eventually there will be a final general meeting.

16.3.15 Company voluntary arrangement

The directors of a company may propose a composition in satisfaction of the company's debts or a scheme of arrangement of its affairs which is to be implemented under the supervision of a qualified insolvency practitioner. That qualified insolvency practitioner may summon meetings of the shareholders to consider the proposal and to approve or modify or reject it.

16.3.16   Application for re-registration of a private company as a public company

A private company may apply to the registrar of companies for re-registration as a public company. Before making such an application the shareholders must pass a special resolution that the company should be so re-registered, and comply with other detailed procedural requirements.

16.3.17   Application for re-registration of a limited company as an unlimited company

A private company registered as a limited company can apply to the registrar of companies for re-registration as an unlimited company. Every shareholder must sign a statutory 'Form of Assent', agreeing to the company being so re-registered.

Note: this is not an exhaustive list.

16.4   COMPANY SEARCHES AND TRADE MARK SEARCHES *

16.4.1   Company searches

It is a simple and quick matter, on payment of a fee, to find out information about companies appearing on the companies' index of England and Wales, Scotland or Northern Ireland, by making a company search at the appropriate Companies House, or any branch of it. Such a search may be carried out personally, or through a lawyer, accountant or company search agent.

It is also possible to access data, or electronic images of documents filed, through various on-line services. Web-based services include Companies House Direct, available via www.companieshouse.gov.uk or JordanWatch, at www.jordans.co.uk.

When making a search, it is crucial that the company name given to Companies House, or to a search agent, is absolutely correct. For example, the names of companies referred to in the financial press are often not the true corporate names of the companies referred to. If the wrong name is given the search will be rejected, or a search may even be made against a company with a similar name, and a fee charged accordingly.

To avoid problems with the name, the company number should, if possible, always be given. A company may have changed its name but it cannot change its company number. Cross-checking of the two should reduce search errors.

The public file of a company at Companies House contains documents which have been filed by, or notices which have been entered against, the company. Such information is either notified to the registrar on official forms, or electronically in a particular format. All company records are therefore consistent, and information is easy to find. Companies House record all such information in their computer. Companies House also have similar records for companies incorporated outside Great Britain or Northern Ireland which have established a place of business or a branch in Great Britain or Northern Ireland. All companies will submit information in three broad classifications:

(1) General information relating to the constitution and management of a company. This includes the original registration documents of the company and the certificate of incorporation. In the case of a public limited company, the register will further show a trading certificate. It also includes all resolutions or orders effecting an alteration to the company's constitution, together with copies of the latest versions, any change in the structure of the share capital of the company, any changes in the registered office and officers of the company, any removal or resignation of the auditors and the appointment of a liquidator.

(2) Financial information relating to a company. This includes the annual accounts of the company and the annual returns as required by the Acts.

(3) Information relating to the registrable charges of a company. This includes the details of charges of the company, including, where applicable, notice of the appointment of a receiver or liquidator.

The public register of an overseas company, as mentioned above, will contain details of the constitution and officers of the company and other details required by the Act.

There is invariably a delay between delivery of documents for registration and their appearance on the public record. However, the registrar of companies will alert the searcher to the existence of certain important documents received but not filmed, by including a 'flag' in the company records. These documents include charges and liquidation documents.

Since the companies index is now computerised, it is possible to ask a company search agent to 'monitor' the companies index daily, to ensure that, in the event that any new companies are formed with a name similar to an existing company name or business name, this is reported to the owners of the existing name. This allows objections to the Secretary of State for the Department for Business, Enterprise and Regulatory Reform, or bringing of, for example, passing-off actions or other name-protection proceedings, to be instituted quickly and effectively against the new company.

16.4.2   Trade mark searches **

Trade marks are a means of identification. They are a sign (which means a word, logo, slogan, colour, sound, shape, smell or 3-dimensional form, or any combination of them) which a sole trader, partnership or company uses in the course of trade, or business, in order that his goods or services may be readily distinguished by the public from similar goods or services provided by others.

A trade mark must be distinctive. For example, in the case of a trade mark for goods, it must be independent of the 'design' of the goods, and of any descriptive wording or purely decorative matter with which it may be associated in ordinary use. For example, no protection will be conferred upon the trader who describes his products as 'good blue butterfly-shaped birthday cards' under the trade marks law. These words are not distinctive, but descriptive words, in ordinary use. In the case of a trade mark for services, it must be different from any sign that others may wish to use in the normal course of their business in relation to the same service.

It used to be the case that it was almost impossible to register geographical or personal names, but these strict rules have been relaxed considerably.

The registration of trade marks is governed by the trade marks legislation. It is quite possible to own a trade mark which is not registered under this legislation through rights acquired by usage of the mark, in which case the mark may be protected by a 'passing-off' action in the courts if another trader uses a mark which is identical or similar to an existing mark. However, registration confers additional protections on the owner.

Registration and search are effected at the Intellectual Property Office in Newport, Gwent which covers the entire UK (www.ipo.gov.uk).

Goods and services are internationally classified into 42 classes. A mark will be registered against one or more classes of goods or service, *and will protect the mark only in respect of classes in which it is registered.* The registrar of trade marks is, quite rightly, very fussy as to the precise class or classes into which a particular product or service falls. It is possible to apply for registration across a range of classes in only one application.

Official registration of a mark is undertaken by the Intellectual Property Office and any searching against a trade mark is carried out there. Once registered, the mark must be renewed every 10 years.

On payment of a fee, anyone may search amongst the representations and indices of trade marks for goods and services in all classes at the trade marks branch of the Intellectual Property Office.

The indices include a classified index of devices and drawings/logos, and alphabetical indices of words occurring as trade marks or parts of trade marks. These are arranged according to their beginnings and endings. The indices include pending applications for registration as well as those marks already protected by registration.

Hearing officers are available for consultation, by appointment, to provide assistance on interpreting search results, among other things, and helping to explore ways of amending a proposed mark to distinguish it from similar marks found during a search. This service is not available for the discussion of marks that are already subject to an application for registration.

Searches of the trade marks register and applications for registration of a trade mark may be made by any member of the public, though it is always prudent to use agents in light of their expertise and knowledge of trade mark law. A search will ensure that a proposed mark, or a mark similar to it, is not already being used by some other person.

It is also possible to register trade marks in other jurisdictions and/or at certain international registers which confer protections in a number of jurisdictions. Searches may also be made in these other jurisdictions or at the international registers. Again, an adviser should be consulted if a registration or search may be required in these other registers.

16.5 STATIONERY AND PREMISES *

16.5.1 Business documents

A company carrying on a business must give particular details on certain of its hard copy and electronic business documents:

ITS NAME   Every company must state its name, exactly as it appears on its certificate of incorporation or any certificate on change of name, on all its hard copy and electronic business letters and on other official documents. These include all its 'notices and other official publications', all 'bills of exchange, promissory notes, endorsements, cheques and orders for money or goods purporting to be signed by or on behalf of the company, and in all its bills of parcel, invoices, receipts and letters of credit', and on their electronic equivalents, and its website.

ITS DESIGNATION The name includes, of course, the words 'Limited', 'Ltd', 'public limited company' or 'plc', or, where appropriate, their Welsh equivalent, and these must be included.

Where such words are included in their Welsh form, the fact that the company is a limited company, or a public limited company, must be stated in English in legible characters on all its prospectuses, bill heads, letter paper, notices and official publications, and on their electronic equivalents, and its website.

Where dispensation has been obtained from the requirement to include the word 'Limited', the fact that the company is a limited company must be stated in legible characters on all its business letters and order forms.

ITS PLACE OF REGISTRATION, REGISTERED NUMBER AND ADDRESS OF REGISTERED OFFICE Every company must print its place of registration (such as 'England and Wales'), the number with which it is registered, and the address of its registered office, legibly, in all its business letters and order forms.

Even where only one address is shown, an indication should be given that this is the registered office of the company. For example, a statement at the foot of a page might say 'registered office as above'.

Whilst there is no requirement to state directors' names on business letters, if one director is named (other than in the text of the letter, or as a signatory) then all must be named.

A Christian name or an initial must be included, and, where another company holds office as a director of the company, the company name of the corporate director must be given.

Whilst there is no requirement to state the share capital of a company on its business documents, if a company does so, it is the company's paid-up share capital which must be specified.

16.5.2 Business premises

ITS NAME A company must keep its name painted or affixed on the outside of every office or place in which its business is carried on, in a conspicuous position, and in legible form.

Where the name of a company or public company includes the equivalent in Welsh of the words 'Limited' or 'public limited company', such words must also be stated in English.

BUSINESS NAME In its registered office and in any premises where a business is carried on by a company and to which the customers or suppliers have access, the company must display, in a prominent position, a notice stating its name and registered office address.

16.5.3 Overseas companies

An overseas company which has established a place of business or a branch in Great Britain or Northern Ireland must state, legibly, its name, the country in which it is incorporated and, if the liability of the members of the company is limited, notice of that fact, in every prospectus inviting subscriptions for its shares or debentures in Great Britain or Northern Ireland, and on all bills, letterheads, notices and other official publications of the company in Great Britain or Northern Ireland.

An overseas company must also display, in any premises where a business is carried on by it, and to which the customers or suppliers have access, in a prominent position, a notice stating its name.

16.6 LEASING

16.6.1 The concept of a lease

It is increasingly difficult to describe accurately what a lease is, as the number of alternative packages available increases almost monthly.

Broadly speaking, a lease is the rental of an asset for a specified period of time. There may be an advance payment (ie deposit) required at the start of the lease, and there may also (or usually instead) be a lump sum due at the end of the period.

Different possibilities could be as follows.

Example 1

Asset cost = £10,000

Leasing payment = 3 × £300 (ie £900) deposit plus 36 × £300

At the end of the period, the asset may be 'leased' for a nominal or peppercorn rent of, say, £5 pa.

In example 1, what has basically happened is that the lessee (the party renting the use of the asset) has paid for the asset over the 3 years. He may continue to use the asset at the end of the period for a nominal amount per year. Depending on the actual agreement, he may be able to purchase the asset from the leasing company at the end of the period. The differences between this type of lease and a hire-purchase type of arrangement are few and subtle and may be summarised as:

(1)   more advantageous cash flow for the lessee as hire-purchase will normally require a higher deposit, as a percentage of the cost price; and

(2)   different tax treatment of the payments in the lessee's tax computation (see below).

Although the cash flow is slightly improved on this type of lease, the lessee will probably pay more out than in a hire-purchase agreement for the same asset over the same period, as more interest will be charged (as part of the leasing payment) on a lease, with the average amount borrowed being higher across the period of borrowing – the period of the lease.

Example 2

Asset cost = £10,000

36 payments of £200 monthly plus lump sum

At end of period the asset would be sold and the lump sum paid off.

This is often termed a residual value lease.

This is basically the same as example 1, the only difference being that the lessee repays less of the cost of the asset (or amount borrowed). An assumption is made on the percentage by which the value of the asset will have fallen by the end of the lease period (ie the depreciation suffered), and some of the borrowing will be deferred and become payable at the end of the lease period.

For example, a car costing £20,000 may be assumed to depreciate by 50% over the 3-year period. Building in a safety margin, the lessor will require the lessee to repay, say, £12,000 (50% × £20,000 plus £2,000 – the safety margin) over the 3 years plus interest on the whole £20,000.

Then, after 3 years, the lease finishes, the car is sold for £9,000 and the lessee has a balance of £1,000 (£20,000 – £12,000 – £9,000) to use as a deposit on another vehicle. This method is very popular for the purchase of expensive motor cars, as they would be very expensive to buy on a straight hire-purchase or loan basis. The lessors do not object to the arrangement because they are lending money against assets which fairly reliably will depreciate at a known rate.

Example 3

Asset cost = £1,000

Monthly rental of £25 for 4 years then returned to leasing company.

The third example would typically be a straight rental of an item such as a television or a photocopier. The lessee would not always wish to own the asset because the items may constantly be updated. A residual lease would not be suitable as the asset when secondhand would have a very low resale value.

16.6.2 Taxation treatment of leasing payments

The taxation treatment of leasing payments is a fairly complex subject and the amount of the payment which may be treated as a deduction from profits is a matter which should be confirmed with the leasing company before the document is signed.

Broadly speaking, for all items except private motor cars, all the leasing payments (except, of course, VAT, which will be reclaimed in the normal way) will be allowable as a deduction against profits.

For motor cars, there is a formula which calculates a restriction on the leasing payments which is currently as follows:

$$\text{Disallowed portion} = \text{leasing payments} \times \left[\left(\frac{\text{cost of car} - £12,000}{2} \right) \div \text{cost of car} \right]$$

so for a car costing (and this refers to the original cost with a secondhand car) £20,000 and annual leasing payments of £4,800, the disallowed portion would be:

$$£4,800 \times \left[\left(\frac{£20,000 - £12,000}{2} \right) \div 20,000 \right]$$

that is to say:

$$£4,800 \times 20\% = £960$$

As can be seen from the example, the original cost of the car can have a significant effect on the allowability of the leasing payments, and therefore the real cost to the company of running that type of car.

As if this is not complicated enough, only 50% of the VAT paid on car leasing payments can be reclaimed.

APPENDIX A

USEFUL ADDRESSES

ACAS

Brandon House
180 Borough High Street
London SE1 1LW
Tel: 020 7210 3613

151 West George Street
Glasgow G2 7JJ
0141 248 1400

3 Purbeck House
Lambourne Crescent
Llanishen
Cardiff CF14 5GJ
Tel: 029 2076 2636

www.acas.org.uk

Advertising Standards Authority

Mid City Place
71 High Holborn
London WC1V 6QT
Tel: 020 7492 2222
www.asa.org.uk

Association of Business Recovery Professionals

8th Floor
120 Aldersgate Street
London EC1A 4JQ
Tel: 020 7566 4200
www.r3.org.uk

Association of Chartered Certified Accountants

29 Lincoln's Inn Fields
London WC2A 3EE
Tel: 020 7059 5000
www.accaglobal.com

The British Chambers of Commerce

British Chambers of Commerce
65 Petty France
London SW1H 9EU
Tel: 020 7654 5800
www.britishchambers.org.uk

British Franchise Association

Thames View
Newtown Road
Henley-on-Thames
Oxon RG9 1HG
Tel: 01491 578050
www.thebfa.org

Chartered Institute of Arbitrators

12 Bloomsbury Square
London WC1A 2LP
Tel: 020 7421 7444
www.arbitrators.org

Citizens Advice Bureaux

(see under Citizens Advice Bureaux in your local telephone directory)

www.citizensadvice.org.uk

Companies House

Crown Way
Maindy
Cardiff CF14 3UZ
Tel: 0870 33 33 636

37 Castle Terrace
Edinburgh EH1 2EB
Tel: 0870 33 33 636

www.companieshouse.gov.uk

Department for Business, Enterprise and Regulatory Reform

Ministerial Correspondence Unit
1 Victoria Street
London SW1H 0ET
Tel: 020 7215 5000
www.dti.gov.uk

Department for Work and Pensions

(see under Work and Pensions Department of, or Social Security Department of, in your local telephone directory)

Equality and Human Rights Commission

3 More London
Riverside Tooley Street
London SE1 2RG
Tel: 020 3117 0235

The Optima Building
58 Robertson Street
Glasgow G2 8DU
Tel: 0141 228 5910

3rd Floor
Capital Tower
Greyfriars Road
Cardiff CF10 3AG
Tel: 02920 663 710

www.equalityhumanrights.com

Financial Ombudsman Service

South Quay Plaza
183 Marsh Wall
London E14 9SR
Tel: 0845 080 1800
www.financial-ombudsman.org.uk

Health and Safety Executive

HSE Infoline
Tel: 0845 345 0055
www.hse.gov.uk

HM Revenue and Customs

(see under HM Revenue and Customs in your local telephone directory)

Information Commissioner's Office

Wycliffe House
Water Lane
Wilmslow
Cheshire SK9 5AF
Tel: 0845 630 6060
www.ico.gov.uk

The Insolvency Practitioners Association

Valiant House
4–10 Heneage Lane
London EC3A 5DQ
020 7623 5108
www.insolvency-practitioners.org.uk

Institute of Chartered Accountants in England and Wales

Chartered Accountants Hall
Moorgate Place
London
EC2P 2BJ
Tel: 020 7920 8100
www.icaew.co.uk

Institute of Chartered Accountants of Scotland

CA House
21 Haymarket Yards
Edinburgh EH12 5BH
Tel: 0131 347 0100
www.icas.org.uk

Intellectual Property Office

Concept House
Cardiff Road
Newport
Gwent NP10 8QQ
Tel: 08459 500 505
www.ipo.gov.uk

The Law Society of England and Wales

113 Chancery Lane
London WC2A 1PL
Tel: 020 7242 1222
www.lawsociety.org.uk

The Law Society of Northern Ireland

40 Linenhall Street
Belfast BT2 8BA
Tel: 028 9023 1614
www.lawsoc-ni.org

The Law Society of Scotland

26 Drumsheugh Gardens
Edinburgh EH3 7YR
Tel: 0131 226 7411
www.lawscot.org.uk

Local Authority Environmental Health Departments

(see under Local Authority in your local telephone directory)

Local Trading Standards Department

(see under Trading Standards in your local telephone directory)

London Enterprise Agency (also known as One London)

New City Court
20 St Thomas Street
London SE1 9RS
Tel: 020 7403 0300
www.gle.co.uk/onelondon

Natural England

Northminster House
Peterborough PE1 1UA
Tel: 0845 600 3078
www.naturalengland.org.uk

Office of Fair Trading

Fleetbank House
2–6 Salisbury Square
London EC4Y 8JX
Tel: 020 7211 8000
www.oft.gov.uk

The Registrar of Companies

1st Floor, Waterfront Plaza
Department of Enterprise, Trade and Investment
8 Laganbank Road
Belfast
BT1 3BS
Tel: 0845 604 8888
www.detini.gov.uk

VAT

(see under HM Customs & Excise in your local telephone directory)

Which?

2 Marylebone Road
London NW1 4DF
0845 307 4000
www.which.co.uk

APPENDIX B

SENSITIVE WORDS AND EXPRESSIONS

You will need the approval of the Secretary of State for Trade and Industry before you use any of the following words or expressions (or their plural or possessive forms) in your chosen company name.

(a)   Words which imply national or international pre-eminence:

British	Great Britain	National	Wales
England	International	Scotland	Welsh
English	Ireland	Scottish	
European	Irish	United Kingdom	

(b)   Words which imply business pre-eminence or representative or authoritative status:

Association	Board	Federation	Institution
Authority	Council	Institute	Society

(c)   Words which imply specific objects or functions:

Assurance	Fund	Reassurance
Assurer	Group	Re-assurer
Benevolent	Holding	Register
Charter	Industrial &	Registered
Chartered	provident society	Re-insurance
Chemist	Insurance	Re-insurer
Chemistry	Insurer	Sheffield
Co-operative	Patent	Stock exchange
Foundation	Patentee	Trade union
Friendly society	Post office	Trust

Words or expressions in the following list need the approval of the Secretary of State. If you want to use any of them in your company name you will need to write first to the relevant body to ask if they have any objection to its use. When you apply for approval to use the name you should tell Companies House that you have written to the relevant body and enclose a copy of the reply you have received.

Word or Expression	Relevant Body for companies intending to have registered office in England or Wales	Relevant Body for companies intending to have registered office in Scotland
Charity, Charitable	Head of Status Charity Commission Woodfield House Tangier Taunton TA1 4BL	*For recognition as a Scottish charity HM Revenue Customs (HMRC FICO (Scotland) Trinity Park House South Trinity Road Edinburgh EH5 3SD*
Contact Lens	The Registrar General Optical Council 41 Harley Street London W1N 2DJ	As for England and Wales
Dentist, Dentistry	The Registrar General Dental Council 37 Wimpole Street London W1M 8DQ	As for England and Wales
District Nurse, Health Visitor, Midwife, Midwifery, Nurse, Nursing	The Registrar & Chief Executive United Kingdom Central Council for Nursing, Midwifery and Health Visiting 23 Portland Place London W1N 3AF	As for England and Wales
Health Centre	Office of the Solicitor Department of Health & Social Security 48 Carey Street London WC2A 2LS	As for England and Wales

Word or Expression	Relevant Body for companies intending to have registered office in England or Wales	Relevant Body for companies intending to have registered office in Scotland
Health Service	Penny Turner Head of Branding Department of Health Room 230B Skipton House 80 London Road London SE1 6LH	As for England and Wales
NHS (National Health Service)	Mike Pattrick Office of the Solicitor Dept of Health Room 518 New Court 48 Carey Street London WC2A 2LS Tel: 0207 412 1225 Email: Mike.Pattrick@dwp.gsi.gov.uk	As for England, Wales and Scotland
Police	Pauline Laybourne Briefing and Honours Team CRCSG Change and Support Unit 3rd Floor A Fry Building 2 Marsham Street London SW1P 4DF	The Scottish Ministers Police Division St Andrew's House Regent Road Edinburgh EH1 3DG
Polytechnic	Department of Education and Science FHE 1B Sanctuary Buildings Great Smith Street Westminster London SW1P 3BT	As for England and Wales
Pregnancy, Termination, Abortion	Department of Health Area 423 Wellington House 133–135 Waterloo Road London SE1 8UG	As for England and Wales

Word or Expression	Relevant Body for companies intending to have registered office in England or Wales	Relevant Body for companies intending to have registered office in Scotland
Royal, Royale, Royalty, King, Queen, Prince, Princess, Windsor, Duke, His/Her Majesty	*(If based in England)* Linda Henshaw Ministry of Justice Constitutional Settlement Division 6th Floor – Point 6B Selbourne House 54 Victoria Street London SW1E 6QW *(If based in Wales)* The National Assembly for Wales Crown Buildings Cathays Park Cardiff CF10 3NQ	Douglas Boyd Protocol Unit St Andrew's House Regent Road Edinburgh EH1 3DG
Special School	Clinton Roche Department for Education and Skills Caxton House 6–12 Tothill Street London SW1H 9NA Tel: 0870 0012345	As for England and Wales
University	Privy Council Office 2 Carlton Gardens London SW1Y 5AA	As for England and Wales

Certain words or expressions are covered by other legislation and their use in company names might be a criminal offence. These are listed below. If you want to use any of these words or expressions in your company name, then you should contact the relevant regulatory authority or ask Companies House for advice before proceeding.

Word or Expression	Relevant Legislation	Relevant Body
Anzac	Anzac Act 1916, s 1	Seek advice of Companies House

Word or Expression	Relevant Legislation	Relevant Body
Architect	Architects Registration Act 1997, s 20	Architects Registration Board 73 Hallam Street London W1N 6EE
Building Society	Building Society Act 1986	Seek advice of Building Societies Commission Victoria House 30–40 Kingsway London WC2B 6ES
Chamber(s) of Business, Chamber(s) of Commerce, Chamber(s) of Commerce and Industry, Chamber(s) of Commerce, Training and Enterprise, Chamber(s) of Enterprise, Chamber(s) of Industry Chamber(s) of Trade, Chamber(s) of Trade and Industry, Chamber(s) of Training, Chamber(s) of Training and Enterprise *or the Welsh translations of these words*	Company and Business Names (Chamber of Commerce etc) Act 1999	Guidance is available from Companies House

Word or Expression	Relevant Legislation	Relevant Body
Chiropodist, Dietician, Medical Laboratory, Technician, Occupational Therapist, Othoptist, Physiotherapist, Radiographer, Remedial Gymnast	Professions Supplementary to Medicine Act 1960 if preceded by Registered or State Registered	Mrs Joan Arnott Department of Health HRD HRB Room 2N35A Quarry House Quarry Hill Leeds LS2 7JE
Chiropractor	Chiropractors Act 1994	The Chief Executive General Chiropractic Council 44 Wicklow Street London WC1X 9HL
Credit Union	Credit Union Act 1979	The Public Records Section Financial Services Authority 25 The North Colonnade Canary Wharf London E14 5HS
Dentist, Dental Surgeon, Dental Practitioner	Dental Act 1984	The Registrar General Dental Council 37 Wimpole Street London W1M 8DQ
Druggist, Pharmaceutical, Pharmaceutist, Pharmacist, Pharmacy	Medicines Act 1968, s 78	The Director of Legal Services The Royal Pharmaceutical Society of Great Britain 1 Lambeth High Street London SE1 7JN *(for Scottish Registered Companies)* The Pharmaceutical Society 36 York Place Edinburgh EH13HU

Word or Expression	Relevant Legislation	Relevant Body
Institute of Laryngology, Institute of Otology, Institute of Urology, Institute of Orthapaedics	University College London Act 1988	Seek advice of University College London Gower Street London WC1E 6BT
Patent Office, Patent Agent	Copyright, Designs and Patents Act 1988	IPPD (Intellectual Property Policy Directorate) Room 3B38 Concept House UK Intellectual Property Office Cardiff Road Newport NP10 8QQ
Olympiad, Olympiads, Olympian, Olympians, Olympic, Olympics, Paralympic, Paralympics, Paralympiad, Paralympiads, Paralympian, Paralympians *translation of these or words so similar to these protected words*	Olympic Symbol etc (Protection) Act 1995 (as amended)* Use of such words may infringe the rights of the British Olympic Association/British Paralympic Association. **Also protects the Olympic symbols of five interlocking rings; the Olympic motto 'Citius Altius Fortius' ('Faster, Higher, Stronger'); the Paralympic symbol of three 'agitos'; the Paralympic motto 'Spirit in Motion'; and anything so similar to them.*	The London Organising Committee of the Olympic Games Limited (LOCOG) 23rd Floor 1 Churchill Place Canary Wharf London E14 5LN

Word or Expression	Relevant Legislation	Relevant Body
	Following London's successful bid to host the 2012 Olympic Games, the London Olympic Games and Paralympic Games Act 2006 has been introduced. This provides further rights for the protection of Olympic words, symbols and marks relating to the Games. In addition to the protected words outlined here, the registration of a company name which includes specific words implying association with the London 2012 Games may infringe the rights of The London Organising Committee of the Olympic Games Limited (LOCOG) under this Act. For further information, please visit: www.london2012.com/about/our-brand/index.php	
Optician, Ophthalmic Optician, Dispensing Optician, Enrolled Optician, Registered Optician, Optometrist,	Opticians Act 1989	The Registrar General Optical Council 41 Harley Street London W1N 2DJ
Red Cross, Geneva Cross, Red Crescent, Red Lion and Sun	Geneva Convention Act 1957	Seek advice of Companies House

Word or Expression	Relevant Legislation	Relevant Body
Solicitor (Scotland)	Solicitors (Scotland) Act 1980, s 31	The Law Society of Scotland 26 Drumsheugh Gardens Edinburgh EH3 7YR
Veterinary Surgeon, Veterinary, Vet	Veterinary Surgeons Act 1966, ss 19, 20	The Registrar Royal College of Veterinary Surgeons 62–64 Horseferry Road London SW1P 2AF

Northern Ireland

You will need the approval of the Department of Enterprise Trade and Investment before any of the following words or expressions (or their plural or possessive forms) is used in a business name.

(a)   Words which imply national or international pre-eminence:

British	Great Britain	National	Wales
England	International	Scotland	Welsh
English	Ireland	Scottish	Northern Ireland
European	Irish	United Kingdom	Northern Irish

(b)   Words which imply business pre-eminence or representative status:

Association	Council	Institution
Authority	Federation	Society
Board	Institute	Government

(c)   Words which imply specific objects or functions:

Assurance	Fund	Reassurance
Assurer	Group	Re-assurer
Benevolent	Holding	Register
Charter	Industrial &	Registered
Chartered	provident society	Re-insurance
Chemist	Insurance	Re-insurer
Chemistry	Insurer	Sheffield
Co-operative	Patent	Stock exchange
Foundation	Patentee	Trade union
Friendly society	Post office	Trust

Words or expressions in the following list need the approval of the Department. If you want to use any of them in your company name you will need to write first to the relevant body to ask if they have any objection to its use. When you apply for approval to use the name you should tell Companies Registry that you have written to the relevant body and enclose a copy of the reply you have received.

Word or Expression	*Relevant Body*
Apothecary	Pharmaceutical Society of Northern Ireland 73 University Street Belfast BT7 1HL
Charity Charitable	Charities Branch Social Development Castle Buildings Stormont Belfast BT4 3PP
Contact Lens	The Registrar General Optical Council 41 Harley Street London W1N 2DJ
Dentist Dentistry	The Registrar General Dental Council 37 Wimpole Street London W1N 8DQ
Health Centre Health Service Pregnancy Termination Abortion	The Office of the Chief Executive Room 3D Department of Health and Social Services Castle Buildings Stormont Belfast BT4 3SQ
Nurse Nursing Midwife Midwifery Health Visitor District Nurse	National Board for Nursing, Midwifery and Health The Registrar & Chief Executive United Kingdom Central Council for Nursing 23 Portland Place London W1B 1PZ

Word or Expression	Relevant Body
Police	The Secretary Northern Ireland Office Stormont House Stormont Belfast BT4 3ST
Polytechnic	Higher Education Branch Adelaide House Adelaide Street Belfast BT2 8FD
Royal Royale Royalty King Queen Prince Princess Windsor Duke His/Her Majesty	Home Office Queen Anne's Gate London SW1H 9AT
Special School	Higher Education Branch Adelaide House Adelaide Street Belfast BT2 8FD

Certain words or expressions are covered by other legislation and their use in company names might be a criminal offence. These are listed below. If you want to use any of these words or expressions in your company name, then you should contact the relevant regulatory authority or ask Companies Registry for advice before proceeding.

Word or Expression	Relevant Legislation	Relevant Body
Anzac	Anzac Act 1916, s 1	Seek advice of Companies Registry
Apothecary		Seek advice of Companies Registry

Word or Expression	Relevant Legislation	Relevant Body
Architect	Architects Registration Act 1938, s 1	The Registrar Architects Registration Council of the United Kingdom 73 Hallam Street London W1N 6EE
Bank Banker Banking	Deposit Banking Act 1987	Authorisation Enquiries Financial Services Authority 25 The North Colennade Canary Wharf London E14 5HS
Building Society	Building Society Act 1986	Building Societies Commission Victoria House 30–40 Kingsway London WC2B 6ES
Chamber(s) of Business, Chamber(s) of Commerce, Chamber(s) of Commerce and Industry, Chamber(s) of Commerce, Training and Enterprise, Chamber(s) of Enterprise, Chamber(s) of Industry Chamber(s) of Trade, Chamber(s) of Trade and Industry, Chamber(s) of Training, Chamber(s) of Training and Enterprise	Company and Business Names (Chamber of Commerce etc) Act 1999	Guidance is available from the Companies Registry

Word or Expression	Relevant Legislation	Relevant Body
Chiropodist Dietician Medical Laboratory Technician Occupational Therapist Othoptist Physiotherapist Radiographer Remedial Gymnast	Professions Supplementary to Medicine Act 1960	Room 12.26 HAP4 Division Department of Health Hannibal House Elephant & Castle London SE1 6TE
Credit Union	Industrial and Provident Societies Act (Northern Ireland) 1969	Seek advice of Companies Registry
Dentist Dental Surgeon Dental Practitioner	Dentist Act 1957, ss 38, 39	The Registrar General Dental Council 37 Wimpole Street London W1M 8DQ
Drug Drugist Pharmaceutical Pharmaceutist Pharmacist Pharmacy	Medicines Act 1968, s 78	The Director of Legal Services The Royal Pharmaceutical Society of Great Britain 1 Lambeth High Street London SE1 7JN
Institute of Laryngology Institute of Otology Institute of Urology Institute of Orthapaedics	University College London Act 1988	Seek advice of University College London Gower Street London WC1E 6BT
Insurance Broker Assurance Broker Insurance Brokers Re-Insurance Broker Re-Assurance Broker	Insurance Brokers (Registration) Act 1977, ss 2, 3	Insurance Brokers Registration Council Higham Business Centre Midland Road Higham Ferrers Northants

Word or Expression	Relevant Legislation	Relevant Body
Olympiad(s) Olympian(s) Olympic(s)	Olympic Symbol etc (Protection) Act 1995	British Olympic Association 1 Wandsworth Plain London SW18 1EH
Optician Ophthalmic Optician Dispensing Optician Enrolled Optician Registered Optician Optometrist	Opticians Act 1958, ss 4, 22	The Registrar General Optical Council 41 Harley Street London W1N 2DJ
Patent Office Patent Agent	Patents Act 1977	IPCD Hazlitt House 45 Southampton Buildings London WC2A 1AR
Red Cross Geneva Cross Red Crescent Red Lion and Sun	Geneva Convention Act 1957	Seek advice of Companies Registry
Veterinary Surgeon	Veterinary Surgeons Act 1966, ss 19, 20	The Registrar Royal College of Veterinary Surgeons 62–64 Horseferry Road London SW1P 2AF

APPENDIX C

THE COMPANIES ACT 1985, TABLE A

Regulations for management of a ([private]) (*public*) company limited by shares[1]

Table A as prescribed by the Companies (Tables A to F) Regulations 1985 (SI 1985 No 805), amended by the Companies (Tables A to F) (Amendment) Regulations 1985 (SI 1985 No 1052), the Companies Act 1985 (Electronic Communications) Order 2000 (SI 2000 No 3372), the Companies (Tables A to F) (Amendment) Regulations 2007 (SI 2007 No 2541) and the Companies (Tables A to F) (Amendment) (No 2) Regulations 2007 (SI 2007 No 2826).

The regulations of Table A to the Companies Act 1985 apply to the Company save insofar as they are not excluded or varied by its Articles of Association.

1   In these regulations—

'the Act' means the Companies Act 1985 including any statutory modification or re-enactment thereof for the time being in force and any provisions of the Companies Act 2006 for the time being in force;

'the articles' means the articles of the company;

'clear days' in relation to the period of a notice means that period excluding the day when the notice is given or deemed to be given and the day for which it is given or on which it is to take effect;

'communication' means the same as in the Electronic Communications Act 2000;

'electronic communication' means the same as in the Electronic Communications Act 2000;

'executed' includes any mode of execution;

'office' means the registered office of the company;

'the holder' in relation to shares means the member whose name is entered in the register of members as the holder of the shares;

'the seal' means the common seal of the company;

'secretary' means the secretary of the company or any other person appointed to perform the duties of the secretary of the company, including a joint, assistant or deputy secretary;

'the United Kingdom' means Great Britain and Northern Ireland.

---

[1]   Save for the words in *italics*, which apply to public companies only, these regulations apply as the articles of association of both private and public companies limited by shares formed on or after 1 October 2007, save to the extent that such companies vary or disapply them.

Unless the context otherwise requires, words or expressions contained in these regulations bear the same meaning as in the Act but excluding any statutory modification thereof not in force when these regulations become binding on the company.

Share Capital

2   Subject to the provisions of the Act and without prejudice to any rights attached to any existing shares, any share may be issued with such rights or restrictions as the company may by ordinary resolution determine.

3   Subject to the provisions of the Act, shares may be issued which are to be redeemed or are to be liable to be redeemed at the option of the company or the holder on such terms and in such manner as may be provided by the articles.

4   The company may exercise the powers of paying commissions conferred by the Act. Subject to the provisions of the Act, any such commission may be satisfied by the payment of cash or by the allotment of fully or partly paid shares or partly in one way and partly in the other.

5   Except as required by law, no person shall be recognised by the company as holding any share upon any trust and (except as otherwise provided by the articles or by law) the company shall not be bound by or recognise any interest in any share except an absolute right to the entirety thereof in the holder.

Share Certificates

6   Every member, upon becoming the holder of any shares, shall be entitled without payment to one certificate for all the shares of each class held by him (and, upon transferring a part of his holding of shares of any class, to a certificate for the balance of such holding) or several certificates each for one or more of his shares of any class, to a certificate for the balance of such holding) or several certificates each for one or more of his shares upon payment for every certificate after the first of such reasonable sum as the directors may determine. Every certificate shall be sealed with the seal and shall specify the number, class and distinguishing numbers (if any) of the shares to which it relates and the amount or respective amounts paid up thereon. The company shall not be bound to issue more than one certificate for shares held jointly by several persons and delivery of a certificate to one joint holder shall be a sufficient delivery to all of them.

7   If a share certificate is defaced, worn-out, lost or destroyed, it may be renewed on such terms (if any) as to evidence and indemnity and payment of the expenses reasonably incurred by the company in investigating evidence as the directors may determine but otherwise free of charge, and (in the case of defacement or wearing-out) on delivery up of the old certificate.

Lien

8   The company shall have a first and paramount lien on every share (not being a fully paid share) for all moneys (whether presently payable or not) payable at a fixed time or called in respect of that share. The directors may at any time declare any share to be wholly or in part exempt from the provisions of this regulation. The company's lien on a share shall extend to any amount payable in respect of it.

9   The company may sell in such manner as the directors determine any shares on which the company has a lien if a sum in respect of which the lien exists is presently payable and is not paid within fourteen clear days after notice has been given to the holder of the share or to the person entitled to it in consequence of the death or bankruptcy of the holder, demanding payment and stating that if the notice is not complied with the shares may be sold.

10   To give effect to a sale the directors may authorise some person to execute an instrument of transfer of the shares sold to, or in accordance with the directions of, the purchaser. The title of the transferee to the shares shall not be affected by any irregularity in or invalidity of the proceedings in reference to the sale.

11   The net proceeds of the sale, after payment of the costs, shall be applied in payment of so much of the sum for which the lien exists as is presently payable, and any residue shall (upon surrender to the company for cancellation of the certificate for the shares sold and subject to a like lien for any moneys not presently payable as existed upon the shares before the sale) be paid to the person entitled to the shares at the date of the sale.

Calls on Shares and Forfeiture

12   Subject to the terms of allotment, the directors may make calls upon the members in respect of any moneys unpaid on their shares (whether in respect of nominal value or premium) and each member shall (subject to receiving at least fourteen clear days' notice specifying when and where payment is to be made) pay to the company as required by the notice the amount called on his shares. A call may be required to be paid by instalments. A call may, before receipt by the company of any sum due thereunder, be revoked in whole or part and payment of a call may be postponed in whole or part. A person upon whom a call is made shall remain liable for calls made upon him notwithstanding the subsequent transfer of the shares in respect whereof the call was made.

13   A call shall be deemed to have been made at the time when the resolution of the directors authorising the call was passed.

14   The joint holders of a share shall be jointly and severally liable to pay all calls in respect thereof.

15   If a call remains unpaid after it has become due and payable the person from whom it is due and payable shall pay interest on the amount unpaid from the day it became due and payable until it is paid at the rate fixed by the terms of allotment of the share or in the notice of the call or, if no rate is fixed, at the appropriate rate (as defined by the Act) but the directors may waive payment of the interest wholly or in part.

16   An amount payable in respect of a share on allotment or at any fixed date, whether in respect of nominal value or premium or as an instalment of a call, shall be deemed to be a call and if it is not paid the provisions of the articles shall apply as if that amount had become due and payable by virtue of a call.

17   Subject to the terms of allotment, the directors may make arrangements on the issue of shares for a difference between the holders in the amounts and times of payment of calls on their shares.

18   If a call remains unpaid after it has become due and payable the directors may give to the person from whom it is due not less than fourteen clear days' notice requiring payment of the amount unpaid together with any interest which may have accrued. The notice shall name the place where payment is to be made and shall state that if the notice is not complied with the shares in respect of which the call was made will be liable to be forfeited.

19   If the notice is not complied with any share in respect of which it was given may, before the payment required by the notice has been made, be forfeited by a resolution of the directors and the forfeiture shall include all dividends or other moneys payable in respect of the forfeited shares and not paid before the forfeiture.

20   Subject to the provisions of the Act, a forfeited share may be sold, re-alloted or otherwise disposed of on such terms and in such manner as the directors determine either to the person who was before the forfeiture the holder or to any other person and at any time before sale, re-allotment or other disposition, the forfeiture may be cancelled on such terms as the directors think fit. Where for the purposes of its disposal a forfeited share is to be transferred to any person the directors may authorise some person to execute an instrument of transfer of the share to that person.

21   A person any of whose shares have been forfeited shall cease to be a member in respect of them and shall surrender to the company for cancellation the certificate for the shares forfeited but shall remain liable to the company for all moneys which at the date of forfeiture were presently payable by him to the company in respect of those shares with interest at the rate at which interest was payable on those moneys before the forfeiture or, if no interest was so payable, at the appropriate rate (as defined in the Act) from the date of forfeiture until payment but the directors may waive payment wholly or in part or enforce payment without any allowance for the value of the shares at the time of forfeiture or for any consideration received on their disposal.

22   A statutory declaration by a director or the secretary that a share has been forfeited on a specified date shall be conclusive evidence of the facts stated in it as against all persons claiming to be entitled to the share and the declaration shall (subject to the execution of an instrument of transfer if necessary) constitute a good title to the share and the person to whom the share is disposed of shall not be bound to see to the application of the consideration, if any, nor shall his title to the share be affected by any irregularity in or invalidity of the proceedings in reference to the forfeiture or disposal of the share.

Transfer of Shares

23   The instrument of transfer of a share may be in any usual form or in any other form which the directors may approve and shall be executed by or on behalf of the transferor and, unless the share is fully paid, by or on behalf of the transferee.

24   The directors may refuse to register the transfer of a share which is not fully paid to a person of whom they do not approve and they may refuse to register the transfer of a share on which the company has a lien. They may also refuse to register a transfer unless—

   (a)   it is lodged at the office or at such other place as the directors may appoint and is accompanied by the certificate for the shares to which it relates and such other evidence as the directors may reasonably require to show the right of the transferor to make the transfer;

   (b)   it is in respect of only one class of shares; and

   (c)   it is in favour of not more than four transferees.

25   If the directors refuse to register a transfer of a share, they shall within two months after the date on which the transfer was lodged with the company send to the transferee notice of the refusal.

26   The registration of transfers of shares or of transfers of any class of shares may be suspended at such times and for such periods (not exceeding thirty days in any year) as the directors may determine.

27   No fee shall be charged for the registration of any instrument of transfer or other document relating to or affecting the title to any share.

28   The company shall be entitled to retain any instrument of transfer which is registered, but any instrument of transfer which the directors refuse to register shall be returned to the person lodging it when notice of the refusal is given.

Transmission of Shares

29   If a member dies the survivor or survivors where he was a joint holder, and his personal representatives where he was a sole holder or the only survivor of joint holders, shall be the only persons recognised by the company as having any title to his interest; but nothing herein contained

shall release the estate of a deceased member from any liability in respect of any share which had been jointly held by him.

30 A person becoming entitled to a share in consequence of the death or bankruptcy of a member may, upon such evidence being produced as the directors may properly require, elect either to become the holder of the share or to have some person nominated by him registered as the transferee. If he elects to become the holder he shall give notice to the company to that effect. If he elects to have another person registered he shall execute an instrument of transfer of the share to that person. All the articles relating to the transfer of shares shall apply to the notice or instrument of transfer as if it were an instrument of transfer executed by the member and the death or bankruptcy of the member had not occurred.

31 A person becoming entitled to a share in consequence of the death or bankruptcy of a member shall have the rights to which he would be entitled if he were the holder of the share, except that he shall not, before being registered as the holder of the share, be entitled in respect of it to attend or vote at any meeting of the company or at any separate meeting of the holders of any class of shares in the company.

Alteration of Share Capital

32 The company may by ordinary resolution—

    (a)   increase its share capital by new shares of such amount as the resolution prescribes;

    (b)   consolidate and divide all or any of its share capital into shares of larger amount than its existing shares;

    (c)   subject to the provisions of the Act, sub-divide its shares, or any of them, into shares of smaller amount and the resolution may determine that, as between the shares resulting from the sub-division, any of them may have any preference or advantage as compared with the others; and

    (d)   cancel shares which, at the date of the passing of the resolution, have not been taken or agreed to be taken by any person and diminish the amount of its share capital by the amount of the shares so cancelled.

33 Whenever as a result of a consolidation of shares any members would become entitled to fractions of a share, the directors may, on behalf of those members, sell the shares representing the fractions for the best price reasonably obtainable to any person (including, subject to the provisions of the Act, the company) and distribute the net proceeds of sale in due proportion among those members, and the directors may authorise some person to execute an instrument of transfer of the shares to, or in accordance with the directions of, the purchaser. The transferee shall not be bound to see to the application of the purchase money nor shall his title to the shares be affected by any irregularity in or invalidity of the proceedings in reference to the sale.

34   Subject to the provisions of the Act, the company may by special resolution reduce its share capital, any capital redemption reserve and any share premium account in any way.

Purchase of Own Shares

35   Subject to the provisions of the Act, the company may purchase its own shares (including any redeemable shares) and, if it is a private company, make a payment in respect of the redemption or purchase of its own shares otherwise than out of distributable profits of the company or the proceeds of a fresh issue of shares.

General Meetings

37   The directors may call general meetings and, on the requisition of members pursuant to the provisions of the Act, shall forthwith proceed to convene a general meeting in accordance with the provisions of the Act. If there are not within the United Kingdom sufficient directors to call a general meeting, any director or any member of the company may call a general meeting.

Notice of General Meetings

38   *An annual general meeting shall be called by at least twenty-one clear days' notice. All other* [G]eneral meetings shall be called by at least fourteen clear days' notice but a general meeting may be called by shorter notice if it is so agreed—

   (a) *in the case of an annual general meeting, by all the members entitled to attend and vote thereat; and*

   (b) *in the case of any other meeting* by a majority in number of the members having a right to attend and vote being a majority together holding not less than [ninety] *ninety-five* per cent in nominal value of the shares giving that right.

The notice shall specify the time and place of the meeting and the general nature of the business to be transacted *and, in the case of an annual general meeting, shall specify the meeting as such.*

Subject to the provisions of the articles and to any restrictions imposed on any shares, the notice shall be given to all the members, to all persons entitled to a share in consequence of the death or bankruptcy of a member and to the directors and auditors.

39   The accidental omission to give notice of a meeting to, or the non-receipt of notice of a meeting by, any person entitled to receive notice shall not invalidate the proceedings at that meeting.

Proceedings at General Meetings

40   No business shall be transacted at any meeting unless a quorum is present. [Save in the case of a company with a single member] two persons

entitled to vote upon the business to be transacted, each being a member or a proxy for a member or a duly authorised representative of a corporation, shall be a quorum.

41   If such a quorum is not present within half an hour from the time appointed for the meeting, or if during a meeting such a quorum ceases to be present, the meeting shall stand adjourned to the same day in the next week at the same time and place or to such time and place as the directors may determine.

42   The chairman, if any, of the board of directors or in his absence some other director nominated by the directors shall preside as chairman of the meeting, but if neither the chairman nor such other director (if any) be present within fifteen minutes after the time appointed for holding the meeting and willing to act, the directors present shall elect one of their number to be chairman and, if there is only one director present and willing to act, he shall be chairman.

43   If no director is willing to act as chairman, or if no director is present within fifteen minutes after the time appointed for holding the meeting, the members present and entitled to vote shall choose one of their number to be chairman.

44   A director shall, notwithstanding that he is not a member, be entitled to attend and speak at any general meeting and at any separate meeting of the holders of any class of shares in the company.

45   The chairman may, with the consent of a meeting at which a quorum is present (and shall if so directed by the meeting), adjourn the meeting from time to time and from place to place, but no business shall be transacted at an adjourned meeting other than business which might properly have been transacted at the meeting had the adjournment not taken place. When a meeting is adjourned for fourteen days or more, at least seven clear days' notice shall be given specifying the time and place of the adjourned meeting and the general nature of the business to be transacted. Otherwise it shall not be necessary to give any such notice.

46   A resolution put to the vote of a meeting shall be decided on a show of hands unless before, or on the declaration of the result of, the show of hands a poll is duly demanded. Subject to the provisions of the Act, a poll may be demanded—

   (a)   by the chairman; or
   (b)   by at least two members having the right to vote at the meeting; or
   (c)   by a member or members representing not less than one-tenth of the total voting rights of all the members having the right to vote at the meeting; or
   (d)   by a member or members holding shares conferring a right to vote at the meeting being shares on which an aggregate sum has been paid up equal to not less than one-tenth of the total sum paid up on all the shares conferring that right;

and a demand by a person as proxy for a member shall be the same as a demand by the member.

47 Unless a poll is duly demanded a declaration by the chairman that a resolution has been carried or carried unanimously, or by a particular majority, or lost, or not carried by a particular majority and an entry to that effect in the minutes of the meeting shall be conclusive evidence of the fact without proof of the number or proportion of the votes recorded in favour of or against the resolution.

48 The demand for a poll may, before the poll is taken, be withdrawn but only with the consent of the chairman and a demand so withdrawn shall not be taken to have invalidated the result of a show of hands declared before the demand was made.

49 A poll shall be taken as the chairman directs and he may appoint scrutineers (who need not be members) and fix a time and place for declaring the result of the poll. The result of the poll shall be deemed to be the resolution of the meeting at which the poll was demanded.

51 A poll demanded on the election of a chairman or on a question of adjournment shall be taken forthwith. A poll demanded on any other question shall be taken either forthwith or at such time and place as the chairman directs not being more than thirty days after the poll is demanded. The demand for a poll shall not prevent the continuance of a meeting for the transaction of any business other than the question on which the poll was demanded. If a poll is demanded before the declaration of the result of a show of hands and the demand is duly withdrawn, the meeting shall continue as if the demand had not been made.

52 No notice need be given of a poll not taken forthwith if the time and place at which it is to be taken are announced at the meeting at which it is demanded. In any other case at least seven clear days' notice shall be given specifying the time and place at which the poll is to be taken.

Votes of Members

54 Subject to any rights or restrictions attached to any shares, on a show of hands every member who (being an individual) is present in person or by proxy or (being a corporation) is present by a duly authorised representative or by proxy, unless the proxy (in either case) or the representative is himself a member entitled to vote, shall have one vote and on a poll every member shall have one vote for every share of which he is the holder.

55 In the case of joint holders the vote of the senior who tenders a vote, whether in person or by proxy, shall be accepted to the exclusion of the votes of the other joint holders; and seniority shall be determined by the order in which the names of the holders stand in the register of members.

56 A member in respect of whom an order has been made by any court having jurisdiction (whether in the United Kingdom or elsewhere) in matters concerning mental disorder may vote, whether on a show of hands or on a poll, by his receiver, curator bonis or other person authorised in that behalf appointed by that court, and any such receiver, curator bonis or other person may, on a poll, vote by proxy. Evidence to the satisfaction of the directors of the authority of the person claiming to exercise the right to vote shall be deposited at the office, or at such other place as is specified in accordance with the articles for the deposit of instruments of proxy, not less than 48 hours before the time appointed for holding the meeting or adjourned meeting at which the right to vote is to be exercised and in default the right to vote shall not be exercisable.

57 No member shall vote at any general meeting or at any separate meeting of the holders of any class of shares in the company, either in person or by proxy, in respect of any share held by him unless all moneys presently payable by him in respect of that share have been paid.

58 No objection shall be raised to the qualification of any voter except at the meeting or adjourned meeting at which the vote objected to is tendered, and every vote not disallowed at the meeting shall be valid. Any objection made in due time shall be referred to the chairman whose decision shall be final and conclusive.

59 On a poll votes may be given either personally or by proxy. A member may appoint more than one proxy to attend on the same occasion.

60 The appointment of a proxy shall be executed by or on behalf of the appointor and shall be in the following form (or in a form as near thereto as circumstances allow or in any other form which is usual or which the directors may approve)—

> '. . . . . PLC/Limited
> . . . .
> I/We, ..., of . . . ., being a member/ members of the above-named company, hereby appoint . . . . of . . . ., or failing him, ... of . . . ., as my/our proxy to vote in my/our name[s] and on my/our behalf at the *annual/any other* general meeting of the company to be held on . . . . 19 . . . ., and at any adjournment thereof.
> Signed on . . . . 19 . . . .'.

61 Where it is desired to afford members an opportunity of instructing the proxy how he shall act the appointment of a proxy shall be in the following form (or in a form as near thereto as circumstances allow or in any other form which is usual or which the directors may approve)—

> '. . . . . PLC/Limited
> . . . .

I/We, ..., of . . . ., being a member/ members of the above-named company, hereby appoint . . . . of . . . ., or failing him . . . . of . . . ., as my/our proxy to vote in my/our name[s] and on my/our behalf at the *annual/any other* general meeting of the company, to be held on . . . . 19 . . . ., and at any adjournment thereof.
This form is to be used in respect of the resolutions mentioned below as follows:
> Resolution No. 1 *for *against
> Resolution No. 2 *for *against.

*Strike out whichever is not desired.
Unless otherwise instructed, the proxy may vote as he thinks fit or abstain from voting.
Signed   this . . . .   day   of . . . .
19 . . . .'

62   The appointment of a proxy and any authority under which it is executed or a copy of such authority certified notarially or in some other way approved by the directors may—

(a)   in the case of an instrument in writing be deposited at the office or at such other place within the United Kingdom as is specified in the notice convening the meeting or in any instrument of proxy sent out by the company in relation to the meeting not less than 48 hours before the time for holding the meeting or adjourned meeting at which the person named in the instrument proposes to vote; or

(aa) in the case of an appointment contained in an electronic communication, where an address has been specified for the purpose of receiving electronic communications—
  (i)   in the notice convening the meeting, or
  (ii)   in any instrument of proxy sent out by the company in relation to the meeting, or
  (iii) in any invitation contained in an electronic communication to appoint a proxy issued by the company in relation to the meeting,

be received at such address not less than 48 hours before the time for holding the meeting or adjourned meeting at which the person named in the appointment proposes to vote;

(b)   in the case of a poll taken more than 48 hours after it is demanded, be deposited or received as aforesaid after the poll has been demanded and not less than 24 hours before the time appointed for the taking of the poll; or

(c)   where the poll is not taken forthwith but is taken not more than 48 hours after it was demanded, be delivered at the meeting at which the poll was demanded to the chairman or to the secretary or to any director;

and an appointment of proxy which is not deposited, delivered or received in a manner so permitted shall be invalid. In this regulation and the next, 'address', in relation to electronic communications, includes any number or address used for the purposes of such communications.

63   A vote given or poll demanded by proxy or by the duly authorised representative of a corporation shall be valid notwithstanding the previous determination of the authority of the person voting or demanding a poll unless notice of the determination was received by the company at the office or at such other place at which the instrument of proxy was duly deposited or, where the appointment of the proxy was contained in an electronic communication, at the address at which such appointment was duly received before the commencement of the meeting or adjourned meeting at which the vote is given or the poll demanded or (in the case of a poll taken otherwise than on the same day as the meeting or adjourned meeting) the time appointed for taking the poll.

Number of Directors

64   Unless otherwise determined by ordinary resolution, the number of directors (other than alternate directors) shall not be subject to any maximum but shall be not less than two.

Alternate Directors

65   Any director (other than an alternate director) may appoint any other director, or any other person approved by resolution of the directors and willing to act, to be an alternate director and may remove from office an alternate director so appointed by him.

66   An alternate director shall be entitled to receive notice of all meetings of directors and of all meetings of committees of directors of which his appointor is a member, to attend and vote at any such meeting at which the director appointing him is not personally present and generally to perform all the functions of his appointor as a director in his absence but shall not be entitled to receive any remuneration from the company for his services as an alternate director. But it shall not be necessary to give notice of such a meeting to an alternate director who is absent from the United Kingdom.

67   An alternate director shall cease to be an alternate director if his appointor ceases to be a director; but, if a director retires by rotation or otherwise but is reappointed or deemed to have been reappointed at the meeting at which he retires, any appointment of an alternate director made by him which was in force immediately prior to his retirement shall continue after his reappointment.

68   Any appointment or removal of an alternate director shall be by notice to the company signed by the director making or revoking the appointment or in any other manner approved by the directors.

69   Save as otherwise provided in the articles, an alternate director shall be deemed for all purposes to be a director and shall alone be responsible for his own acts and defaults and he shall not be deemed to be the agent of the director appointing him.

Powers of Directors

70   Subject to the provisions of the Act, the memorandum and the articles and to any directions given by special resolution, the business of the company shall be managed by the directors who may exercise all the powers of the company. No alteration of the memorandum or articles and no such direction shall invalidate any prior act of the directors which would have been valid if that alteration had not been made or that direction had not been given. The powers given by this regulation shall not be limited by any special power given to the directors by the articles and a meeting of directors at which a quorum is present may exercise all powers exercisable by the directors.

71   The directors may, by power of attorney or otherwise, appoint any person to be the agent of the company for such purposes and on such conditions as they determine, including authority for the agent to delegate all or any of his powers.

Delegation of Directors' Powers

72   The directors may delegate any of their powers to any committee consisting of one or more directors. They may also delegate to any managing director or any director holding any other executive office such of their powers as they consider desirable to be exercised by him. Any such delegation may be made subject to any conditions the directors may impose, and either collaterally with or to the exclusion of their own powers and may be revoked or altered. Subject to any such conditions, the proceedings of a committee with two or more members shall be governed by the articles regulating the proceedings of directors so far as they are capable of applying.

Appointment and Retirement of Directors

73   At the first annual general meeting all the directors shall retire from office, and at every subsequent annual general meeting one-third of the directors who are subject to retirement by rotation or, if their number is not three or a multiple of three, the number nearest to one-third shall retire from office; but, if there is only one director who is subject to retirement by rotation, he shall retire.

74   Subject to the provisions of the Act, the directors to retire by rotation shall be those who have been longest in office since their last appointment or reappointment, but as between persons who became or were last reappointed directors on the same day those to retire shall (unless they otherwise agree among themselves) be determined by lot.

75   If the company, at the meeting at which a director retires by rotation, does not fill the vacancy the retiring director shall, if willing to act, be deemed to have been reappointed unless at the meeting it is resolved not to fill the vacancy or unless a resolution for the reappointment of the director is put to the meeting and lost.

76   No person *other than a director retiring by rotation* shall be appointed or reappointed a director at any general meeting unless—

(a)   he is recommended by the directors; or

(b)   not less than fourteen nor more than thirty-five clear days before the date appointed for the meeting, notice executed by a member qualified to vote at the meeting has been given to the company of the intention to propose that person for appointment or reappointment stating the particulars which would, if he were so appointed or reappointed, be required to be included in the company's register of directors together with notice executed by that person of his willingness to be appointed or reappointed.

77   Not less than seven nor more than twenty-eight clear days before the date appointed for holding a general meeting notice shall be given to all who are entitled to receive notice of the meeting of any person *(other than a director retiring by rotation at the meeting)* who is recommended by the directors for appointment or reappointment as a director at the meeting or in respect of whom notice has been duly given to the company of the intention to propose him at the meeting for appointment or reappointment as a director. The notice shall give the particulars of that person which would, if he were so appointed or reappointed, be required to be included in the company's register of directors.

78   *Subject as aforesaid,* [T]he company may by ordinary resolution appoint a person who is willing to act to be a director either to fill a vacancy or as an additional director and may also determine the rotation in which any additional directors are to retire.

79   The directors may appoint a person who is willing to act to be a director, either to fill a vacancy or as an additional director, provided that the appointment does not cause the number of directors to exceed any number fixed by or in accordance with the articles as the maximum number of directors. *A director so appointed shall hold office only until the next following annual general meeting and shall not be taken into account in determining the directors who are to retire by rotation at the meeting. If not reappointed at such annual general meeting, he shall vacate office at the conclusion thereof.*

80   *Subject as aforesaid, a director who retires at an annual general meeting may, if willing to act, be reappointed. If he is not reappointed, he shall retain office until the meeting appoints someone in his place, or if it does not do so, until the end of the meeting.*

Disqualification and Removal of Directors

81   The office of a director shall be vacated if—

(a)   he ceases to be a director by virtue of any provision of the Act or he becomes prohibited by law from being a director; or

(b)   he becomes bankrupt or makes any arrangement or composition with his creditors generally; or

(c)   he is, or may be, suffering from mental disorder and either—

   (i)   he is admitted to hospital in pursuance of an application for admission for treatment under the Mental Health Act 1983 or, in Scotland, an application for admission under the Mental Health (Scotland) Act 1960, or

   (ii)   an order is made by a court having jurisdiction (whether in the United Kingdom or elsewhere) in matters concerning mental disorder for his detention or for the appointment of a receiver, curator bonis or other person to exercise powers with respect to his property or affairs; or

(d)   he resigns his office by notice to the company; or

(e)   he shall for more than six consecutive months have been absent without permission of the directors from meetings of directors held during that period and the directors resolve that his office be vacated.

Remuneration of Directors

82   The directors shall be entitled to such remuneration as the company may by ordinary resolution determine and, unless the resolution provides otherwise, the remuneration shall be deemed to accrue from day to day.

Directors' Expenses

83   The directors may be paid all travelling, hotel, and other expenses properly incurred by them in connection with their attendance at meetings of directors or committees of directors or general meetings or separate meetings of the holders of any class of shares or of debentures of the company or otherwise in connection with the discharge of their duties.

Directors' Appointments and Interests

84   Subject to the provisions of the Act, the directors may appoint one or more of their number to the office of managing director or to any other executive office under the company and may enter into an agreement or arrangement with any director for his employment by the company or for the provision by him of any services outside the scope of the ordinary duties of a director. Any such appointment, agreement or arrangement may be made upon such terms as the directors determine and they may remunerate any such director for his services as they think fit. Any appointment of a director to an executive office shall terminate if he ceases to be a director but without prejudice to any claim to damages for

breach of the contract of service between the director and the company. A managing director and a director holding any other executive office shall not be subject to retirement by rotation.

85   Subject to the provisions of the Act, and provided that he has disclosed to the directors the nature and extent of any material interest of his, a director notwithstanding his office—

(a)   may be a party to, or otherwise interested in, any transaction or arrangement with the company or in which the company or in which the company is otherwise interested;

(b)   may be a director or other officer of, or employed by, or a party to any transaction or arrangement with, or otherwise interested in, any body corporate promoted by the company or in which the company is otherwise interested; and

(c)   shall not, by reason of his office, be accountable to the company for any benefit which he derives from any such office or employment or from any such transaction or arrangement or from any interest in any such body corporate and no such transaction or arrangement shall be liable to be avoided on the ground of any such interest or benefit.

86   For the purposes of regulation 85—

(a)   a general notice given to the directors that a director is to be regarded as having an interest of the nature and extent specified in the notice in any transaction or arrangement in which a specified person or class of persons is interested shall be deemed to be a disclosure that the director has an interest in any such transaction of the nature and extent so specified; and

(b)   an interest of which a director has no knowledge and of which it is unreasonable to expect him to have knowledge shall not be treated as an interest of his.

Directors' Gratuities and Pensions

87   The directors may provide benefits, whether by the payment of gratuities or pensions or by insurance or otherwise, for any director who has held but no longer holds any executive office or employment with the company or with any body corporate which is or has been a subsidiary of the company or a predecessor in business of the company or of any such subsidiary, and for any member of his family (including a spouse and a former spouse) or any person who is or was dependent on him, and may (as well before as after he ceases to hold such office or employment) contribute to any fund and pay premiums for the purchase or provision of any such benefit.

Proceedings of Directors

88   Subject to the provisions of the articles, the directors may regulate their proceedings as they think fit. A director may, and the secretary at the

request of a director shall, call a meeting of the directors. It shall not be necessary to give notice of a meeting to a director who is absent from the United Kingdom. Questions arising at a meeting shall be decided by a majority of votes. In the case of an equality of votes, the chairman shall have a second or casting vote. A director who is also an alternate director shall be entitled in the absence of his appointor to a separate vote on behalf of his appointor in addition to his own vote.

89   The quorum for the transaction of the business of the directors may be fixed by the directors and unless so fixed at any other number shall be two. A person who holds office only as an alternate director shall, if his appointor is not present, be counted in the quorum.

90   The continuing directors or a sole continuing director may act notwithstanding any vacancies in their number, but, if the number of directors is less than the number fixed as the quorum, the continuing directors or director may act only for the purpose of filling vacancies or of calling a general meeting.

91   The directors may appoint one of their number to be the chairman of the board of directors and may at any time remove him from that office. Unless he is unwilling to do so, the director so appointed shall preside at every meeting of directors at which he is present. But if there is no director holding that office, or if the director holding it is unwilling to preside or is not present within five minutes after the time appointed for the meeting, the directors present may appoint one of their number to be chairman of the meeting.

92   All acts done by a meeting of directors, or of a committee of directors, or by a person acting as a director shall, notwithstanding that it be afterwards discovered that there was a defect in the appointment of any director or that any of them were disqualified from holding office, or had vacated office, or were not entitled to vote, be as valid as if every such person had been duly appointed and was qualified and had continued to be a director and had been entitled to vote.

93   A resolution in writing signed by all the directors entitled to receive notice of a meeting of directors or of a committee of directors shall be as valid and effectual as it if had been passed at a meeting of directors or (as the case may be) a committee of directors duly convened and held and may consist of several documents in the like form each signed by one or more directors; but a resolution signed by an alternate director need not also be signed by his appointor and, if it is signed by a director who has appointed an alternate director, it need not be signed by the alternate director in that capacity.

94   Save as otherwise provided by the articles, a director shall not vote at a meeting of directors or of a committee of directors on any resolution concerning a matter in which he has, directly or indirectly, an interest or duty which is material and which conflicts or may conflict with the

interests of the company unless his interest or duty arises only because the case falls within one or more of the following paragraphs—

(a)   the resolution relates to the giving to him of a guarantee, security, or indemnity in respect of money lent to, or an obligation incurred by him for the benefit of, the company or any of its subsidiaries;

(b)   the resolution relates to the giving to a third party of a guarantee, security, or indemnity in respect of an obligation of the company or any of its subsidiaries for which the director has assumed responsibility in whole or part and whether alone or jointly with others under a guarantee or indemnity or by the giving of security;

(c)   his interest arises by virtue of his subscribing or agreeing to subscribe for any shares, debentures, or other securities of the company or any of its subsidiaries, or by virtue of his being, or intending to become, a participant in the underwriting or sub-underwriting of an offer of any such shares, debentures, or other securities by the company or any of its subsidiaries for subscription, purchase or exchange;

(d)   the resolution relates in any way to a retirement benefits scheme which has been approved, or is conditional upon approval, by the Board of Inland Revenue for taxation purposes.

For the purposes of this regulation, an interest of a person who is, for any purpose of the Act (excluding any statutory modification thereof not in force when this regulation becomes binding on the company), connected with a director shall be treated as an interest of the director and, in relation to an alternate director, an interest of his appointor shall be treated as an interest of the alternate director without prejudice to any interest which the alternate director has otherwise.

95   A director shall not be counted in the quorum present at a meeting in relation to a resolution on which he is not entitled to vote.

96   The company may by ordinary resolution suspend or relax to any extent, either generally or in respect of any particular matter, any provision of the articles prohibiting a director from voting at a meeting of directors or of a committee of directors.

97   Where proposals are under consideration concerning the appointment of two or more directors to offices or employments with the company or any body corporate in which the company is interested the proposals may be divided and considered in relation to each director separately and (provided he is not for another reason precluded from voting) each of the directors concerned shall be entitled to vote and be counted in the quorum in respect of each resolution except that concerning his own appointment.

98   If a question arises at a meeting of directors or of a committee of directors as to the right of a director to vote, the question may, before the

conclusion of the meeting, be referred to the chairman of the meeting and his ruling in relation to any director other than himself shall be final and conclusive.

Secretary

99   Subject to the provisions of the Act, the secretary shall be appointed by the directors for such term, at such remuneration and upon such conditions as they may think fit; and any secretary so appointed may be removed by them.

Minutes

100   The directors shall cause minutes to be made in books kept for the purpose—

(a)   of all appointments of officers made by the directors; and

(b)   of all proceedings at meetings of the company, of the holders of any class of shares in the company, and of the directors, and of committees of directors, including the names of the directors present at each such meeting.

The Seal

101   The seal shall only be used by the authority of the directors or of a committee of directors authorised by the directors. The directors may determine who shall sign any instrument to which the seal is affixed and unless otherwise so determined it shall be signed by a director and by the secretary or by a second director.

Dividends

102   Subject to the provisions of the Act, the company may by ordinary resolution declare dividends in accordance with the respective rights of the members, but no dividend shall exceed the amount recommended by the directors.

103   Subject to the provisions of the Act, the directors may pay interim dividends if it appears to them that they are justified by the profits of the company available for distribution. If the share capital is divided into different classes, the directors may pay interim dividends on shares which confer deferred or non-preferred rights with regard to dividend as well as on shares which confer preferential rights with regard to dividend, but no interim dividend shall be paid on shares carrying deferred or non-preferred rights if, at the time of payment, any preferential dividend is in arrear. The directors may also pay at intervals settled by them any dividend payable at a fixed rate if it appears to them that the profits available for distribution justify the payment. Provided the directors act in good faith they shall not incur any liability to the holders of shares

conferring preferred rights for any loss they may suffer by the lawful payment of an interim dividend on any shares having deferred or non-preferred rights.

104 Except as otherwise provided by the rights attached to shares, all dividends shall be declared and paid according to the amounts paid up on the shares on which the dividend is paid. All dividends shall be apportioned and paid proportionately to the amounts paid up on the shares during any portion or portions of the period in respect of which the dividend is paid; but, if any share is issued on terms providing that it shall rank for dividend as from a particular date, that share shall rank for dividend accordingly.

105 A general meeting declaring a dividend may, upon the recommendation of the directors, direct that it shall be satisfied wholly or partly by the distribution of assets and, where any difficulty arises in regard to the distribution, the directors may settle the same and in particular may issue fractional certificates and fix the value for distribution of any assets and may determine that cash shall be paid to any member upon the footing of the value so fixed in order to adjust the rights of members and may vest any assets in trustees.

106 Any dividend or other moneys payable in respect of a share may be paid by cheque sent by post to the registered address of the person entitled or, if two or more persons are the holders of the share or are jointly entitled to it by reason of the death or bankruptcy of the holder, to the registered address of that one of those persons who is first named in the register of members or to such person and to such address as the person or persons entitled may in writing direct. Every cheque shall be made payable to the order of the person or persons entitled or to such other person as the person or persons entitled may in writing direct and payment of the cheque shall be a good discharge to the company. Any joint holder or other person jointly entitled to a share as aforesaid may give receipts for any dividend or other moneys payable in respect of the share.

107 No dividend or other moneys payable in respect of a share shall bear interest against the company unless otherwise provided by the rights attached to the share.

108 Any dividend which has remained unclaimed for twelve years from the date when it became due for payment shall, if the directors so resolve, be forfeited and cease to remain owing by the company.

Accounts

109 No member shall (as such) have any right of inspecting any accounting records or other book or document of the company except as conferred by statute or authorised by the directors or by ordinary resolution of the company.

Capitalisation of Profits

110 The directors may with the authority of an ordinary resolution of the company—

(a) subject as hereinafter provided, resolve to capitalise any undivided profits of the company not required for paying any preferential dividend (whether or not they are available for distribution) or any sum standing to the credit of the company's share premium account or capital redemption reserve;

(b) appropriate the sum resolved to be capitalised to the members who would have been entitled to it if it were distributed by way of dividend and in the same proportions and apply such sum on their behalf either in or towards paying up the amounts, if any, for the time being unpaid on any shares held by them respectively, or in paying up in full unissued shares or debentures of the company of a nominal amount equal to that sum, and allot the shares or debentures credited as fully paid to those members, or as they may direct, in those proportions, or partly in one way and partly in the other: but the share premium account, the capital redemption reserve, and any profits which are not available for distribution may, for the purposes of this regulation, only be applied in paying up unissued shares to be allotted to members credited as fully paid;

(c) make such provision by the issue of fractional certificates or by payment in cash or otherwise as they determine in the case of shares or debentures becoming distributable under this regulation in fractions; and

(d) authorise any person to enter on behalf of all the members concerned into an agreement with the company providing for the allotment to them respectively, credited as fully paid, of any shares or debentures to which they are entitled upon such capitalisation, any agreement made under such authority being binding on all such members.

Notices

111 Any notice to be given to or by any person pursuant to the articles (other than a notice calling a meeting of the directors) shall be in writing or shall be given using electronic communications to an address for the time being notified for that purpose to the person giving the notice. In this regulation, 'address', in relation to electronic communications, includes any number or address used for the purposes of such communications.

112 The company may give any notice to a member either personally or by sending it by post in a prepaid envelope addressed to the member at his registered address or by leaving it at that address or by giving it using electronic communications to an address for the time being notified to the company by the member. In the case of joint holders of a share, all notices shall be given to the joint holder whose name stands first in the

register of members in respect of the joint holding and notice so given shall be sufficient notice to all the joint holders. A member whose registered address is not within the United Kingdom and who gives to the company an address within the United Kingdom at which notices may be given to him, or an address to which notices may be sent using electronic communications, shall be entitled to have notices given to him at that address, but otherwise no such member shall be entitled to receive any notice from the company. In this regulation and the next, 'address', in relation to electronic communications, includes any number or address used for the purposes of such communications.

113   A member present, either in person or by proxy, at any meeting of the company or of the holders of any class of shares in the company shall be deemed to have received notice of the meeting and, where requisite, of the purposes for which it was called.

114   Every person who becomes entitled to a share shall be bound by any notice in respect of that share which, before his name is entered in the register of members, has been duly given to a person from whom he derives his title.

115   Proof that an envelope containing a notice was properly addressed, prepaid and posted shall be conclusive evidence that that the notice was given. Proof that a notice contained in an electronic communication was sent in accordance with guidance issued by the Institute of Chartered Secretaries and Administrators shall be conclusive evidence that the notice was given. A notice shall be deemed to be given at the expiration of 48 hours after the envelope containing it was posted or, in the case of a notice contained in an electronic communication, at the expiration of 48 hours after the time it was sent.

116   A notice may be given by the company to the persons entitled to a share in consequence of the death or bankruptcy of a member by sending or delivering it, in any manner authorised by the articles for the giving of notice to a member, addressed to them by name, or by the title of representatives of the deceased, or trustee of the bankrupt or by any like description at the address, if any, within the United Kingdom supplied for that purpose by the persons claiming to be so entitled. Until such an address has been supplied, a notice may be given in any manner in which it might have been given if the death or bankruptcy had not occurred.

Winding Up

117   If the company is wound up, the liquidator may, with the sanction of a special resolution of the company and any other sanction required by the Act, divide among the members in specie the whole or any part of the assets of the company and may, for that purpose, value any assets and determine how the division shall be carried out as between the members or different classes of members. The liquidator may, with the like sanction, vest the whole or any part of the assets in trustees upon such

trusts for the benefit of the members as he with the like sanction determines, but no member shall be compelled to accept any assets upon which there is a liability.

Indemnity

118 Subject to the provisions of the Act but without prejudice to any indemnity to which a director may otherwise be entitled, every director or other officer or auditor of the company shall be indemnified out of the assets of the company against any liability incurred by him in defending any proceedings, whether civil or criminal, in which judgment is given in his favour or in which he is acquitted or in connection with any application in which relief is granted to him by the court from liability for negligence, default, breach of duty or breach of trust in relation to the affairs of the company.

INDEX

References are to paragraph numbers.